From Camden Town to Camden Lock:
AD 1800-2000

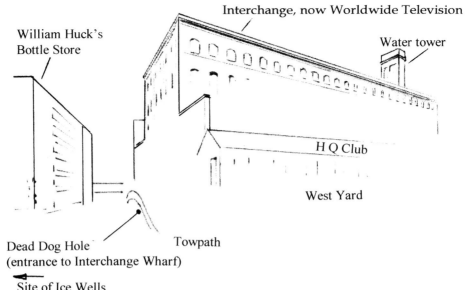

Interchange, now Worldwide Television

William Huck's
Bottle Store

Water tower

H Q Club

West Yard

Dead Dog Hole
(entrance to Interchange Wharf)

Towpath

Site of Ice Wells
(off picture).

KEY TO THE BACK COVER

Camden Lock viewed from the Diagonal Bridge, looking west.

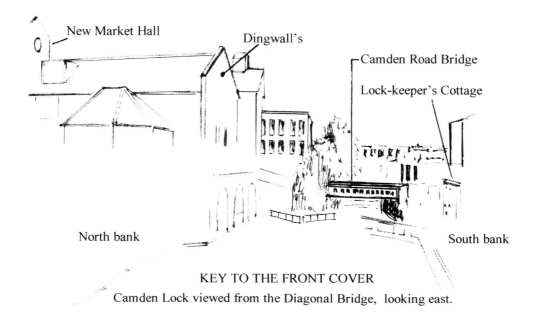

New Market Hall

Dingwall's

Camden Road Bridge

Lock-keeper's Cottage

North bank

South bank

KEY TO THE FRONT COVER
Camden Lock viewed from the Diagonal Bridge, looking east.

The Growth of Camden Town:
AD 1800 - 2000

ISBN 0 9509362 9 4
First published 1999
Copyright © Jack Whitehead, 1999
The author declares his moral right to this book

Printed by
Biddles Limited
Guildford,
Surrey GU1 1DA

Published by Jack Whitehead
55, Parliament Hill, London NW3 2TB
0171 435 3302

Orders and enquiries by post or telephone only please.

Acknowledgements

First I would like to thank my wife and son for reading the various chapters and making valuable suggestions, Tom Whitehead for his photography, Keith Robinson for his professional help, and Malcolm Tucker for his specialist historical advice.

I would like to thank the archivists at Camden Local History Library, City of Westminster Archive, Greater London History Library, London School of Economics, the National Film Institute, the Royal Veterinary College, London Transport Museum, and the following individuals and firms:-

Aimimage Ltd., Bob Baker of T.P.Bennett Partnership, architects, Nigel Baldock of Baldock Quick Partnership, Bamboo Film & Television Productions, Grace Beckett, Ruth Blum, Camden Planning Dept., Kevin Brownlow of Photoplay Productions Ltd., Chris Bryant of Pickfords, Chrysalis Sport, Classic FM, Luke Swanson of Diageo, John Dickinson, architect, Moira Duncan of Thompson Travel, Ivy Durrant and the late Sid Durrant and Harry Durrant, Eurocrew, Terry Farrell & Partners, architects, Jo Aren of Getty Images, Neil Gilchrist of Kerr-Gilchrist, Philip Goodman of Xanthus Fine Art, who bought the Clark picture at auction, Piers Gough of CZGW, architects, Fanny Bostock of Jim Henson Co., Robin Heare, Henry Hertzberg, of Chapman Taylor Partnership, architects, Hilltop Pictures, S.W. Holloway of Hunting Gate Construction, Malcolm Holmes, Ben Hume-Paton of Image Dynamic, International Distillers & Vintners, Julie Jack of Community Housing Association, Sarah Jones, jeweller, Fred Le Grys, Mr King, Fred Monson of Worldwide Television, Mrs Moore, MTV, Torquil and Caspar Norman, Eric Reynolds and Cathy Palmer of Northside Developments, Chris Papaloisou, architect, Keith Patterson-Browne, Red Pepper Film Co., Heinz Richardson of Jestico-Whiles, architects, Pat Rigg, Nick Roberts of Chelsfield plc, Eric Robinson, Safeways, Sainsburys plc, Geoff Saul, Helen Scott-Lidgett, the management team of Stables Market, Moira Duncan of Thompson Travel, Tony Stone Images, Judith Tranter of J.C.M.T., architects, Twenty Twenty Television, Harvey Van Sickle, Mark Wadhwa of North London House, Werner Forman Archive, W.G.Wright, Hon. curator of the Gilbey Archive, Bishop's Stortford,

To Susie, Paul and Tom,
who will recognise
some of the stories.

Contents

Introduction

I have travelled through Camden Town all my life and now I walk in its packed streets daily, yet each time I see Camden Town it is different. As a child it was the way to the Zoo, with a peep into Palmer's Pet Shop in Parkway first, as a taste of what was to come. Later, Camden Town was on the way to the West End, shops and theatres. For years it was on my way to work.

To the thousands of tourists who see it for the first time, it is a unique experience. A place on holiday – crowded, vibrant, thrusting, with a spirit of well-being. It has all the exhilaration of a street market and yet the goods are not trash. There are serious artists here, doing serious work. The food is good. There are plenty of restaurants and interesting shops and the music scene is alive. Fantastic fibre glass figures climb up the buildings. There is champagne in the air.

To other people it is a centre for the media, full of TV studios, picture libraries and camera crews. Yet all of this has been true for only the last few years, and was undreamed of before. In earlier years Camden Town was a hub of transport; the centre of the biggest drinks firm in the world; a place of factories making a thousand things; an area noisy day and night with carts and vans, railway engines and the tread of factory and railway workers. To the navigators, the men who built the Canal two centuries ago, it was just another length of canal to be dug and puddled with clay. Even to the railway builders, Camden Town was still set in lush meadows. Earlier again it had been just five streets of a New Town, planted well outside London, with the nearest house in Bedford Square, Bloomsbury.

And two hundred years ago it did not exist. Camden Town was not even a name. There had been an ancient village of Kentish Town, but no old village of Camden. Instead, there were just a few fields of heavy clay Two muddy trackways, one to Highgate and one to Hampstead, forked at what is now the Tube Station.

We each have our own starting point when looking at Camden Town. I have seen it in many moods over the years and indeed they are the subject of the book. I hope that readers will begin where they like in the story, working forwards and backwards as they choose. The history of Camden Town illustrates two hundred years of change in Britain. The laying out of Camden Town as a New Town; the expansion of Industry in the period from 1820 when Britain was becoming dominant and made goods for the whole world, and its decay, which had begun well before the Second World War. All these periods are reflected in Camden Town. The piano trade faded early. The destruction of heavy industry began when the country sold every-thing to pay for the Second World War Then came its final collapse in the 1960s, when accountants took charge and said that it was more profitable to asset strip than to modernize the factories. At the same time, canal and railway transport died. Camden Town became a place of depression - bleak, empty of work, dead.

However, from 1973, when Camden Lock opened, the first glimmerings of a revival could be seen. A few market stalls – some young people selling original fashions – a few artists making and selling their goods – new music (and Rock began in Camden Town they say) – clubs which opened late. Then came the media invasion. It is a story of an area finding a new path, a new way to earn a living, and a new purpose. Those few market stalls started it all, and today land values have rocketed.

'In the beginning it was not even a name' - - -. Now read on.

Early Camden Maps

Ogilby's 1672 map of Middlesex names Hampstead, Childe Hill and Highgate, all remote villages far outside London, while Camden Town was nothing but an open space. I have marked its position with a C in this map. Westminster and London are clustered as separate cities on the north bank of the Thames. Tottenham Court was a large house set in a private estate, in the fields to the north.

In 1804, well over a century later, Tompson's Parish map of St Pancras, 1804, printed on page 2, shows the Fleet River coming down from Hampstead and Highgate in two tributaries which meet just north of Camden Town. The river flowed under Kentish Town Road, through the fields east of Great College Street and past the Veterinary College to King's Cross. The centuries old roads to Hampstead and Highgate are shown and Parkway is called The Crooked Lane. Camden Road had not been cut at this time.

A modest network of five streets had been laid out behind the High Street and a few houses erected. Before this could be done, the streets laid out and money borrowed to lay drains etc., an Act of Parliament was required. As Camden Town did not yet exist and Kentish Town was a very old village indeed, the houses were built under the

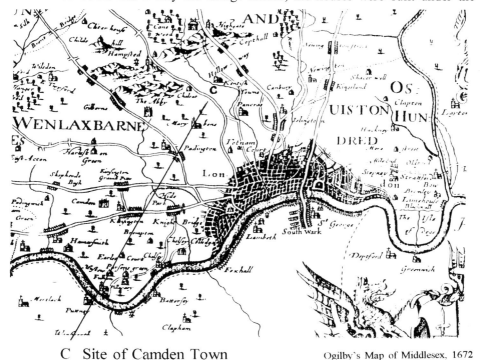

C Site of Camden Town   Ogilby's Map of Middlesex, 1672

1

Kentish Town Act of 1788. Camden Town was to be a New Town, laid out by a speculator who hoped to sell building lots and harvest ground rents, but the leases he could offer were for only forty years.

Builders had no inducement to erect expensive houses on those terms, because after forty years the houses would become the property of the ground landlords. Therefore they built only modest houses, most of which have not survived but a few can still be seen at the High Street end of Pratt Street. Nos. 4, 6 and 8 show an extraordinary array of doorways. The first has the original round-headed doorway and transom of about 1800; the second was given a 'gothic' entrance, probably in the 1860s; while No. 8 is fronted with a formidable iron-work grille – our 1990s way of welcoming strangers.

By 1804, Gloucester Place had been built on the site of what is now the Camden Theatre, in Crowndale Road. There were houses on either side of the High Street, some of which survive as shops, but the site where Waterstones now stands was still a brickfield making bricks from the local clay. Originally they were very simple three-

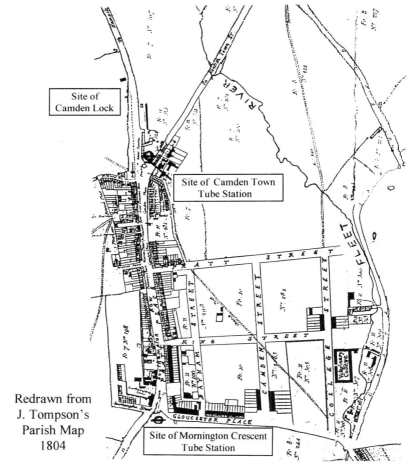

Redrawn from
J. Tompson's
Parish Map
1804

2

storey houses, but their front gardens have long been built over to form single-storey shops. There was also a tiny development around what is now Camden Tube Station, and the corner by the Midland Bank was then the village pound.

This water-colour by Thomas Clark shows the rural nature of Camden Town at this time. Thomas Clark was a landscape and architectural engraver who lived at 42 Pratt Street, Camden Town, when the houses there were still surrounded by open fields. It must have been a good place for an artist to live, on the edge of the country, yet within walking distance of the galleries and print shops of the City and West End. There was a similar colony of artists in Lisson Grove at the time, also next to open fields.

View from Chalk Farm, by Thomas Clark, dated 1824[3]

Clark is better known for his steel engravings of other people's work than for his own watercolours. He was awarded the Large Silver Medal of the Society of Arts for his engraving of Chichester Cross, in 1831, and he engraved for any number of books of travel - 'Views of the Rhine', etc.[1] Nevertheless, his water-colour landscapes are quite common.[2] At one time he was even confused with Constable, but so much is known about Constable today that experts can separate them quite easily. Everything in Constable relates to something else, so that a particular feature - perhaps a cart, or a boat - can normally be traced back through other drawings and paintings, to a tiny sketchbook of many years earlier. There is no such history to the pieces of Clark's watercolours. They are direct studies, often rather empty compared with Constable. They can be thought of as Clark's notebooks and all the more valuable topographically.

This one is called 'From Chalk Farm' and indeed the lower slopes of Haverstock Hill, just above the present Chalk Farm Station, must have been Clark's nearest vantage point for viewing the landscape. From this position in 1824, with the canal only a few years old and the railway still in the future, he could have watched the new fringes of London being built in Bloomsbury and Regent's Park

In the centre of the picture is a domed building, but it may perhaps not be St Paul's as there are no towers. It could be The Colosseum, on the site of the present

Colosseum Terrace in Regent's Park. However, the dates do not quite match. The Colosseum did not open until 1829, while this drawing is dated 1824. Perhaps the drawing was dated later from memory. However, the dome shape is very like the dome of St Paul's, so perhaps Clark simply forgot to draw the towers.[3]

OLD CHALK FARM IN 1730.

CAMDEN TOWN, FROM THE HAMPSTEAD ROAD. MARYLEBONE, 1780.

[1] Dictionary of Steel Engravers, by Basil Hunnisett, 1980.
[2] Dictionary of Water-colour Painters, by Mallalieu.
[3] I am grateful to Mr Goodman of Xanthus, Fine Art dealers, for permission to print the picture.

The Almshouses in Bayham Street, Camden Town

J.W. 94

St Martin's in the Fields, the parish church near Trafalgar Square, owned various almshouses which gave shelter to 'poor, old women'. Rents from other properties supported their daily needs. There are records of this charity stretching back to 1681. However, by the beginning of the eighteenth century the houses in Crown Street, near Hoxton Square, had 'so fallen much in decay' that it was necessary for the parish to rebuild them.[1] Soon after 1800, St Martin's had bought a new burial ground far out in the country, in Pratt Street, Camden Town, and resolved to build new almshouses there. An Act of Parliament gave permission for the Church to remove the almswomen from Crown Street to new almshouses at the corner of Bayham Street and Pratt Street, and sell off the old land.

The new site was 280 feet in length and 45 feet in depth. There they built nine houses, designated by the letters A - I. The central house, E, contained four rooms on the ground floor and two upstairs. There was also a large room which was reserved as a committee room. Each of the other houses had eight rooms, so the new buildings provided no less than seventy rooms. The whole expense of erecting and completing the new almshouses was £4,069, fifteen shillings and fivepence and the trustees were able to sell the Crown Street property for £4,102, 10 shillings.

The Bayham Street houses are still standing, behind a row of pleached lime trees. The central entrance has a triangular pediment and four almshouses on each side. There was not quite enough room for four full houses on each side, so the fourth one from the left is narrower and has lost its blind windows.

In 1887-8[2] the accounts show that £1,070 - fourteen shillings were paid to the almswomen, so the houses were still housing only women. The Church also paid out £1,453 to other pensioners, showing what a lot of the charity work was still in the hands of the church and explains why Charles Booth's Survey on Poverty took so much evidence from church people.[3]

---

[1] Report of Commissioners of Charities & Education of England and Wales, Vol. 22, p.710

[2] Annual Report of St Martin's in the Fields, 1887-8, Westminster City Archive

[3] See chapter on the Booth Survey later in the book.

The Arrival of the Grand Junction Canal at Paddington

The Regent's Canal, which seems so old to us, was in fact the very last section of a much earlier and larger canal development. The rivers of the Midlands manufacturing towns had been linked by a series of canals to form the Grand Junction Canal. By 1804, when Tompson drew this map, it had already reached Paddington, connecting the industries of the Midlands to London. Bulk goods could now be brought easily and cheaply to the very edge of London.

A large Canal Basin had been created in an open field at Paddington, with a single loading building. It was a timber structure with a taller central section to house the crane and a large over-hanging roof where barges could be loaded under cover, but at first there was nothing else. At some time this timber building, shown on page 218, was replaced by a brick one with a slate overhanging roof. This second building can still be seen at the Edgware Road end of the Basin. Until 1998 it was hemmed in by warehouses, now demolished, but the Metropole Hotel still towers immediately above. This loading building (page 220) is now listed Grade II. By perhaps AD 2005, when the Paddington Basin has been fully redeveloped, this old building will have been dismantled and rebuilt at the other end of the Basin, as part of a boat facility for touring canal boats..

The Grand Junction Canal and Paddington Basin before the Regent's Canal was built and Little Venice was formed.

The map shows the planned second Canal Basin in black. It was never built.

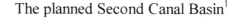

The planned Second Canal Basin[1]

At the start of the nineteenth century Paddington suddenly became the terminus for goods and passengers from all over the Midlands. Road transport was so slow and expensive that frequently the quickest and cheapest way to travel even for passengers was by canal barge, while goods and minerals moved far faster than by road. By using four horses and travelling at a trot, Pickford's could take a barge from London to Birmingham in two and a half days. Large furniture depositories arose around the Paddington Basin. Wharves held piles of building materials, coal, hay, pottery and for the return journey, manure from the fields and household rubbish to fuel brickyard kilns. While Camden Town still slept in her fields, Paddington was becoming an industrial centre. Indeed Paddington was so self-confident that a second canal basin was planned on what is now the St Mary's Hospital site in Praed Street, Paddington.

However, most firms wanted their goods carried beyond Paddington, to the centre of London and especially to the docks, yet all goods arriving at Paddington had to be carried from there expensively by cart. Very soon there was a demand for the canal to be extended to the Port of London and the deep-sea ships. Soon there was a plan to build the Regent's Canal to link Paddington to the open sea.

Before Little Venice was created

Faden's map of 1810, showing the Grand Junction Canal terminating at Paddinton.

Bartlett and Britton's map of 1834, showing the Regent's Canal and Little Venice.

7

Faden's map of 1810 is the only one I know which shows the canal system terminating at Paddington. Thereafter the Regent's Canal was always shown on maps because by 1811 the idea of a canal from Paddington to Wapping had been forced through. Bills had been put through Parliament and soon the surveyors were tramping the fields.

The Regent's Canal Company

The map shows the route of the Regent's Canal, while the section on page 10 reveals some of the problems faced by the engineers. The canal company had to tunnel under Maida Hill and again at Islington, skirt the newly developing Regent's Park in a deep, expensive cutting, create locks at Camden Town and elsewhere, and negotiate with reluctant landowners. The shareholders had to spend far more money than they had planned..

Paddington wharf owners and contractors, Paddington Vestry and all those profiting by the success of Paddington as the canal terminus, protested at the idea of the Regent's Canal being built, as it would drain away their livelihoods. Other people were concerned at the loss of open space in Marylebone Farm (now Regent's Park). This was public land and would be covered with private houses, becoming the preserve of the rich. Still others feared that the Prince Regent, who was promoting the development of this Crown land, would squander money on grandiose building, as he had squandered money before, and leave Parliament to settle the bills.

The Grand Junction Canal Company had brought the canal to Paddington along the 100 foot contour (30 metres) sweeping round the lower slopes of Maida Hill into Paddington Basin. To continue, they wished to stay at the same level, or fall lower. It would have been simplest to have continued under Edgware Road and through Marylebone Farm, but this was very valuable property indeed.

Nash was just starting to create Regent's Park on the old Marylebone Farm. He did not want a canal to separate his new estate from Regent's Street and his wealthy clients in the West End. He was creating an enclosed estate, cut off from the working world, difficult to enter except from Portland Place and a few chosen gateways. On the other

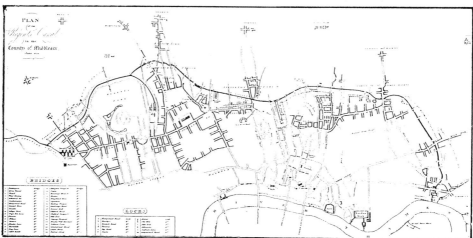

The Plan of the Regent's Canal, from Paddington to the Thames at Limehouse.

8

hand, Nash liked the idea of the canal bordering his Park on the north in a well-wooded valley, insulating it silently and romantically from the outside world. The effect of that policy, and its influence on public debate, on the separation of classes and the positioning of areas of public and private housing, we shall see continuing into the 1980s and beyond.

The route involved many bridges. Where possible the canal was narrowed to only one barge width, allowing a shorter, cheaper bridge, but on the Regent's Park stretch where the long bridges had to fly high above to span the wide cutting, there was no advantage in narrowing the canal so it remained full width.

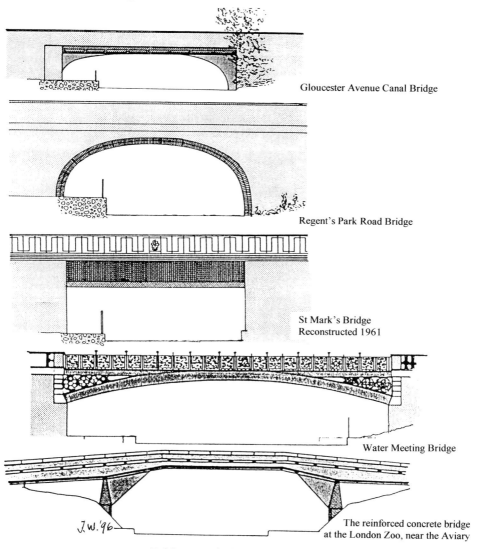

Gloucester Avenue Canal Bridge

Regent's Park Road Bridge

St Mark's Bridge
Reconstructed 1961

Water Meeting Bridge

J.W.'96

The reinforced concrete bridge
at the London Zoo, near the Aviary

Bridges on the Regent's Canal

Section of the Intended Canal

The section shows the path of the Regent's Canal straightened out. The distance from Broad Water, now called Little Venice, to the River Thames at Limehouse, is about six and a half miles as the crow flies, but the canal winds for nearly nine. It falls 86 feet as it passes through two tunnels and thirteen locks. There had been no locks all the way from Uxbridge to Paddington, and the Regent's Canal was able to continue on this level course as far as Camden, Here there was a sharp fall in ground level which made locks necessary.

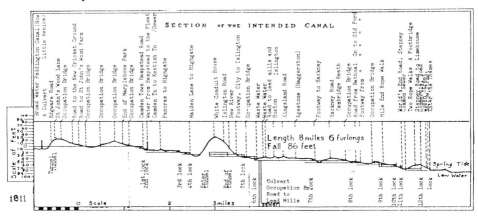

Section of the Regent's Canal

In reality the canal winds along the contour, but this section has been straightened out. It shows tunnels at Maida Hill and Islington and the fall of the land between Paddington and Limehouse.

Saving water was very important. An average lock on the Grand Junction Canal holds 50,000 gallons of water, lost each time a boat passes through.. Water from the higher reach flows down to the lower level and fresh water has to be provided from somewhere to replace it. The Welsh Harp, for example, like many other apparently natural stretches of water, is nothing less than a reservoir built to top up the canal. There is no Welsh Harp on the first Ordnance Survey map. Water was also fed into the canal from Hampstead Heath, through a pipe near the Stationary Engine Vaults.

On 14 October 1812 work began on experimental locks at Camden Town, designed by Sir William Congreve (the inventor, not the dramatist). These were 'hydro-dynamic locks', planned to save water. Two large water-tight steel boxes (or caissons) were connected by chains and pulleys. These failed at a cost of £12,000 and had to be replaced in 1814 at yet more expense. Instead, the Company installed double locks with an inter-connecting paddle, a system which saved nearly half a lock of water each operation. By 1816 the canal had reached Camden Town and opened a branch (now filled in) to Cumberland Market, but troubles persisted.

When the canal reached Agar Town, near King's Cross, there was a pitched battle with pick-axe handles between canal navvies and the workmen employed by Agar. He was the grasping lawyer-landlord who had built Agar Town as a speculative venture, and now saw yet another way of making money. He sued the Canal Company for trespass, won £1,500, holding up work for several months. Then Thomas Hosmer, the

Treasurer and one of those who first proposed the canal, ran off with the Company's funds, was caught and transported. There was still no through route to the Thames and until there was, the canal could not hope to make a profit. The board had to raise still more money, but they also faced another problem.

The Water Companies had opposed the canal vigorously from the start. Hampstead Water Company had two sets of ponds on Hampstead Heath and a pumping station in East Heath Road. From the Lower Pond in East Heath Road ran a line of pipes supplying water to Fleet Road, Camden Town and along Hampstead Road to a reservoir at what is now Tolmer's Square. A similar pipe ran from the Highgate ponds to supply Kentish Town. Further along the proposed canal route, Rennie, of the New River Company, which had no fewer than sixty pipes radiating from New River Head, opposed the cutting of the canal vociferously.

Water pipes were then mere elm tree trunks, bored out, joined end to end and laid only a hand's breadth below the surface, so a canal several feet deep would destroy the pipes. As the water flowed by gravity, the pipes could not be raised or lowered without much leaking. At this period water could not be carried to the upper floors of houses because of lack of pressure, so raising or lowering the pipe would not have helped. Nor would pumping have solved the problem as the water would have sprayed out at every joint. Eventually the Canal was forced through by Act of Parliament and from that time on the Hampstead Water Company supplied water to the district north of the Canal only.

All this controversy cost the Canal Company litigation, time and money. In the end it was only mass unemployment and the threat of violent public disorder that finally got the job done. By 1817 the country was in a post-war slump because, with the defeat of Napoleon at Waterloo in 1815, all war work stopped. Supply contracts were terminated overnight. For example, Isambard Brunel, father of Isambard Kingdom Brunel, who built the Great Western Railway, had built a factory to mass-produce army boots and was left with nobody to buy them. Other manufacturers were in a similar plight. There was no work for the returning soldiers, who became vagrants and a heavy weight on their local parishes. In Paddington, a hundred years earlier, after another war, the church wardens recorded, 'Two shillings paid for bread and cheese to 24 poor sailors on their travels'. Anything to get them out of your parish and pass on the responsibility to someone else. The provision for destitute people had not changed in the following century, so local parishes were feeling the strain.

It was in this setting of ex-soldiers roaming the country looking for jobs that the Poor Employment Act of 1817 was passed and the government agreed to lend the Regent's Canal Company £200,000 to complete the canal. A century later, similar agitation at the end of yet another long war, brought about the Russian Revolution. It is true that in 1817 the British government was more concerned to create work and so buy peace for itself than to complete the Canal, but it served to finish the project.

By 1820 the Canal was finally open. Midlands manufacture could be carried smoothly to the waiting ships in the London Docks and from there to the whole world. Even so, the Canal was never to be a financial success because it was swamped by its accumulated debts. Earlier canals had made a lot of money, but the Regent's Canal arrived too late. In a few years the railways would thunder into London and gradually steal the canal's trade.

Camden Lock

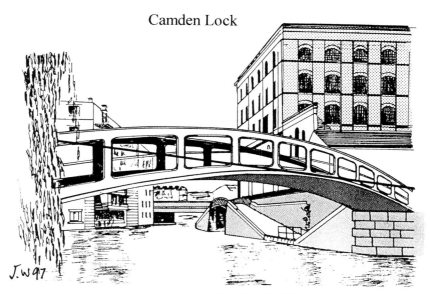

The Diagonal or Roving Bridge

The drawing shows the Diagonal Bridge, with the Interchange building behind to the right. William Huck's bottling store is on the left. The barge entrance to Interchange, below the towpath is called the Dead Dog Hole, for reasons which will become clear.

Regent's Canal bridges are in all shapes and sizes, some narrowed to take only a single barge, while others are high and free-flying, spanning the valley near the Zoo. By far the best known is the Roving, or Turnabout Bridge, in the middle of Camden Lock. Here one lingers to survey the scene north and south and wonder why such a long bridge was built when a short one would have cost less. All the other bridges go straight across. Why the difference?

The bridge is cast in four pieces. Each side of the bridge consists of two halves, joined at the centre with large bolts. At the ends of the bridge the top rails swell into massive blocks, each of which carries two 1.25 inch diameter steel bars, seen in the drawing above and on the next page. They run from the top of the bridge, but the curvature carries them down to below the footpath at the centre. They are threaded at 12 threads to the inch, a very shallow thread for a bar of this diameter, more like a thread used for a pipe than solid metal. The bars must have been threaded by hand and this shallow thread was the only one available. The whole bridge is an interesting example of engineering before the more powerful machines required by the Railway Age were developed.

But why a diagonal bridge? The answer is in the granite cobbles, steeply pitched to give a grip to horses' hooves. Each one is polished by wear as if ready for a geologist's lens. This surface has been produced by a couple of centuries of hard wear by workmen in industrial boots, shod heel and toe with iron studs and especially by the heavy shoes of cart horses, for horses knew this bridge well. The canal towpath is on the north bank only, so consider the problem of moving a mass of horse-drawn barges travelling in both directions through two locks.

A barge coming down-stream from Regent's Park was towed by the barge's own horse. The tow rope was released as the boat approached the locks and, while it still had enough forward movement, it was steered into whichever lock was being lowered at the time. On the other hand, barges travelling up-stream were raised by the water to the level of the Lock Basin but when they reached the top they had no forward motion. These barges stayed still and had to be towed. It was easy to attach a rope to the barges near the north bank as it was next to the towpath and then for the horse to continue the tow towards Paddington. However, the barges which had come up in the south lock had to be towed across to the towpath bank before they could continue their journey. This was the purpose of the Roving Bridge.

A horse drew the barge from the south lock to the foot of the bridge and the tow rope was then detached. A second rope was lowered from the bridge and another horse pulled the barge across to the opposite bank. The tow rope dragged against the the thick top rail of the bridge, slowly hauling the barge over to the north bank against the flow of the current. This was hard work and it would have been even more difficult if the bridge had been at right angles to the canal. As it was, the ropes cut deep grooves into the bridge rail and into the stones of the towpath bank.

Grooves worn in the handrail of the bridge by innumerable tow ropes.

Arrived on the towpath side, the bargeman quickly unfastened the rope without slowing the boat and freed the horse. The man who had been leading the horse, turned it round and, with a slap on its flank, sent it back unattended across the bridge to the other bank. There it waited patiently to tow yet another boat across the bridge. Meanwhile, the barge horse took over again for the level walk to Uxbridge.

This towing problem was so complicated that special horses were used. Ordinary barge horses towed their barges to and from the lock, but at Camden Town the barges had to be worked by specially trained horses. These were so familiar with the routine that they crossed Chalk Farm Road and went down the slope to the lower level, or went back across the Roving Bridge to the southern bank, unattended.

A view from the south bank, with the market beyond

Park Village East

In 1995, two fine houses from the beginning of the nineteenth century were carefully restored. They are in Park Village East and can be seen from the Gloucester Road Bridge, at the top of Parkway. Numbers 2 and 4, the first two houses in the road were built in the 1830s but, owing to the unusual pattern of short-term tenancies, very few changes had been made to them over a hundred and seventy years. Perhaps officers in the Barracks nearby leased them for short periods and then moved on, forming a moving tenancy. The houses had been just patched, so that they survived in almost their original form. This, and the fact that the buildings are listed Grade II, meant that they had to be restored with care and made it possible for them to be examined closely.

The modern view from Gloucester Road Bridge is a puzzle. The bridge, elaborately built with trefoil, terracotta sides, bridges only a shallow trench. The houses stand in a slight valley and the gardens go down in steps. Originally, the houses were built with short rear gardens, immediately above a tow path and a Navigable Cut. This Cut was a branch canal from the Regent's Canal to Cumberland Basin. It was all part of John Nash's plan for Cumberland Basin to replace the original Haymarket, just south of Piccadilly Circus. This had become valuable housing land, so a replacement was required and Cumberland Basin was ideally positioned for bringing in hay by barge. Robert Bevan painted the hay carts in Cumberland Market several times.

During the Second World War the Navigable Cut was filled in with bomb debris, so that the Cut and the Cumberland Basin ceased to function. After the War, the Crown gave the pieces of canal bed and tow path behind the different houses to the house-holders. Thus their rear gardens took on a three-stepped form – garden, tow-path and canal bed. Over half a century these unusual gardens have matured and trees planted immediately after 1945 are now well grown. The rear of the houses continues to be 'picturesqe', in the fashion of the late eighteenth century. From the Gloucester Road bridge, which now spans a shallow wooded valley instead of a canal, the houses could be on some Bavarian hillside.

2 and 4 Park Village East, South Elevation

The further garden level

The canal bed level

The tow path level

The original garden level

The three-stepped gardens after the canal was filled in.

2 and 4 Park Village East, North Elevation

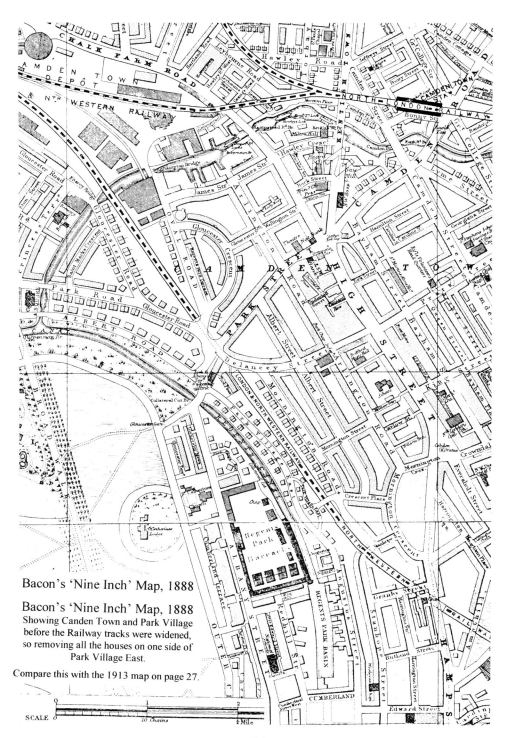

Bacon's 'Nine Inch' Map, 1888

Bacon's 'Nine Inch' Map, 1888
Showing Camden Town and Park Village
before the Railway tracks were widened,
so removing all the houses on one side of
Park Village East.

Compare this with the 1913 map on page 27.

SCALE

16

The History

Nash's Regent's Park development incorporated an entire range of house sizes and styles. Within the Park were large villas set in their own grounds for the very rich, and imposing stucco terraced palaces for the wealthy. Outside the Park were middle class villas in Park Village and the markets and barracks, each with their working class housing, near the Cumberland Basin. It was built as a complete new town on the edge of London. Park Village, Camden Town, Harlow – New Towns will be a theme of this book.

John Nash saw the romantic possibilities of the new Regent's Canal which was being built around the northern edge of his new Regent's Park. On the way to the new hay market which he was planning in Cumberland Basin, would be a secluded, peaceful valley bordering the canal. He envisaged a pretty 'village' on its banks, as an annexe to his noble Corinthian terraces in Regent's Park itself. In stucco, with tall windows leading out to wooded gardens overlooking the canal. On the edge of London, they would be the equivalent of Blaize Hamlet, which Nash had already built on the outskirts of Bristol in 1810.

He wrote to the Office of Woods and Forests:-

> ' --- These 2 plots being without the pale of the park and in the vicinity of the Barracks are only calculated for houses of the smallest class (4th rate houses) and it has occurred to me that if they were considered together as one plot of ground and the Houses, though small, scattered about in an irregular manner as Cottages with plantations between them, a very delightful Village might be formed through which the Canal would pass, and if arranged with Taste and the Buildings truly partake of the Cottage Character, the whole would be an ornamental feature and command, though humble, yet the better class of people who require such small buildings.'[1] [1]

Thus there would be two villages, East and West, separated by the Canal. Many years later, before the Second World War, a ferryman with a small stone hut on the towpath used to ferry people from one bank to the other. By then the canal was so quiet that kingfishers nested in the bank, and there can have been little demand for the ferryman's services. He must have taken on the traditional role of the hermit in a eighteenth century Romantic landscape. John Nash would have savoured that.

The two villages were built over a period of about fifteen years, the earliest houses by Nash and the later ones by his stepson Pennethorne. In the event the designs were altered from the 'humble cottages' first mentioned,[i] to larger, middle-class residences. More closely packed and in more orderly rows than his first layout suggested, they soon became popular.

Architectural historians have tended to be interested almost exclusively in the villas at the north end of street, those designed by Nash himself. John Summerson describes them as 'a quaint set of variations on the styles, starting at the north with Nos. 2 and 4, castellated Tudor, going on to the broad-eaved Italian (Nos. 6 and 8), and then something with eaves of the sort usually considered Swiss, then various versions of the classical vernacular and so rapidly descending to the nondescript'. [2]

In the two years 1828 and 1829, Thomas Courtney Lancefield took 99 year leases on no fewer than twenty-two house sites in Park Village East. This was a speculative venture which would take a number of years to complete and helps to account for the variety of designs to be found along the road. (Public Record Office, Ref: MPZ 14)

Nos. 2 and 4 Park Villlage East

Nos. 6 and 8 Park Village East were built in 1824, while Nos. 2 and 4, which had been planned and leased at the same date, were not built until the 1830s. Thus the latter are probably not the work of Nash, but of Pennethorne.

Originally each house had only a narrow garden, with the towpath and canal below. Thus when the first tenants moved into the houses their furniture and probably they themselves, with their children and servants, pots and pans and the remains of yesterday's dinner, may have arrived by canal. One of Pickford's barges could have brought them from far away, tied up immediately below the house and the men carried in the furniture through the garden doors.

The York and Albany public house, named after the dukedoms of George III's second son, Frederick Augustus, was built between 1824 and 1826, but when the railway came in the 1830s, it ceased to be a Picturesque country pub on the edge of the country. Later it was extended and then completely destroyed in 1878. When the Gloucester Road Bridge was rebuilt on a northern alignment, to straighten out the connection with Parkway, a new York and Albany was built in glazed Doulton Ware. About 1900 a Riding Academy was built at the rear of the pub. This was later taken over by the London Zoo as a quarantine building, so that giraffes overtopping the fences, the roaring of wild cats and the screeching of parrots, added a bizarre touch to the area.

Park Village West, being nearer the Park and away from the railway, had always been better regarded than Park Village East, which was to develop a rather unsavoury reputation about the turn of the century, as Gillian Tindall has recorded.[3] The Booth Survey of Poverty, of 1889, had some hard things to say, as will be seen in that chapter (p. 70).

The most famous occupant of No. 4 Park Village East was Sidney Webb. Sidney and Beatrice Webb, founders of the London School of Economics and early members of the Labour movement, first started corresponding in 1881. Sidney Webb, still trying to establish himself as a journalist, lived with his father at No 4 from 1890 until his marriage in 1892. For years Beatrice had had to nurse her father in distant Minchinhampton and it was not until his death that she felt free to marry. Thus some of Sidney's letters were addressed to her from Park Village. When they married they took a lease on a house, 41 Grosvenor Road, Pimlico, on the Embankment, 'with a wide view across the river to Lambeth Palace and St Paul's,' but apparently they still retained some control over No 4 Park Village East.

The picturesque effect of Park Village East was partly destroyed when the four-track line of the London and North-Western Railway was widened between 1900 and 1906. One side of Park Village East was demolished and a huge retaining wall built. From Hampstead Road, Park Village now looks like some distant hill-top village seen glistening in the sun, across the great valley of railway tracks. For years the road was a cul-de-sac and children could ride horses there in safety, but there is now a connection across the railway bridge, with Hampstead Road.

From 1903-1912 No 4 was used as the headquarters of a Yeomanry regiment. After the First World War the lease was taken by Mrs Ethyl Mary Wood, the then recently widowed daughter of Quintin Hogg and sister of the first Viscount Hailsham. Mrs

Wood, a progressive woman in her own right, was a governor of Regent Street Polytechnic, which had been founded by her father, and was awarded a CBE in 1920.

The branch canal was filled in with bomb debris, so that today there appears to be no reason for a bridge at Gloucester Road. From the Regent's Park side of the bridge it could be a mere 'folly', put up by some landscape gardener like Repton, to close off a view; or designed by Nash himself to keep the outside world away from his exclusive Regent's Park estate. Today the bridge rises only a couple of metres above the turf, but up to 1941 it was a canal bridge like all the others, standing high above the canal.

Some people can remember as children being perched on the parapet of the bridge to see the barges go past. Far below was the water, with grimy boat children waving back – children who lived in a different world, travelling on long voyages to distant towns and bringing their mysterious cargoes back to Cumberland Basin. Children who walked familiarly with horses, seldom going to school, living a wandering life far removed from settled Camden Town. These were children of romance.

One can stand there on Gloucester Road Bridge, at the junction with Albany Street, with the traffic swirling behind, and look over into the wooded valley of the canal. These peaceful Pennethorne houses seem unaffected by the din. It is Osbert Lancaster's 'Drayneflete Revealed', come to life.

Local children played by the canal and swam in it. From above, gentlemen threw in pennies for the brave boys to dive for and clapped when they came to the surface again, holding up the coin in triumph. If someday the land below the bridge is excavated, a careful archaeologist will find the old towpath and the canal bed lined with puddled clay. In the silt above there may be a few pennies which were never retrieved, old bicycles, stolen purses emptied of their contents, a knife, or some other instrument which could once have been a murder weapon.

The Construction of the Houses

Examination of Numbers 2 and 4 Park Village East showed that parts of the houses were poorly built originally. John Nash was often criticised for his workmanship but it was always pressure on price that really drove the industry. For economy reasons, brick-layers were not allowed to throw away any bricks, or pieces of brick, so some walls were made up of half-bricks and odd ends, with no bonding between them. Only the mortar was holding up parts of these buildings. When the houses were restored in 1995, the builders had to be particularly careful with the walls holding the conical spire. When removing the outside rendering, half bricks began to fall out and the situation became extremely dangerous.. At one time the Clerk of Works had eleven steel pins inserted through the walls below the spire and did not leave the room during working hours for three weeks. His food was brought in to him as he refused to leave the room while anyone else was in there. Strain gauges in all the walls would reveal any movement vertically or horizontally, but they had to be watched continuously, as any movement would have been sudden and people could have been killed.

Instead of removing the rendering in the modern manner, with pneumatic hammers, all the work had to be done by hand, exposing a small part without juddering the building, replacing with new bricks properly bonded, waiting for the mortar to set, and only then moving on to another small area. It would have been far cheaper to have demolished the conical roof and rebuilt, but this was a Grade II building, so demolition was out of the question.

The Gutter Construction

When the houses were built, it was the fashion to conceal the gutters behind fretted wooden barge boards. The original gutters were made of oak lined with sheet lead, but because they were concealed, the damage caused by this type of construction was hidden from view. Lead always 'creeps', because it is heavy. When it expands in the heat of summer, it moves downwards. In winter it contracts, but again downwards because of its weight. With this downward creeping movement, the lead slowly pulled away from its nails. After a time the sheet lead had become completely detached from the oak support and water penetrated behind the lead, saturating the walls. They became so wet that when the house was restored and a new damp proof course had been inserted, it took months for the building to dry out, despite the fact that 1995 was a particularly dry summer.

Finding a good modern solution to the gutter problem was not easy. The fretted bargeboards had to be retained, so the new gutters would still be hidden. What would happen in the next hundred years and how could the architect ensure that the gutter would not fail again? After much searching, a very deep aluminium gutter protected by an impervious plastic coating and with neoprene joints, was found in France. This gutter is as near indestructible as can be, while the deep section will cope with flash downpours. It should keep the walls dry for years to come

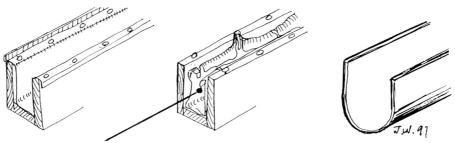

The gutter in 1950, with the lead pulled away by 'creeping'.

The new double-depth gutter in aluminium coated in plastic and with neoprene joints.

East Elevation

The Window Construction

The window construction came as a great surprise. When these houses were built, architects were really designers. Builders knew their materials well and built in traditional ways, so that architects could leave the actual building to them. Architects provided the overall design drawings, but at that time no architect would have thought of providing details of window construction. Given the shape and position of the windows, the builder was expected to get on with it. However, this was a strange moment in architectural history – a short moment when the builder did not know what to do.

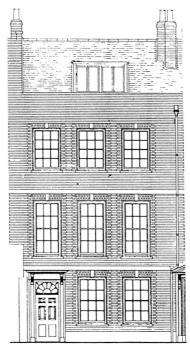

Typical Regency windows with brick piers between them
All sashes can be raised and lowered.

The shape of the windows in Park Avenue East is Tudor, with four-centre tracery, but instead of being casement windows, they are sashes. The joiner who made them would have served his apprenticeship in the Regency period and learnt to build sash windows between brick piers. The Regency house had a range of single windows on each floor in which both the top and bottom halves of each window could be raised and lowered. Each sash had counter weights, one on either side, running in hollow boxes. The pair of weights exactly equalled the weight of the sash, so that the sash would stay in any chosen position without rising or falling. This window system had worked well for the whole of the eighteenth century. When, at the beginning of the nineteenth century, the architect gave the builder these particular drawings, with several windows side by side, the joiner tried to build them as sashes but could not find room for enough weights.

21

A Regency window always has a brick pier on either side and therefore room for four sash weights. The Park Village East had several windows side by side, with only solid mullions between them. There were only two brick piers outside the set of two, three, or four windows, instead of two piers for each single window. Each moving sash needs a pair of weights, one on each side, so only two sashes in the complete array could move, however many windows there were in a row. One sash cord ran in the box next to the sash, but the other had to run across the complete window to the further wall.

It was not until Pugin built the House of Commons, with casement windows similar to the casements used by Tudor builders instead of sashes, that we had a true Tudor Gothic Revival building. Over the years, many windows in the two Park Villages have been converted to casements as these give better ventilation. These few survivors are rare and represent a strange period in the history of joinery.

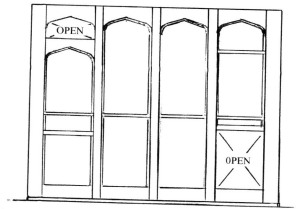

Picturesque Tudor Gothic windows at 2-4 Park Village East.
Only the top left and bottom right sashes can open.

Plan showing the two pairs of weights in their boxes and solid mullions between the sashes, with no room for more weights.

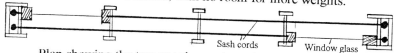

Plan showing the two opening sashes with their sash cords.   J.w97.
Other sashes have been omitted.

From the hall rises a fine staircase with very restrained iron banisters and a Cuban Mahogany handrail. Much ironwork is elaborate, ornate, but these banisters are simple rectangular bars with just a few decorated by shallow casting. The hall has an eigthteenth century quietness and elegant restraint. The upper floors are even more simple, in painted wood, while the stairs down to the kitchens are cut York Stone, with a mere iron handrail as thin as a fishing rod. Below again, the steps down to the cellar reveal that the York Stone steps, which have straight cut edges above, have been left rough below. As a result, going down into the cellar is like venturing down into some Megalithic tomb.

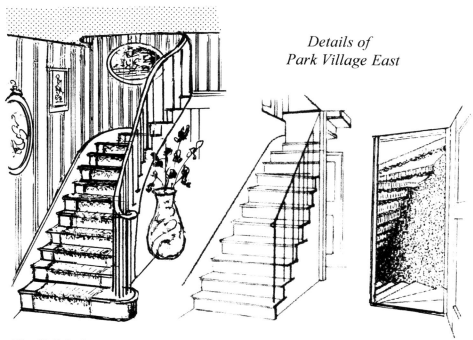

*Details of
Park Village East*

The Hall Staircase
with a Cuban Mahogany
handrail and iron banisters

The Kitchen Staircase
with York Stone steps and
wrought iron banisters

The Cellar Steps with
York Stone steps undressed
on the undersides

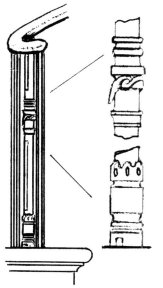

The Banister Curl, with a detail
of the central cast iron post

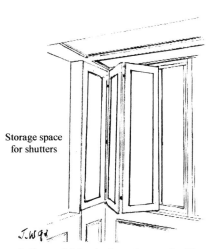

Storage space
for shutters

A three-fold window shutter half open,
with its storage space on the left The
shutters fold back and become part
of the room panelling.

Plans for Cumberland Basin and the Park Village houses

This map shows that Park Village West had been built, but only three pairs of houses had been started in Park Village East. The two Park Villages were designed as a more modest area of housing outside the 'pale' of Regent's Park itself. Cumberland Market would be an area of trading and business, but the sketched outlines of streets show that houses were planned to spread seamlessly from Park Village West to Mornington Crescent. When the railway line to Euston cut the deep ravine between the two, it separated them surgically. They would become different worlds.

Cumberland Market

Cumberland Basin attracted many factories over the years. A vinegar works, piano factories, gramophone record makers ----. The list goes on and on. Many servants who worked in the large houses in Regent's Park lived in the small, terraced houses round the basin. These were among the Camden Town houses which were to become so over-crowded because of the demolition of houses elsewhere. Streets disappeared to make room for Euston, King's Cross, and St Pancras railway stations, and then for the rebuilding of the City of London in the 1860-80 period. Hundreds of homeless people had to crowd in wherever they could.

Looking at the area today, it is difficult to imagine the contrast with the old, industrial past. When the branch canal was filled in with bombing debris during the Second World War, the canal trade which

Bartlett & Britton map of 1834

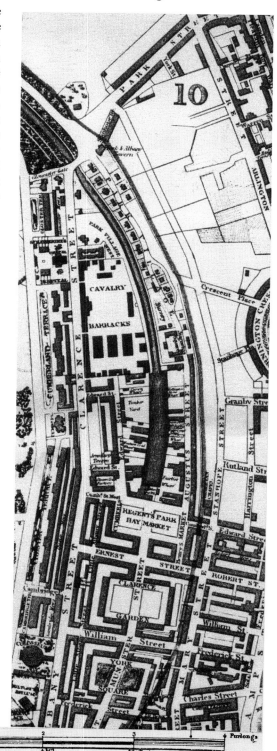

SCALE

had been slowing down for years, finally stopped. The Basin became allotments and the whole area was transformed into a vast housing estate. Now traffic rushes past in Hampstead Road on one side and Albany Street on the other. Between the two is a peaceful mass of flats, virtually free of traffic. It is a strange, isolated landscape, like a calm oasis between two traffic corridors, with its allotments cultivated as neatly as any garden.

The World of Elegance and the World of Work

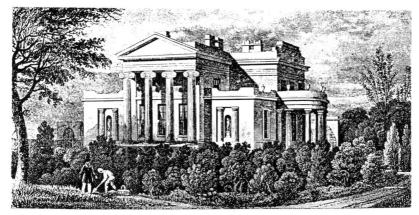

A Regent's Park villa. Grove House, now Nuffield Lodge.

Cumberland Market, by Robert Bevan. Private collection.

25

Contrasting Camden Town and Regent's Park

Walk from Portland Place Station along Albany Street, curve behind Park Village and Camden Town High Street to Inverness Market and Camden Lock and even today, you have two worlds all the way along, one on your left and one on your right. In Albany,there are blocks of working class flats and the Barracks on the right. The flats replaced dilapidated three-storey houses built round Cumberland Market – the workaday world of wharves, vinegar distillers, piano manufacturers, and servants. Today the street is wide, but its colours are drab.

Slip through one of the narrow openings on the left, go up the stairs and you find yourself in the stucco splendour of Nash's Regent's Park Terraces. It is like emerging from the backstage gloom of a theatre, stumbling past the rows of props and stays supporting the scenery, into a flood-lit stage of double-height plaster columns and Corinthian capitals, with a singer in centre stage hitting top C. The contrast is overwhelming. Today one can still experience the difference between the Regent's Park palaces, built in the 1820s to be approached by horse and carriage from Westminster, along the newly built Regent's Street, sweeping through Portland Place, round Park Crescent and so into the Park; and the working class district next door, built to house the servants.

The same contrast continues. Walk from Hampstead Road along Mornington Street and you are suddenly in the ornate stucco of Park Village, built by Nash and Pennethorne. The fact that the Village was later sliced in half by the railway makes the change even more dramatic. Half way along Camden High Street, is the narrow tunnel which used to be the side entrance to the Bedford Music Hall. Go through and you reach Arlington Road and Albert Street, larger, brighter and more expensive.

In Inverness Street Market you walk from the stalls and typical three-storey Camden Town houses, now shops and cafes, into the large stucco houses of Gloucester Crescent beloved by media people. From there on, the railway and Camden Lock divide Primrose Hill from Chalk Farm as a cordon sanitaire, as they have done for over a hundred and fifty years. In 1995 a new road was tunnelled under the North London railway from Ferdinand Street, but it never penetrated through to Primrose Hill. The contrast remains. Chalk Farm is still literally on the wrong side of the tracks.

[1] Public Record Office, CES 2/778

[2] Summerson, Life and Work, p.128.

[3] The Fields Beneath, by Gillian Tindall, Pub. Temple Smith, London, 1977.
Information from Mrs Elizabeth Hoare, Simon Marks, of Purcell Miller Triton, and Mr W. H. H. Van Sickle.

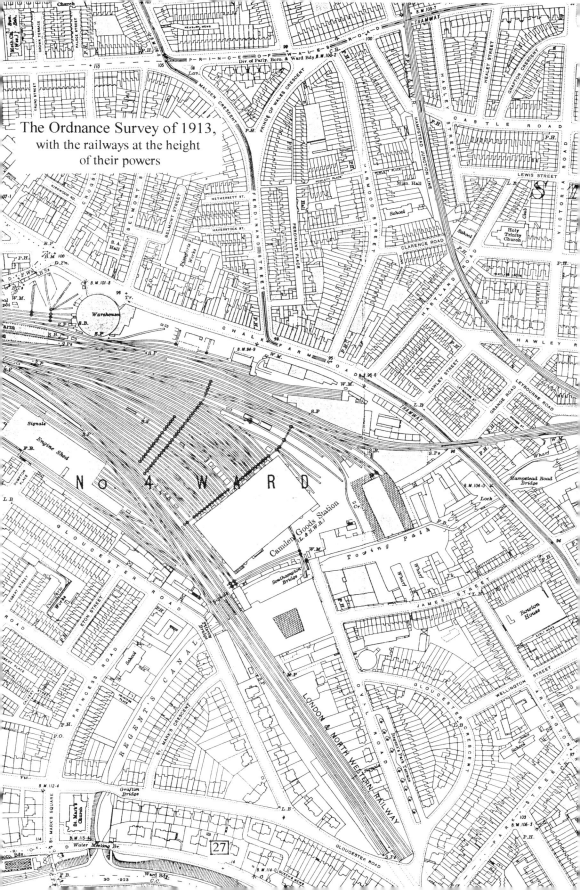

The Ordnance Survey of 1913,
with the railways at the height
of their powers

The London and Birmingham Railway

At first, the Regent's Canal made very little difference to the locality. Camden Town was a new town laid out in the fields on the road to Hampstead. Hampstead had been well known as a health resort for many years, but Camden Town was just one of a number of new towns being created round London. Camden Town, Agar Town, Somers Town, there were any number of hopeful landlords poised around London, waiting eagerly for the builders to arrive and make their fortunes. Canal barges passed by to the north of them all, but at first few barges stopped, except perhaps to unload some bricks or timber. There was no industrial life.

The Gas Works, the tile kilns and two dust scavenging yards in Maiden Lane were not far away to the east, but at Camden Town there was no real industry. People living in the new town enjoyed their green suburb and looked towards the City of London for work. To canal bargees, Camden Town was a place of anonymous fields somewhere on the way to the docks. Only when the railway arrived and Camden Town became the natural exchange point for canal and rail, did the situation change. Suddenly Camden had an industrial future.

When the London & Birmingham Railway set up offices at 69 Cornhill EC3, in 1830, the Company announced that the railway was to terminate at Camden Town. Rails would pass either under or above existing roads and never be at the same level, so that road traffic would not be inconvenienced. In fact, the London & Birmingham was built on an embankment at Camden Town and had no railway arches or viaducts except over the canal. Later, Primrose Hill was linked to the London Docks and the North London Line via Camden Road Station. Since Primrose Hill was so high, the new railway had to be built on arches and these arches were to play a large part in the industrial development of the area.

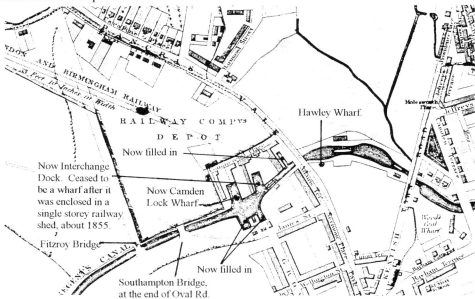

Britton, Bartlett & Davies' map of the [Parliamentary} Borough of St Marylebone, 1834

The original announcement by the company said that railway lines would be carefully fenced everywhere and opposite 'gentlemen's residences' the fencing would be ornamental. It claimed that carriages made little noise, while the engines were so clean and silent that nobody would notice they were there. The Act specified that trains must not make smoke. Therefore coke, which burns cleanly, was used. Only later, when engines were invented which could consume their own smoke within the length of the boiler flue, was coal used as a fuel. Thus there was some substance in the claim about cleanliness. Railway engines at this period were no larger than a good-sized lorry and capable of drawing 600 tons at twelve miles an hour.

The Britton, Bartlett & Davies map shown opposite

The 1834 map shows the triangle of land bought by the Railway Company, with the proposed London & Birmingham line marked in. It was then to terminate north of the canal. Only a year later, in 1835, an Amending Act was passed authorising the Company to extend its line 'to a certain place called Euston Grove on the North side of Drummond Street, near Euston Square'. Trains would have to cross the Canal at a height which allowed boats to pass below. Height was no problem to civil engineers, who were used to carrying canals and viaducts across great gorges, but the ground between Camden Town and Euston already dropped sharply. The fact that the railway had to be raised at Camden Town and lowered to go under the roadway at Hampstead Road, increased the slope considerably. The engineers would finish with a gradient of 1 in 69. This was very steep indeed for a locomotive of that period, so the Company decided to detach the locomotives at Camden Town and allow the carriages to free-wheel down to Euston under the control of a brakeman, or 'Bankrider'. On the journey out of Euston the carriages would be man-handled as far as the bridge just outside Euston Station and there be attached to a 7 inch circumference continuous rope 12,240 feet long, to pull them up to Camden Town. There were two ropes, one up and one down, driven by two stationary condensing engines, built into great vaults at Camden.

The Stationary Engine House under construction, April 1837, with the Passenger Engine House behind.   Lithograph by J.C.Bourne

The Stationary Engine House under construction, April 1837

Bourne's drawing on the previous page shows the Stationary Engine House being built, with huge wooden centring frames for the brick vaults and massive retaining walls.[1] The engines were in the underground vaults, with two huge chimneys which were to dominate the scene for years. Behind is the Locomotive Engine House.

Robert Stephenson, the company's chief engineer, designed both of these, but he did not design the Roundhouse, which was not erected until 1846-7.

Keeping the Incline ropes tight

The continuous loops of rope which raised and lowered the trains had to be kept taut at all times if they were to work properly, yet they expanded as soon as strain was put on them. They also contracted and expanded according to the weather. Robert Stephenson's solution to this problem is shown here. Each loop ran round a sheave mounted on a moveable trolley and the rope was pulled tight by a heavy weight which was free to rise and fall in a deep shaft.

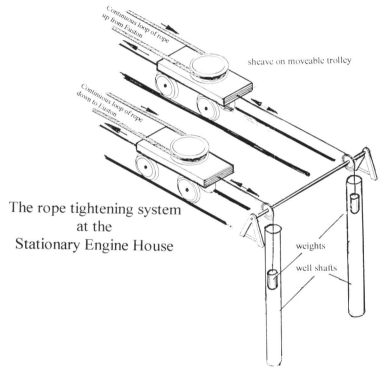

Continuous loop of rope up from Euston

sheave on moveable trolley

Continuous loop of rope down to Euston

The rope tightening system
at the
Stationary Engine House

weights

well shafts

The Incline from Camden Town to Euston was not straight so (to accommodate the curve) the rope ran through both vertical and sloping sheaves. These were fixed in cast-iron cases bedded in the ballasting.[2] The winding engine remained in service until 1844 when more powerful locomotives were able to take the trains into and out of Euston and the rope winding system could be abandoned.

Plan of the Stationary Engine House

Key

B   Four boilers
C   Two chimneys
D   Two driving wheels
E   Two engines
P   Four pulley wheels. The pulley wheels were unequally sized, with the inner ones 12 ft in diameter and the outer ones 20 ft
T   Tightening sheave mounted on a truck
W   Well for Counterbalance Weight.

These engines hauled the continuous ropes which raised and lowered the trains from Camden to Euston. The engines were stationary: only the ropes moved. They were completely different from the locomotive engines which normally pulled the trains.

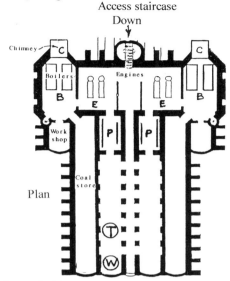

Plan

The San Francisco Cable Cars

The cables have long gone from Camden Town but American visitors will know of a system like it which is still in operation. Andrew Smith Hallidie was born in London in 1836 and as a young lad he probably watched the railway carriages being hauled up the slope from Euston. His father, Andrew Smith, was an engineer and inventor who held a patent for making wire rope. Hallidie later took this name in honour of his godfather and uncle, Sir Andrew Hallidie, who had been physician to King William IV and to Queen Victoria.

Hallidie trained as a mechanic, moving in 1852 to San Francisco, where he tried his luck in the goldfields, did blacksmithing work, built various cable systems for transporting ore, and cable suspension bridges over a number of rivers, including the Sacremento. In the end he devoted his time solely to the manufacture of wire rope.

In 1873 he tested the first of the famous San Francisco Cable Cars which are pulled up the steep hills by cables. A continuous cable runs underground in a narrow channel, where it can be heard grinding away all day. A 'grip' below the car holds it on to the cable. Where the route curves, the cables pass round a pulley and the Gripman up above has to release the grip, allow the momentum of the car to carry it beyond the pulley and then re-grip the cable. This calls for such great strength and alertness that most applicants for the job fail the test.

As motor cars developed, the cable cars became obsolete. However, public protest kept them running, partly as a tourist attraction, and in the Cable Car Barn in Washington Street, visitors can still see the same system of keeping the cables taut, with a pulley on a moving wagon, as Hallidie probably watched and remembered in Camden in the eighteen-forties.

The Highgate Cable Tramway, 1884

In 1873, the year Hallidie tested his first cable car in San Francisco, horse-drawn trams linked the City of London with Highgate Archway, but Highgate Hill was far too steep for horse trams. Encouraged by the success in San Francisco, the Highgate Cable Tramway was opened in 1884, the first in Europe. Thus the cable system, which had become obsolete on the railway between Camden and Euston, was repatriated from the other side of the world. As in San Francisco, the cables were below the ground, under a third rail and for some years the line worked well. However, after a horrific accident in which a cable snapped, the line was suspended and only reopened in 1909 after electrification [3]

After this digression, let us return to the early days of the London and Birmingham Railway.

The First Railway Engine House

The First Engine House can be seen in the background of the engraving of 'The Stationary Engine House under construction', which was shown on page 29. The two buildings were completely different, with different jobs to do. One hauled the engines up the slope from Euston, while the other was an engine storage house. The Engine House, designed by Robert Stephenson and built by William and Lewis Cubitt in 1836-7, is the subject of three lithographs by John C. Bourne. The building, with access through two large archways, was about 180 feet square and could hold up to 30 engines.

The First Railway Engine House seen from the north, in 1838.
Sketch made from the J. C. Bourne lithograph

In the distance are the twin chimneys of the Stationary Engine House, with the Locomotive Engine Shed to the left. The main line curves round to the right between the two chimneys, while the line to the Locomotive Engine House branches off it and then branches again towards the two arched entrances to the shed.. This area is now covered by the Gilbey's Yard and Juniper Crescent housing, and Safeway's supermarket.

The London & Birmingham Railway Incline under Park Street (now Parkway) 1836, by J. C. Bourne. Note the curved cast-iron roof girders of the cut-and-cover tunnel.

The London & Birmingham Railway Bridge at Camden Town under construction.
By J.C.Bourne, pub. September 1838 [4] (Drawn from the vicinity of the later Oval Road)

J.C.Bourne.

J.C.Bourne, who was called 'the Piranesi of the railways', made a most impressive lithograph of the Fitzroy Railway Bridge being built across the Canal. Today it is just one bridge lost among a long succession of bridges. Then, the meadows still came down to the edge of the water. This bridge was a foreign, industrial structure invading an almost rural landscape. To build it, men worked from barges, or in the open fields.

By 1837, Southampton Bridge, the road bridge at the end of Oval Road had been built, but it has been rebuilt since. On the other side of the railway, the bridge

33

intended for Gloucester Avenue, and called Fitzroy Bridge, had also been built. Hampstead Road Bridge had been there from the opening of the canal, but the Roving Bridge (Diagonal Bridge) had not yet been built. The horses towing the barges still had to pass via Commercial Place (now Camden Lock Place) and Hampstead Road to get from one bank to the other.

Artesian Wells

To obtain water for their engines the Company sunk an artesian well at Camden, 10 feet in diameter and 140 feet deep. The water obtained was pumped by a 27 horse power, high pressure steam engine into two large cisterns 110 feet above the level of the rails at Euston, to supply all Euston Station, all the Company houses and two hotels at Euston with 'the most beautiful water.' The only things which could not stomach the water were the boilers of the locomotives, which became thickly encrusted with the soda contained in the artesian well water. As a result the Company had to obtain purer water from The West Middlesex Water Works Company at great expense. Ordinary water for the engines was also taken from the canal.

There appear to have been two generations of wells. Bourne (1839) describes a well and tank at the original locomotive house. Another was sunk at the Passenger Engine house in 1846-7. This was at Camden Town, opposite the Roundhouse. Hence the high elevation quoted for the roof-top cisterns above Euston.

The East End of Primrose Hill Tunnel, October 1837 [5]

Pickfords at Camden Town, 1841

Pickfords were established as important carriers in the Canal Age, so that when the railways appeared, it was natural for them to carry goods by rail as well. Transport by Canal was reliable, but painfully slow. London to Birmingham, 110 miles as the crow flies, though far longer by the circuitous routes taken by the canals, took at least two and a half days. At twelve miles an hour, the early trains took about ten hours, so rail traffic was bound to increase.

Pickford's London headquarters were then at City Road Basin, but this was not suitable for future goods carriage, as it did not connect with any railway line. A completely new centre was required. Baxendale, the new manager who had come into Pickford's and was regenerating it, bought a plot of land on the south side of the Regent's Canal, at the top of Oval Road. He asked William Cubitt (1791-1863) to create a special building which could transfer goods efficiently between road, water and rail. [6]

Thomas Cubitt (1788-1885) was the famous master-builder who developed enormous areas of Clapham Common and Clapham Park, Bloomsbury, and Belgravia, while William split off from him in 1828 and developed particular expertise as a contractor for industrial buildings. His firm's name is frequently mentioned in connection with Pickford developments at this period. To add to the complication of Cubitt names, Lewis Cubitt (1799-1883) worked with both of his brothers. He had architectural training and became noted as a railway architect. There was also the other (Sir) William Cubitt, (1785-1861) a distant kinsman who was a noted civil engineer and worked alongside Lewis Cubitt. William and Lewis were the contractors for Euston Station and took over the work on the Camden depot when the previous contractor failed. Today, the more fashionable Thomas Cubitt is best known and may often be credited with work done by the whole family.

A portion of the upper works of Pickford's Depot, Camden Town [7]
Lithograph by Thomas Allom

The Construction

Pickford's building was erected on open ground adjacent to the railway line from Euston and on the southern edge of the canal. On the one acre site, William Cubitt created a building with hoists on the canal edge to load and unload from barges below. There was a private railway across the canal to the rear of the Railway's Goods Sheds. Originally erected in 1841-2, and extended in 1847, it had a main floor at railway level, with stables for the cartage horses at canal wharf level, beneath a vaulted floor. (See the illustration and also the map on the next page).

Inside the building were railway lines with turntables, so that wagons could be manoeuvred in all directions. Outside, the railway lines continued across the canal to the northern bank on two private bridges. One of these bridges ran shoulder to shoulder with the railway bridge, while the other stood on the site of the Pirate's Castle footbridge at the end of Oval Road. When Pickford's bridges reached the northern bank they joined the London North Western railway lines at two turntables. One of these turntables and a length of rail are now embedded in the cobbles in front of the modern Gilbey's Yard houses. The name 'Gilbey's Yard' is not quite correct as this was always railway land, not Gilbey's.

The idea of connecting road, rail and canal traffic in one building appears to have been originated by Pickfords and copied by many others. Indeed, Pickfords were so quick off the mark that the directors were able to celebrate the opening of their new building with an elaborate meal in 1841,[12] only six years after the railway opened.

As a carrier, the firm was responsible by law for goods for the whole journey, door to door. The Company had its own wagons, horses, and barges and warehouses. It also hired railway wagons and paid tolls by weight to each railway whose lines they used. Pickfords depended heavily on the London to Birmingham line and by 1846 was handling 1,600 tons a week, or 85,000 tons a year, about one tenth of all the goods the line handled.[13]

Pickford's shed burnt down in a dramatic fire in 1857 and was rebuilt, but the horses, which were rescued from the fire only in the nick of time, were rehoused in new stables in Gloucester Avenue, behind the Engineer public house. The Goad map of 1891 (four pages ahead) shows the horse tunnel which ran from the stables, under the road and the railway tracks to the horse slope on the north bank of the canal. It was a completely integrated system centred round the Railway Bridge and Oval Road. The Pickford building was the largest purpose-built warehouse on the railway at that date and cost about £40,000.

PICKFORD & CO.

FOREIGN AND GENERAL CARRIERS,

RAILWAY AGENTS,

Town
Carmen,
Furniture
Removers,
and
Wharfingers;

Also
Shipping,
Insurance,
and
Forwarding
Agents

Changes at Camden

At the start of any new industry there is always rapid change. Many designs quickly become obsolete; invention races ahead and everything is in a state of flux. Camden Station was built in 1837, just before Paddington, 1838, well before King's Cross in 1850, and far earlier than St Pancras in 1868.

Early engines were small and could be manoeuvred separately from their lightly-built tenders. At first the four-wheel engine was enough, but soon the heavier six-wheeled ones, with more weight and friction, and thus more traction, became necessary. This and other technical developments caused changes at Camden Town which other stations, built later, did not have to face.

The map below shows the positions of a number of buildings which are discussed later and may help the reader to keep track of events.

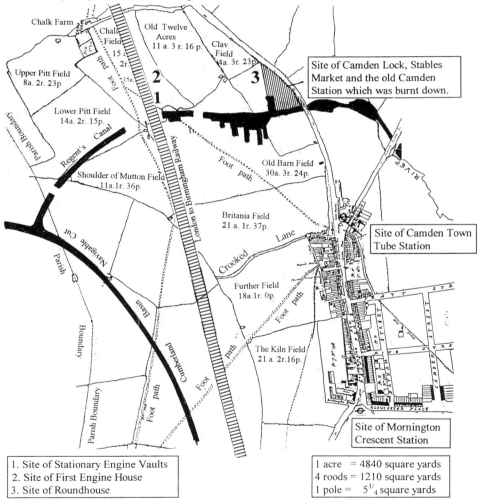

1. Site of Stationary Engine Vaults
2. Site of First Engine House
3. Site of Roundhouse

1 acre	= 4840 square yards
4 roods	= 1210 square yards
1 pole	= 5¼ square yards

A composite map of Camden Town Based on Tompson's Parish map of 1804, with later developments marked in.

Camden Town at the height of its industrial power.
At this time it conveyed goods by rail and water to the whole world.

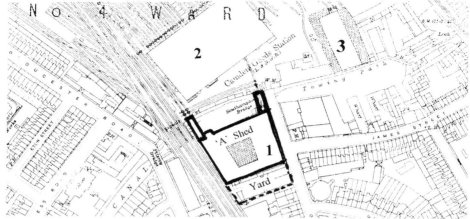

The Pickfords building (site 1) but in 1913, after they had left.

This Ordnance Survey map shows the situation long after Pickfords had left the building and when Gilbeys owned the site. By 1913 it very different from the early layout and has changed dramatically since, but explains some of the varied history of the site, including the two private bridges across the canal, which Gilbey's used to great advantage.[14]

Key to the map

1 **Site of Pickford's building** but when it had been rebuilt by Gilbey's and called 'A' Shed. The Pickfords building covered 1 acre and was enlarged in 1847. Enlarged again to 1½ acres when it was rebuilt in 1857 to fill the whole plot (as shown on this OS map).

2 **London & North Western Goods Shed**. Built in 1864 to replace several smaller goods sheds built in the 1840s, it had a plan area of 100,000 sq. ft. It was then the largest in the country and was further enlarged in the 1930s.

3 **Interchange Warehouse**. Present building was erected circa 1901-1905, over the top of the canal dock. 3 floors of warehousing above a railway goods shed with communication through trap doors to the canal dock below. It is discussed later in the text. The present building replaced a two-storey transport shed erected circa 1854-56 when the dock was enlarged. Before that, in the 1840s a railway line had been carried on a ramp down to cranes at the dockside.

New Buildings are Planned in 1846

Although in the original Act of 1833, before the Euston extension Act was passed, a passenger station was envisaged, there was never a Camden passenger station. Camden had a very different future. Despite the outspoken antagonism between the canal company and the railways, Camden Town was bound to expand rapidly as it was the natural exchange point between water and rail. For this reason, and because of the difficulty of dragging trains back up the slope from Euston, the railway Goods Department developed at Camden. Very little of the goods traffic continued through to Euston.

Soon a vast complex of lines had been built beside Chalk Farm Road. A goods station was opened in 1839, at the corner of Chalk Farm Road and Commercial Place, but it was destroyed by fire. When, in 1845, the Board of the London and Birmingham Railway decided to adopt the heavier and more powerful six-wheel engines, the turntables in the original Engine House, near Gloucester Avenue, had become too small. In 1846-7 two new buildings were planned: the New Passenger Engine House and the Luggage Engine House (now called the Roundhouse).

The Design of the Roundhouse

The Roundhouse is circular, with a span of 160 feet diameter, built in 9 inch white Suffolk brick and strengthened on the outside by a series of buttresses each 3 feet wide and about 14 feet apart. The roof is supported by a circle of 24 columns 80 feet in diameter, set in the centre of the building. These columns are 21 feet 9 inches high

'The New Great Circular Engine House', or 'Luggage Engine House', built for the London & Birmingham Railway.   From the illustrated London News, 1847

The edge of the turntable can be seen in the centre of the ring of pillars, with the rails running up to it. A fireman standing in the pit between the rails is shovelling out the ash from the previous engine.

and are interconnected to form a polygon of 24 sides. A lantern covered with rough plate glass is raised 4 feet 3 inches off the roof, with wooden louvres at the sides to exhaust steam and smoke. The building was designed to hold 23 engines, one between each pair of columns, with the 24th track left clear for entrance and exit. Each bay took one engine and its tender, with below it a long pit used for maintenance purposes and the removal of ash.

In the centre was a turntable 36 feet in diameter, the very reason for the building. All engines had to run on to the turntable in order to turn into their respective berths, which were a little longer than 36 feet. When supplied with coke and water each weighed about 50 tons. This weight, carefully balanced on the turntable, was pivoted round and the engine driven into its bay.

Earlier turntable houses had been polygonal. The one at Derby, for example, had sixteen sides, but in 1847 R.B.Dockray erected this circular building which was later called 'The Roundhouse'. The shape has advantages both economic and aesthetic. It is unlikely that it would have achieved such affection if it had been a more usual square or oblong.

Robert Benson Dockray

The Roundhouse seems to have been built in the far distant past and yet, while researching for this book in Camden History Archives, I met the grandson of a man who worked with Dockray. Mr Philip Sykes, a New Zealander, was in England and wanted to consult the file on the Roundhouse which I was already using. His maternal grandfather, William Murray, had been an assistant engineer to Dockray at the time when he was building the Roundhouse. William Murray later went to Australia, where he continued to build railways. Philip Sykes, father of the present Philip Sykes', arrived from New Zealand as Murray's assistant engineer, married Murray's daughter and carried her back to New Zealand with him. Here was I, in London, talking to the grandson of a man who had helped build the Roundhouse. Suddenly the building came alive and was new again.

Robert Dockray[9] was born in 1811, four years before the Battle of Waterloo, just about when the Regent's Canal was being planned. He came from a Quaker family and was educated in schools of the Society of Friends, at Kendal and Darlington, and of course Darlington was a famous railway town. He became an assistant engineer in the Stockton & Darlington Railway in 1835 and five years later, at the age of 29, became the resident engineer (under Robert Stephenson as consulting engineer). When the London and North Western Railway was formed, Dockray became responsible for its Southern Division. He supervised the construction of branches to Leamington, Peterborough, Banbury and Oxford. This was onerous work. Clearly he was a hardworking, conscientious man who made great demands on himself. The strain brought on neuralgia and he lost an eye. He resigned because of ill-health in 1852, at the age of only forty. He retired to Ramsgate, but returned to a railway house in Haverstock Hill, overlooking his Roundhouse. Later he removed to Lancaster, where he died in 1871, at the age of sixty.

On one occasion when a railway engine in the Roundhouse was building up steam ready for departure, the spindle of the regulator slipped out of its socket and the engine drove straight through the outside wall. It demolished a large section of the wall, causing people to scatter in all directions in case the whole building should collapse.

The same accident was repeated shortly afterwards. Only then was the throttle mechanism on the engines modified to prevent further accidents.

One of the great pleasures in looking at the Roundhouse is its functional nature. It was so well designed that not a brick, not a pillar, not a slate was wasted. Everything did its job in the most economical way possible. Below were brick vaults which raised the turntable and engine storage bays to the railway level. Simple, functional and not used at first for any other purpose, such as for storage or stables. In the centre of the railway level was the circular turntable leading to bays of similar length all round. These were surrounded by a circular brick wall and a circle always encloses the largest area for the fewest bricks. No wasted corners or land. Above was a conical roof requiring the smallest quantity of timber as rafters and the fewest slates. Above again was an open lantern, so that the hot air and steam would rise and escape, giving natural ventilation. Robert Stephenson himself said that it could not be better.

However, the Roundhouse ceased to be used for engines quite soon. The received wisdom is that the Roundhouse became unusable because the turntable became too small for the later, bigger engines. Malcolm Tucker points out that, while 'the 36 ft turntable was becoming a little small it was still useable by the largest goods locomotives'. Other turntables in use elsewhere were only slightly larger.

A new cross-over line was built at Camden Town in 1851, enabling goods locomotives to use the Passenger Locomotive House. At the same time new engine houses were being built at other stations along the line and an additional engine house was provided at Wolverton, the works and staging post half way between London and Birmingham.' Thus the combination of the cross-over line at Camden and extra facilities elsewhere, may have made it more economical to pension off the Roundhouse. and concentrate work at the Passenger Locomotive house.[10] Perhaps more significantly, removing the cattle pens freed the space around the Roundhouse for coal

North View of the Camden Goods Yard, with the Roundhouse behind.

41

and goods traffic, as there was a pressing need at this time (1854) to provide longer marshalling sidings and more unloading and storage facilities at Camden.

The woodcut, on page 41, of Camden Goods Yard from the north (undated and of unknown origin) is from the Camden Local History Collection. "it shows a Stephenson "Patentee"design with the characteristic 'Gothic' top to the firebox, like a groined vault, which is to be seen in many of Stephenson's locomotives."[11]

Incidentally, people may think that this 'Gothic' shape was chosen purely for artistic reasons, but is more likely to have been an engineer's solution to a problem. It would have been far quicker and cheaper to make, as four metal plates shaped on a bending machine and the corners rivetted up, than would a hammered dome like the one in the Whishaw drawing below.

From Whishaw's 'Railways of Great Britain and Ireland'

The North London Railway

In June 1846 a Royal Commission decided that no more railway termini should be built in London as there were already enough lines radiating from the centre. Instead, what was needed were some circular lines joining the various main-line routes.

On 26 August 1846 an Act was passed permitting the construction of an eight mile long railway from the West India Docks at Blackwall to Camden Town to carry goods. On early maps it is called The West India Docks Railway. Passenger traffic was not even considered. Building made such slow progress that it took until September 1850 for the stretch from Islington to Bow Junction to open and then a 15 minute passenger service from Fenchurch Street to Islington proved very popular. In December the line reached Camden Town and was extended to Hampstead Road by June 1851. By the time that the stretch from Bow to the West India Docks was opened on 1 January 1852, the North London Line had built up a valuable passenger traffic almost by accident. (This was not the Northern Line of the Underground, which was built much later).

With the through line from Camden, goods could be moved directly to and from the London docks and the railway was a real rival to the Regent's Canal at last.

New Coal Yards

A Plan of Camden Depôt of 1848, too black and fragile to be reproduced here, shows a Cattle Landing area and cattle pens near to the Roundhouse. These were for live cattle which would then have been driven to Smithfield Cattle Market. In 1854, these pens were relocated to Maiden Lane on the North London Line, in good time for the opening of the Caledonian Cattle Market the following year. This made space for the replanning of the goods yard. When the North London Railway was first built, in 1850-51, it ran south of these cattle pens, but in 1854 the line was moved northwards, closer to the Roundhouse, as it is today.

The land up to Chalk Farm Road east and west of the Roundhouse was raised to railway level behind a new retaining wall, to provide space for much needed coal sidings. This redevelopment is shown on a large scale site plan of 1856, not reproduced here.[13] The sideways movement of the line obliterated the cattle pens and increased the area of the marshalling yards near the Goods Station. By the 1870s Camden Town lay in a sea of railway lines. The North Western Railway and the North London Line crossed the district, belching smoke and coal dust day and night.

The Great Wall of Camden

Creating the new marshalling yards involved building one of the most notable features of the area, the Yellow Brick Wall. When this was built, about 1846, it stretched along Chalk Farm Road from the railway bridge to the Roundhouse. Today half of it has been demolished to create the petrol station and the new access road to Safeway's.

A short length of the wall which still remains has been cleaned, so that it appears attractive, a very Judy Garland of a wall, yet it was not always like that. For well over a century it was dark, forbidding, blackened with the coal dust and soot which filled the air. David Thompson, in his book, 'In Camden Town', describes his intense dislike of this 'prison wall'. In the nineteen-sixties it still gloomed interminably along Chalk Farm Road, casting a shadow on the brightest day, driving him to walk on the other side of the road, away from its baleful influence. He describes the Camden Town Riots of 1848, where gangs of Irish and Cockney labourers forced the gate and fought each other so fiercely that the police from three local police stations were overwhelmed. Eventually the military had to be brought from the Albany Road Barracks. 1848 was the year of revolutions throughout Europe, so there were probably other conflicts and aspirations in the air besides racial abuse, but this wall and gate seems to recall the brutality of the scene. One would hardly guess from its appearance today, when for most people Camden Town is a place for fun, at this darker industrial history.

It was this industrial history which created such an extraordinary wall - The Great Wall of Camden. From Chalk Farm Road the wall appears to be uniform, but in fact it changes dramatically along its length, as one can see from inside the Stables Market. At the Market entrance it is a normal vertical wall, eighteen inches thick, with a heavier pier at the end (see Fig.1). At the Horse Hospital the wall changes slowly into a massive buttress wall up to 6 ft 9 ins thick (see Fig.2) with a stepped parapet wall above. This heavy, buttress wall is needed to support the steeply sloping road which used to lead to the Goods Yard above. The cobbled slope is lined with heavy blocks of Millstone Grit, now worn and smashed by the rims of hundreds of iron-shod cartwheels. In 1991, when the new road to Safeway's supermarket was cut through and the length from the present garage to the Roundhouse was demolished, Malcolm Tucker made a sketch. It is redrawn here as Fig.3.

The wall leans back at a slope of 1 in 15, or about 4° to take the thrust of the raised road and then the new marshalling yards. As the sloping road starts, it becomes six bricks thick at its thinnest part and the Millstone Grit kerbs continue right to the top. Above the kerb, the parapet wall is vertical. Below the cobbles of the roadway are 3 feet of hard-core and then London Clay. At the back of the wall is a layer of broken blue and white 19th century pottery and oyster shells, clearly all sieved from household rubbish and set aside to be sold as drainage material. It is shown in Fig. 3. When, in the 1990s, the wall was turned at right angles along the new Safeway's road, it was built in massive concrete faced with yellow brick.

It is possible to *experience* the size of this wall. Step up from the roadway, over the huge kerb, and stand on top of the buttress wall with the parapet wall on one side. The parapet wall is substantial, but nothing to the thickness and sheer bulk of the wall below your feet.

In 1998 the top end of the old roadway has become a quiet viewing platform. The land as far as the Roundhouse has been scooped out, back to the level of the old 'Clay Field' which is shown on the 1804 Parish Map. For over a century this was a level stretch of marshalling yards, raised above Chalk Farm Road and held in place by the buttress wall. Horses and carts toiled up the slope with goods to be loaded on to the

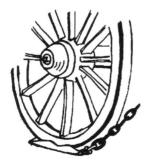

A wooden cart wheel with a steel drag under the wheel to act as a brake. These skids created sparks as they slid down the hill and wore away the granite setts to the state we see today.

railway trucks, or slid down again with heavy loads, held back only by the screaming steel skid under the wheel. These stones have suffered far more damage than similar ones elsewhere. Most are merely polished by wear, while these granite setts have been ground away by a century of laden wagons.

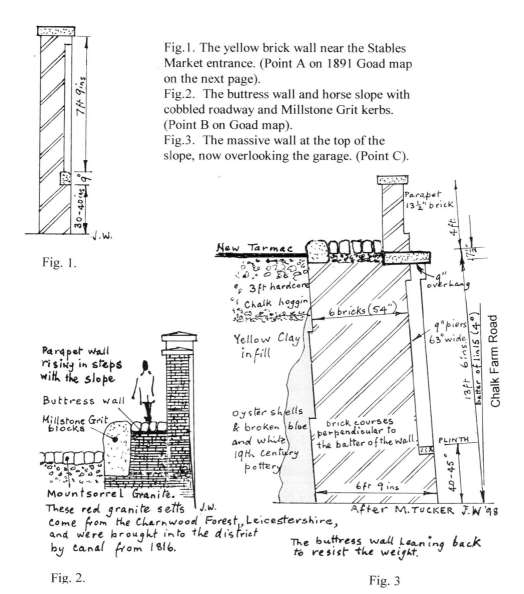

Fig.1. The yellow brick wall near the Stables Market entrance. (Point A on 1891 Goad map on the next page).
Fig.2. The buttress wall and horse slope with cobbled roadway and Millstone Grit kerbs. (Point B on Goad map).
Fig.3. The massive wall at the top of the slope, now overlooking the garage. (Point C).

Fig. 1.

Parapet wall rising in steps with the slope

Buttress wall

Millstone Grit blocks

Mountsorrel Granite.
These red granite setts come from the Charnwood Forest, Leicestershire, and were brought into the district by canal from 1816.

New Tarmac

3ft hardcore

Chalk hoggin

Yellow Clay infill

oyster shells & broken blue and white 19th century pottery

6 bricks (54")

brick courses perpendicular to the batter of the wall

6ft 9ins

Parapet 13½" brick

4 ft

9" overhang

9" piers 63" wide

Chalk Farm Road

PLINTH

40-45°

After M. TUCKER J.W '98

The buttress wall leaning back to resist the weight.

Fig. 2.

Fig. 3

Three sections through the Yellow Brick Wall in different positions.

45

New Stables, 1854-56

The building of the North London Railway line also affected the redesign of Camden Goods Yard. When the line cut through the site of the old goods station in 1851, it left a triangular space to the north, between the line and Chalk Farm Road. Here, as part of the remodelling of the goods yard, the stables with semicircular windows were built between 1854 and 1856. The stables were in four blocks, 1½ storeys high, but mostly raised in height since then. At that time they stabled 148 horses and today are used as part of the market.

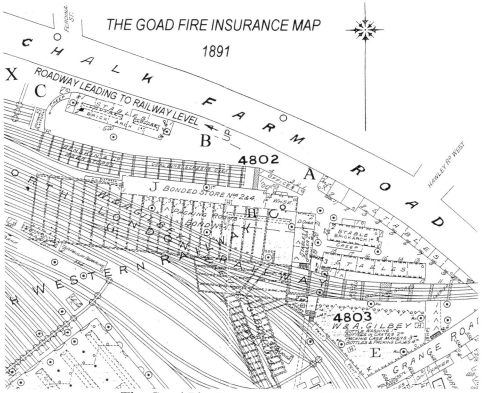

The Goad Fire Insurance map, 1891

This shows the new stables, 1854-56; the vaults with Gilbey's Bonded warehouses and the North London Line above them; and the curved creep of the Horse Hospital at the top of the map. Commercial Place is called Grange Road, with Gilbey's Bottle Store, which was later burnt down, at the end.

The artist's impression of the 1998 planned redevelopment which is printed at the end of this book, would have been drawn from about point X, in the top left.

The New London North Western Goods Shed

Built in 1864 to replace several sheds, the building had a plan area of 100,000 square feet. This was still its area in 1891 when the Goad map was drawn, but it was enlarged in the 1930s. It was built on brick arches, had 8 platforms with ridge and furrow roofs above, and there was a narrow row of offices on the second floor. At the time of this drawing, Samuel Allsopp & Sons, the brewers, stored their beers in the vaults below. Later Gilbey's occupied them.

The railway lines from Gilbey's A Shed, on the other side of the canal, ran past one end of the goods shed to the normal marshalling yard and also directly to No 6 platform. A special Gilbey's train departed from the latter every evening for decades.

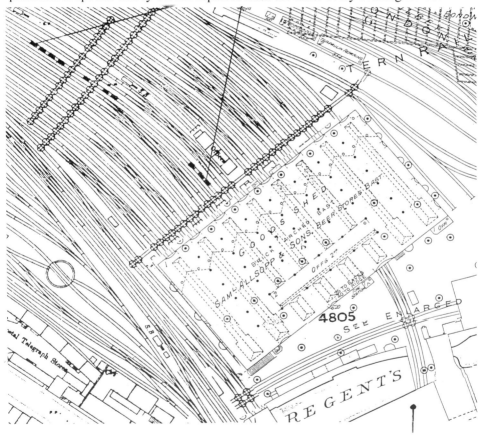

Site of Gilbey's 'A' Shed

The Goad Fire Insurance map of 1891

It shows the mass of tracks and turntables. One goods train being assembled on the tracks has been added to illustrate the method.

Shunting Yard

A length of the railway line and a turntable have been retained in Gilbey's Yard (the new prize-winning housing development by the Pirates' Bridge). This turntable was used to turn a railway wagon through a right-angle and shows how small the early railway wagons were and continued to be until the 1960s.

The Goad Fire Insurance map of 1891 shows no fewer than thirty-two turntables immediately north of the Goods Shed and there are two similar arrays only a few yards further on. These were used to move filled trucks into position, ready to form complete trains. The trucks were juggled by complicated, zig-zag routes so that when the time came, each would be in its position at the rear of the line of trucks, ready for dropping off at the correct station. One set of trucks has been added on the drawing in this book to show the process of assembly. The three rows of turntables allowed the shunters to move a particular truck to the front, or back, of any group on any particular line, so that they were each in the correct final position. Only when each truck was in its place was the whole line linked up to form a complete train.

Much of this work would have been done by horses and, with so many trucks being moved, different gangs of shunters working side by side at different tasks, the work going on twenty-four hours a day, it was a complicated, noisy affair. On the site where people now quietly sleep, there was noise and clatter day and night. The noise is not entirely finished. The new work to convert the main line track for modern high-speed trains, due to be carried out before the year AD 2000, will once again disturb the peaceful sleep of the neighbourhood.

The Effects of the Clean Air Act

It is difficult now to think back to before diesel trains, the electrification of the railways, and the Clean Air Act, to the smog and pollution of that time. One typical young man was diagnosed as having tuberculosis. His family had died of it and he was infected. The Second World War probably saved his life, taking him abroad to the dry atmosphere of Egypt where he appeared to be cured. A year after returning to live in Camden Town, the pollution had brought back the disease.

This is not the place for a serious study of railways in general, but the effect of the railways on Camden Town was dramatic, influencing its whole future. The London and Birmingham Railway, which ran through Camden Town to Euston, split the area in two. Park Village, which had been linked to Mornington Crescent and the Hampstead Road, was suddenly cut off. This division became a social division – 'within the pale' and 'outside the pale' of Regent's Park.

In the 1960s, the railway goods traffic disappeared and the development of the redundant land was to change the face of Camden Town.

Gilbey' Yard, Chalk Farm, London NW1, 1997
Award winning development by Community Housing Association

This is the north bank of the canal today, opposite the site of William Cubitt's building, which burnt down, and of its replacement which became Gilbey's 'A' Shed, which has also been demolished and replaced by the Pirate's Castle. The picture was taken from the present Pirates' Bridge, looking west. One railway line and a turntable are still in place at the top of the wall. Although the present houses are called Gilbey's Yard, Gilbeys never had a direct connection with this particular site. It was, in fact, the site of the large goods shed built by the LNWR in 1864.

[1] Camden History Archive

[2] Francis Whishaw, "The Railways of Great Britain and Ireland", London; Simkin Marshall & Co, 1840.

[3] Highgate and Muswell Hill, by Joan Schwitzer and Ken Gay, 1995

[4] Camden Local History Archive

[5] Camden Local History Archive

[6] Traffic and Transport: an economic history of Pickford's, by Gerald L. Turnbull, Allen & Unwin, 1979

[7] Railway Times, Dec. 1841

[8] Map modified by Chris Bryant to show bridges.

[9] A Hampstead Victorian, by Michael Robbins, Camden History Review No 8, 1989

[10] Comments by Malcolm Tucker, June 1998, based on London & Birmingham Railway minutes.

[11] Malcolm Tucker

[12] Camden Local History Archive

[13] LNWR Plan of Camden Station, 1856, 40 ft to 1inch.PRO; Rail 410/2072

The Camden Ice Wells

In 1995, developers who wished to erect a block of offices at 34/36 Jamestown Road, could not decide where to place the pilings for their heavy building. Down below were some nineteenth century ice wells but exactly where, nobody knew. The ice wells were somewhere below ground, economically useless, capped over and forgotten. Now they had become a problem. Malcolm Tucker, who is a specialist in industrial archaeology, looked first at the historical evidence. He was then present to record what was found when the larger ice well was opened, and an ablseiler went down to measure it[1]

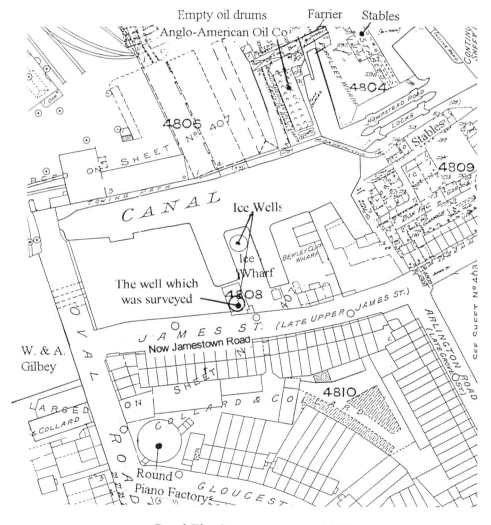

Goad Fire Insurance map. 1891

Modern refrigeration allows us to freeze water into ice at will, anywhere in the world. In the nineteenth century things were very different. Then ice had to be collected in the winter from frozen lakes or canals and stored throughout the rest of the year. Large houses had ice wells in the grounds, or cut into a hillside, where winter ice could be stored. The wells were used too, as cool stores for meat and butter, so dairies and butchers in town often had ice wells. One was found in Gray's Inn Road a few years ago. They can be found all over the country and architects in London come across them quite frequently when they begin to build on old sites.

Canals, shallow and slow-moving, became a common source of ice. One can imagine that boatmen, with their boats fast-frozen and no money coming in, were only too happy to supply the demand. Thus canal ice, full of dead dogs and other impurities, arrived in restaurant kitchens and in the drinks at London clubs. William Leftwich, a confectioner and pastry-cook, who probably also made ice cream, set up business to supply ice to high-class West End restaurants and customers.

His first ice well was at Cumberland Basin, conveniently close to the wealthy Regent's Park houses. Dug in 1825, it was 82 feet deep, 34 feet across and had a capacity of 1,500 tons. It was egg shaped, with a drainage well extending to the chalk, 300 feet below. The Camden Town wells were built in the 1830s and still Leftwich was the only ice seller in the London directories.

It was not until 1857-8, that the man who was to become the biggest competitor, appeared on the scene. He was Carlo Gatti, who also came from the catering and confectioery trade. Gatti set up an ice house at New Wharf Road, near King's Cross, in the premises now occupied by the Canal Museum and where his two ice wells are open to the public.

Instead of canal ice, Leftwich began to import ice from lakes in the clean Norwegian countryside. This was crystal clear, and soon became very popular. The frozen lakes were ploughed in two directions with narrow cutters to divide the ice into blocks. These were then wrapped and brought by sea to Limehouse and along the Regent's Canal. Besides ordinary ice, Leftwich advertised Ice Pyramids, large blocks of ice carved to shape and decorated with flowers. These were used as table decorations at banquets and, as they melted, served to keep the air cool.

The Survey

In April 1839, Leftwich was given permission to construct a dock, later called the Ice Wharf, on the south side of the Canal. Earlier, two wharfs had been cut slightly to the east, but the site of the present 34-36 Jamestown Road was then still farmland.

Two ice wells are shown on the 1891 Goad Fire Insurance maps, one at the canal end of the Ice Wharf and the larger one near Jamestown Road. An old photograph shows the Ice Wharf with two cranes, one over each well. In 1912 the wells were capped with reinforced concrete. On 21 November 1995, the reinforced capping over the larger ice well was opened up and an abseiler descended, with a strong torch in his helmet and a measuring tape. The well was a deep brick cylinder with a domed roof and a small sump below, so that melt water could be pumped away. At the bottom was a wooden platform of heavy timber on which the ice blocks used to stand. These blocks, weighing from two to four hundredweight each, were separated from each

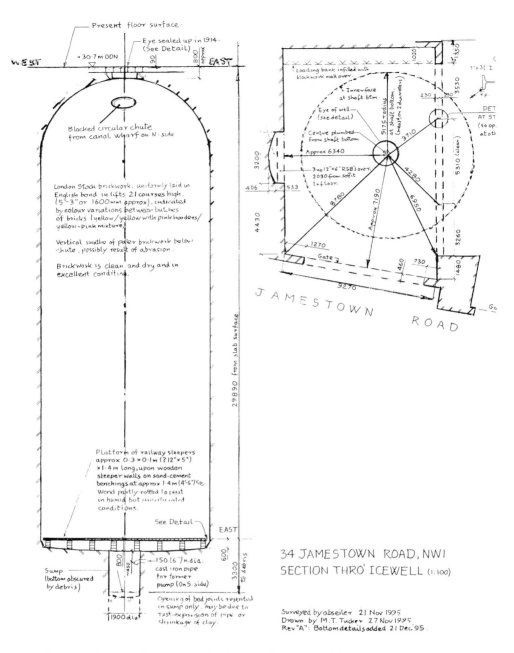

Present floor surface.

W. E ST

Eye sealed up in 1914.
(See Detail)

+30.7m ODN

EAST

Blocked circular chute
from canal wharf on N. side

London Stock brickwork uniformly laid in
English bond in lifts 21 courses high
(5'-3" or 1600mm approx), indicated
by colour variations between batches
of bricks (yellow/yellow with pink headers/
yellow-pink mixture)

Vertical swathe of paler brickwork below
chute, possibly result of abrasion.

Brickwork is clean and dry and in
excellent condition.

29890 from slab surface

Platform of railway sleepers
approx 0·3 × 0·1 m (?12"×5")
× 1·4 m long, upon wooden
sleeper walls on sand-cement
benchings at approx 1·4 m (4'-6") c/c
Wood partly rotted to peat
in humid but unsaturated
conditions.

See Detail

EAST

Sump
(bottom obscured
by debris)

150 (6")n.dia.
cast iron pipe
for former
pump (On S. side)

Opening of bed joints reported
in sump only, may be due to
rust-expansion of pipe or
shrinkage of clay.

1900 dia.

Loading bank infilled with
blockwork wall over

Inner face
at shaft btm.

Eye of well
(see detail)

Centre plumbed
from shaft bottom

Approx 6340

3 no 12"×6" RSB's over
2030 from soffit
to floor.

5175 radius
at shaft bottom
(mean of 2 diameters)

3710

4280

6650

3260

Gate

JAMESTOWN   ROAD

34 JAMESTOWN ROAD, NW1
SECTION THRO' ICEWELL (1:100)

Surveyed by abseiler 21 Nov 1995
Drawn by M.T. Tucker 27 Nov 1995
Rev "A": Bottom details added 21 Dec'95.

other and from the brick walls, by layers of straw, which insulated them and allowed the melt water from the ice to escape. By 1995, the wooden platform was like peat.

The walls, which appear to have been in very good condition and dry, are in London Stock brick-work, laid in English bond. They may have been built from the top downwards, in a series of 'lifts' each about 1.6 metres high. These bands of brick-work vary slightly in colour - yellow, yellow with pink borders, yellow-pink mixture, etc. – depending on the different firings of the bricks in the kiln. First, a hole would

52

have been excavated about five metres deep and a circular dome built, like an igloo, with a small hole at the top and a second one on the edge of the Ice Wharf, through which the ice would be lowered into the chamber.

This was 5.175 metres (almost 17 feet) in diameter. Then the hole was excavated to a further 1.6 metres and the spoil lifted out in a bucket through the top entry hole. The London Clay was stiff enough to support itself while the next circle of twenty-one courses of bricks were being laid. Further 'lifts' were excavated and built until the full depth of 29·890metres (approximately 100 feet) was reached. This is the equivalent of a ten storey building below ground. In 1873, an article in The Standard reported that the well held no less than 4,000 tons of ice and that it 'was said to be the biggest in London'. It also reported that that the well was 100 feet deep and 44 ft in diameter. When opened in 1995 it was found to be only 34 feet diameter, so the visible brickwork may be a later relining of a larger well.

The drawings, reproduced by kind permission of Mr Tucker, show a section through the ice well, with the two entrances at the top and the sump below, with the remains of the pipe through which melt water was drawn off by pumping and so drained into the canal. The plan shows the circular well with the sump below, only a few inches off centre. Surrounding the well is shown the open fronted brick building where the ice was loaded into carts, for daily delivery to customers. This brick building was still in existence in 1995 when the survey was made.

A second, smaller, ice well lies slightly to the north of the first. Later the canal basins along Jamestown Road were filled in, and the site of the Ice Wells became garaging. The proposed building has not yet been built and the ice wells themselves are still there, capped over, ready for whatever may befall.

A typical Carlo Gatti ice cart [2]

The Ice Trade

Norwegian ice imports by Leftwich and others grew rapidly, so that by 1880, nearly 175,000 tons were coming into London alone. Ice carts, especially the yellow and black one belonging to Carlo Gatti, were a feature of London streets right up to the Second World War.[2]

The ice men descended into the well in the early mornings by a steel ladder and spent up to two hours winching up the ice blocks to the surface. These could weigh from 2 to 4 hundredweight each and might have to be lifted fifty feet or more. The ice was laid in the 'ice table', where each man had to split his blocks with an ice pick into smaller pieces, suitable for the customers. These blocks, carefully swathed in sacking for insulation, were then delivered by cart to restaurants, fishmongers, and private houses. The men arrived back at the ice well for a second delivery by 8.30 in the morning. In hot weather, when the demand was high, they could deliver up to four loads a day.

There are many stories of the ice men walking all the way to London each Spring, from their villages in Switzerland, and back again when the cold weather set in. This, and the importation of ice, have long ceased. Thus the economies of both Norway and Ticino, the Italian part of Switzerland, where the men were traditionally forced to go abroad for work, were both disrupted by the invention of the common refrigerator.

PLOUGHING AND STORING ICE ON THE HUDSON RIVER, NEW YORK, C. 1870[3]
A complete section of the river ice is being ploughed into blocks, the blocks broken off, poled to land and winched up a slope into a warehouse, for storage and distribution.

[1] Historical Report on 34-36 Jamestown Road, NW1, by Malcolm Tucker, Sept. 1995 (Camden Hist. Archive).
[2] Breaking the Ice, by Felicity Kinross, Country Life, 18 October 1980
[2] Breaking The Ice, by Felicity Kinross, Country Life, 18 October, 1990
[4] Old engraving, reprinted in Cold Storage and Ice-making, by B.H.Springett, Pitman, 1921.

Piano Manufacture in Camden Town

The piano was first demonstrated in London by Charles Dibden, who is most famous for his sea songs. Between the acts of a performance of The Beggar's Opera at Covent Garden, on 16th May 1767, Dibden accompanied Miss Bricklet on the 'new pianoforte'. So besides all his other skills as singer, composer, novelist and above all composer, he played the piano. The youngest of eighteen children, he was trained as a singer and later created many entertainments, performing especially at Drury Lane. He wrote and composed upwards of 1400 popular songs mostly to do with the sea. 'I sailed from the Downs in The Nancy, Saturday Night at Sea, T'was in the Good Ship Rover, and dozens of other patriotic songs, including the immortal Tom Bowling, written on the death of his eldest brother Captain Thomas Dibden.

Charles Dibden lived in Arlington Road, Camden Town and is buried in the church-yard between Bayham Street and Camden Street. It is a strange coincidence that the piano industry should later have grown up in his own back yard. Piano manufacture, which had started in the West End, moved first to Tottenham Court Road and when Collard & Collard and other famous firms like Brimsmead, and Challen, moved to Camden Town it encouraged other firms to set up nearby.

Mario Clementi, who was called the first composer for the pianoforte, lost a lot of money when the piano firm of James Longman & Co failed. This company was managed by Clementi's friend Frederick William Collard, who immediately formed a partnership with his brother and opened a new firm called Clementi & Co. When Clementi died, in 1832, they became Collard & Collard, a very famous name in piano history[1]

Camden Town was a very suitable centre for piano manufacture. The Regent's Canal could be used for transporting heavy and bulky goods like pianos cheaply, either to the west and so to the complete canal system which covered the Midlands, or east to the docks and from there all over the world. Camden Town was also near the rail-heads of King's Cross, Euston and St Pancras, so transport conditions by water and rail were ideal. Soon the area became a centre of the piano industry.

The fortunes of one man may be taken as typical of many. John Sandon, my grandfather, was born in 1851 and at the age of thirty-one he went into partnership as

Collard & Collard's piano factory in 1998

55

a piano manufacturer with a man called Steadman Neither appears in the Post Office Directory before this, so presumably it was a first-time venture for both of them. They took premises at 54 Queen Street, Camden Town. By the time Sandon & Steadman set up their business, London had over two hundred piano making firms, three quarters of them north of the river. Manufacture in North London developed early and by the time the southern suburbs were built, the piano industry was well established along the Regent's Canal, in Stoke Newington, Islington and especially in Camden Town. Some were large firms, making complete instruments on a mass production system, moving them from department to department as the work progressed, as Collard & Collard did in their famous circular factory in Oval Road. Twenty-two windows with a bench under each to give good light and a central lift to move the instruments from floor to floor. The circular shape gave the maximum floor space for the minimum bricks and the maximum light. It is strange the Camden Town has two fine circular buildings, this and the Roundhouse.

The Goad Fire Insurance map shows that Collard & Collard had a concentration of factories at the end of Oval Road. Each part of the process had its own space. Case-making, fall-making, the 'ware room', and 'bellying' (whatever they were) 'finishing' and others. Behind the Oval Factory, in the triangle bounded by the houses in

A Camden Town piano maker in the nineteen thirties, years later than this story.

Gloucester Crescent, Arlington Road and Jamestown Road (now occupied by the flats built by Community Housing) was a range of other buildings, each with its specialist use. Veneer store, timber stores, engineers' shops, french polishing, fret-cutting and wood turning, glue boiling, stringing shops, key loading, where the keys were balanced with lead weights to make them return rapidly, and further rooms where a dozen other specialist skills were performed.

Other firms were little more than small assembly shops in back kitchens, with parts bought in ready made. One old piano maker said, "Sometimes, on a Friday afternoon, you could meet the boss of one of these small factories hawking a piano round the district in the hope of selling it for cash, twenty pounds or so, to pay the wages and the rent. Piano firms were in all sizes - whales and minnows."

Besides manufacturers there were small-part makers, clustering round the big firms. Piano key makers; wrench pin makers; sellers of key leads; hammer coverers; incisors, who cut the fretted wooden fronts; truss carvers; gilders; marquetry workers; french polishers, veneer, timber and ivory suppliers; makers of piano castors; candle-sconce makers; piano stool, music cabinet, piano-back makers; piano movers, storers, tuners and salesmen. All these found a living in and around Camden Town and along the Canal.

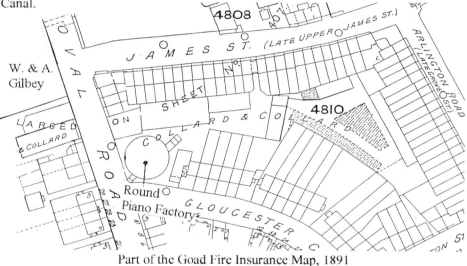

Part of the Goad Fire Insurance Map, 1891

It was in this atmosphere that Sandon & Steadman had set up business in 1883. In 1884 they took extra premises at 14 Charlton Street, Somers Town, between Euston Station and St Pancras. Perhaps the lease was running out, because they left Queen Street in 1885 and took further premises in Drummond Street, Somers Town. The firm must have prospered for, by 1890, they had taken a showroom in Berners Street, off Oxford Street. Clearly it was a flourishing business at this time. John Sandon had a growing family, Britain had come out of the 1887 slump and the future must have looked propitious.

The firm continued in these three premises until 1889. John Sandon's son, John Edward Sandon, the oldest of the children, had joined the firm as a salesman. He showed off the pianos to customers at Berners Street but, when he was only twenty-one, his father died.

57

The death must have come as a shock to everyone, for John Sandon was only forty-nine. His son was not a manufacturer and we know nothing of Steadman's abilities. At that time, when German pianos were flooding into the country, competition was becoming fierce. John Sandon's photograph shows a powerful, self-confident man, bald, with a flowing beard, older than his age. He was the driving force behind the firm, which never recovered after his death

They retrenched immediately. By 1900 they had abandoned both Berners Street and Drummond Street, but it was not enough. The firm lasted only another eight years. The name does not appear in the Post Office Directory after 1908: nor does Steadman's name appear alone, so it was the end. German competition had driven them out of business, but no doubt the untimely death of one of the founders before his son was capable of taking over, may have hastened the result. In 1911 there were still 136 piano firms in Britain, all but three manufacturing in London. With all these surviving in Islington, Camden Town and Stoke Newington, there seems no reason why Sandon & Steadman too could not have weathered the economic conditions for a while, but the firm would not have survived for ever.

After 1900 the British piano industry became cut-throat, insecure. Everything was short-term and without vision, so that the standard of workmanship fell. Training schemes were introduced by some firms to attract young workers, but the market continued to shrink and young people refused to enter an industry which offered so few prospects. By 1912, German exports of pianos and piano parts were sixty-five times as large as Great Britain's.[2] Germany dominated the piano industry rather as Japan was to dominate the electronics industry after the Second World War.

There was a small revival in the piano industry immediately after the First World War, though this was soon affected by the rise of the gramophone, cinema and radio. Collard & Collard left in the 1920s and their round factory was occupied by garment firms, engineers and printers over the years. Output recovered somewhat in the 1930s, reaching 60,000 pianos in 1936. During the Second World War there was a reprieve for one small Kentish Town firm. Every ship in the fleet had to have a small organ which could be used for entertainment and for playing hymns on a Sunday morning, but this boost was short lived. After the War, piano and organ making were still declining, threatened this time not by Germany, but by Korea.

In the 1960s, the Koreans had begun to make pianos. Their first ones hardly worked, yet in a very few years they were producing splendid instruments. They approached piano manufacture not as a craft industry, but as a modern engineering problem, using the latest machines and production methods. Traditionally piano parts were made by small-batch production and the parts then fitted together. Indeed a fitter is a man who takes other people's parts and makes them fit. The Koreans insisted on modern machining accuracy. They were machining parts to 3 microns, so that every part fitted first time. The skill and time of the fitter were no longer required, so that pianos could be assembled, not fitted. The drop in production costs was enormous. Soon the Royal Academy of Music began buying Korean pianos.

In 1993 the local telephone book listed a few piano shops in North London, piano removers and tuners, but no piano manufacturers at all. Heckscher & Co, in Bayham Street, is almost the sole survivor of the piano industry in Camden Town. This firm began in Germany in 1869 and moved to England in 1883, where they set up as maufacturers in the West End. Today they are suppliers of piano parts, not manufacturers of pianos. Repairers write for the hundreds of different parts which go to make a piano – replacement wires of all gauges, lengths of green baize an inch wide, new keys, or any of the other parts needed to keep a piano in order. A very necessary service, but not the same as manufacture.

About 1970, when industry in Camden Town was almost defunct, I cleared out part of an old piano factory. There were off-cuts of American Black Walnut and mature Japanese Oak which had been seasoning for over thirty years and cut like butter – all the unremarked debris from an old factory. The owner was retiring because of rising rents and falling business. His mews factory was being refurbished and restored as part of an urban renewal programme. This included a new roof of Welsh slates at £3 each. At a time when huge new factories and trading estates were being erected on green-field sites, with roofs in corrugated iron, this inner-city factory was being treated like a stately home and priced out of any future manufacture. The owner, a man of long experience, knew it was time to get out.

The planners were working to the ideas current at the time. Industry should be zoned away from housing, preferably in a New Town beyond the Green Belt. Old buildings in London had to be restored to their original condition, in materials used at the time they were built. The fact that those materials had become extremely expensive was irrelevant. Authentic restoration came first. No industry could have supported this cost. With the best will in the world and hoping to improve people's lives, planners were destroying industry. The same thing was happening all over London. Planners and industrialists were living in different worlds, but nobody had thought through the consequences.

Within a few years the delicate network of local employment was shattered. London, which in Victorian times had been the biggest industrial city in the British Isles, had lost its industry. Instrument making in Islington and Clerkenwell, gunsmiths in Paddington, furniture in Hoxton, metal casting in Bayham Street, brewing in Hawley Street - industry withered or fled.

The site of Collard and Collard's piano factory in Oval Road has a history typical of the area. Once a state of the art factory, the firm closed down when public demand for pianos fell and new production methds were introduced.. The part of the site to the west of Oval Road was redeveloped by Gilbey's, who themselves later left for Harlow. On the east side, the Round Factory had stood, not derelict but dejected and unloved, for years. It housed printers and other firms for several years. By 1994, now listed grade II, it had been restored, renamed The Rotunda, and housed design consultants Jones, Knowles, Ritchie and the Virago Press. The rest of the Collard & Collard site has become new low-rent housing. This typified the change which was happening all over Camden Town. It was becoming a centre for TV companies, publishers, designers, and the media in general, or being redeveloped for housing, as we shall see.

THE PIANOFORTE INDUSTRY

1. Made in St Pancras: British Pianos and their Story, by C. D. Howkins, St Pancras Journal, Vol. 19, No. 10
2. & 3 The Piano Makers, David Wainwright, Hutchinson , 1975, pp 122

Walter and Alfred Gilbey

In 1856, two young men discharged at the end of the Crimean War, were in need of jobs. Walter, aged 26 and Alfred 24, returned to England without capital or special skills, but into a rapidly expanding economy. Their older brother, Henry Parry Gilbey, was a partner in a wholesale wine merchants, Southard, Gilbey & Co. and he advised them to set up as retail wine merchants. Less than a year later they leased some cellars in Oxford Street, at the corner of Berwick Street.

They concentrated on good, cheap wines from Cape Town as these could be imported at half duty. The wine was so good and so cheap that Gilbey's had 20,000 customers within months and two years later new premises were opened. Extra branches were opened in Dublin, Edinburgh and Belfast. Relations were drawn in to run the new branches, so that it expanded as an interlinked family business from the start, with the names Gold, Blyh and Grinling recurring time and again over the generations.

In 1861, Gladstone, as part of his foreign policy, reduced the duty on French wine, which had been prohibitively high. The tax fell from twelve shillings to two shillings per dozen bottles. Clearly this would undercut South African wines with their greater transport costs. Gilbey's immediately changed tack and concentrated on importing cheap Bordeaux wines at the expense of their South African ones. South African trade was not to recover for a generation. Gilbeys, unlike their competitors, promised to

The Pantheon, Oxford Street

Now the site of Marks & Spencer's

pass on the full reduction in duty to their customers. As a result, Gilbey's French wines fell to 18 shillings a dozen, far below the prices their competitors were offering. Imports from France rose from a quarter of a million gallons to four and a half million in eight years. The firm's expansion was so rapid that they were able to take over the Pantheon in Oxford Street, the site of the present Marks & Spencer's building.

The Pantheon had opened in 1772 as a place of entertainment, with an enormous hall and domed roof, painted pillars, the walls spectacularly decorated with frescoes and lit with green and purple lamps, it had quickly became the rage. James Wyatt, the architect, had built an exotic extravaganza. Everyone flocked to it. Later it was a theatre and an opera house, but was destroyed by fire in 1792. Rebuilt as a theatre it failed, became a bazaar and then an art gallery. Gilbey's bought it in 1867 for £67,000.

Gilbeys began distilling gin in London in 1872. Cheap and easy to produce, in Hogarth's day it had an appalling reputation. 'Drunk for a penny and dead drunk for twopence.' London Gin was flavoured with juniper berries, coriander and other herbs. That Juniper name was to be revived in the 1990s.

The firm had always concentrated on the mass sale of reliable wines - not top vintage, but good quality. As this depended on the bulk purchase from dependable suppliers, they decided to deal with the French wine growers direct, cutting out the middle-man. Henry Parry Gilbey, the older brother who had first advised Walter and Albert, now joined the firm, bringing with him his expertise as a wholesaler.

James Blyth and Alfred Gilbey toured French and other Continental vineyards, buying and shipping direct to England for bottling at the Pantheon, and later at Camden Town. They also visited cork growing districts in Portugal, where again the firm bought direct from the growers. As a result of these annual excursions, the family ties became even more complicated. No less than three of the Gilbey family married into Spanish wine firms and soon their wines too were on the Gilbey lists.

In their travels Alfred Gilbey and James Blyth discovered the sparkling wines of the Lower Loire valley. These were cheap, not unlike champagne, and became highly popular in Britain. In 1875, Gilbeys bought the 470 acre Chateau Loudenne, in the Gironde, north of Bordeaux, which produced claret. Here they made their own wine and stored purchases from elsewhere.

Bottling in Gilbey's 'A' Shed

The Roundhouse from Chalk Farm Road after Gilbey's took over.

This engraving is very inaccurate. The complete section between the end of the vaults and the Roundhouse, now occupied by the access road and garage, has been omitted. Secondly, the yellow brick wall is far too low. In reality, people were dwarfed by it as they are today.

WINE AT THE REDUCED DUTY.

W. & A. GILBEY, Wine, Spirit, & Liqueur Importers and Distillers, will send, on application, their detailed price list of the peculiar Wines and Spirits of every country; and any can be tasted at each of their Establishments in England, Ireland, and Scotland; at either of the London Docks, and Bonded Warehouses; at their large cellarage under the Princess's Theatre; or at their Counting-house and sample-rooms, 357. Oxford-street, London (three doors from the Pantheon).

W. & A. G.'s connexion—extending to 18,000 Families, and upwards of 80 of the Chief Hospitals, Military Messes, and Public Institutions—offers every reasonable guarantee to inspire confidence in their mode of doing business.

WINES from FRANCE at the Reduced Duty.

Clarets, Vin Ordinaire. 18s. and 24s., also Medoc 24s. St. Emilion 28s., and St. Julien 30s. per doz.

Bordeaux White Wines—Sauterne 18s. and 24s., also Vin de Graves 24s., and Barsac 24s. per doz.

Burgundy Red Wines—Macon 24s., Beaune 24s., Pomard 30s., Aloxe 30s., and Volnay 36s. per doz.

Burgundy White Wines—Chablais 18s. and 24s., also Pouilly 24s., and Meursault 36s. per doz.

Sparkling Champagne, 33s. per doz. quarts, and 18s. per doz. pints. Also other Champagnes, 48s., 54s., and 66s. per doz.

Sparkling White Burgundy 42s., and sparkling St. Peray, 42s. per doz.

WINES from the RHINE at the Reduced Duty.

White Wines—Hocheimer 18s. and 24s., also Marcobruner 26s. per doz.

Sparkling Hock 38s., also Sparkling Moselle 38s. per doz. quarts, and 21s. per doz. pints.

WINES from SPAIN at the Reduced Duty.

Sherry (pale or gold) 26s. per doz., or in cask, £4 7s. 6d. per 7 gall., £8 13s. 3d. per 14 gall., and £17 3s. per cask of 28 gall.

WINES from PORTUGAL at the Reduced Duty.

Port, 8 years in the wood, 30s. per doz. or in cask, £5 1s. 6d. per 7 gall., £10 1s. 3d. per 14 gall., and £19 19s. per quarter cask of 28 gall.

Port, 11 years in the wood, 36s. per doz., or in cask, £5 19s. per 7 gall., £11 11s. 6d. per 14 gall., £23 2s. per 28 gall. cask.

WINES from the CAPE of GOOD HOPE.

Port, Sherry, Madeira, &c., all first growth, 20s. per doz., £3 6s. 6d. per 7 gall. cask, £6 11s. 3d. per 14 gall. cask, and £12 19s. per quarter cask of 28 gall.

Also first growths with age 24s. per doz., £4 0s. 6d. per 7 gall. cask, £7 19s. 3d. per 14 gall. cask, £15 15s. per 28 gall.

WINES from MARSALA at the Reduced Duties.

Marsala, 20s. per doz., £3 6s. 6d. per 7 gall. cask, and £6 11s. 3d. per 14 gall cask, and £10 3s. 6d. per cask of 22 galls.

This is old Bronte Wine, and considered by many superior to the finest Sherries.

Foreign and British Spirits at the Reduced Duty.

	Per gall.
BRANDY, U.V. brand, very fine ...	16s. 6d.
Do. the finest Cognac ...	22s.
Do. very old	26s.
RUM, finest Jamaica	16s.
WHISKY, pure old Scotch	18s.
Do. pure old Irish	18s.
GIN, excellent Household	11s.
HOLLANDS, Geneva,"Silver Stream"	14s.

Do. in the original green Cases and square Bottles as imported ... 32s. per doz.

A small sample of most of the above Wines will be forwarded for 6d.

A detailed Price List on application of the particular Wines of every country.

In England, Cheques to be crossed to our bankers, the BANK of ENGLAND, and Post Office Orders made payable to the General Post Office, LONDON; in IRELAND, the BANK of IRELAND, and General Post Office, DUBLIN; in SCOTLAND, the BANK of SCOTLAND, and General Post Office, EDINBURGH.

W. & A. GILBEY, 357, Oxford-street, London.
31, Upper Sackville-street, Dublin.
12, St. Andrew's-square, Edinburgh.

Quickly even the Pantheon was outgrown. It was to remain as the administrative centre until 1937, when Chermeyeff built Gilbey House in Jamestown Road, but the bottling department was moved to Camden Town and Gilbey's long association with Camden Lock began. In the railway arches, always at a cool, even temperature, were butts of sherry holding 108 gallons and pipes of port holding 117 gallons, together with butts of whiskey and rum, so that Camden Town became a veritable lake of wines and spirits.

The Roundhouse, long after the engines had gone, became a bonded warehouse. Fifteen gigantic vats of whiskey and other spirits were maturing there under the control of the Customs Service. As orders came in, vats were tapped, bottles labelled and duty levied. Until this was paid not a dram could be moved. What a place for a party.

By 1905, Gilbey's had bought three whisky distilleries, Glen Spey, Knockando and Strathmill, all in the Glenlivet district of Strathspey, where they produced nearly 300,000 gallons of proof spirit. At the same time they held large stocks of Irish whiskey in Dublin and had opened plants in Canada and Australia.

In 1997 I went to a secure documents store where I presented a letter from Gilbey's giving me permission to see the Camden Town files. Two large men carried in a huge wooden box with a hinged lid. I was warned not to move it or I would give myself a hernia. Instead, they carried in a table and chair so the I could work in comfort. Inside was album after album. The first contained whisky labels. Dozens of different

The Roundhouse from the north
By this time the building was a bonded store and the round-arch entrance was closed.

whisky labels. The second album had more whisky labels and so had the third. Every village in Scotland must have had its own distillery and Gilbey's seemed to have bought them all. Almost every album in the box had whisky labels and those that did not, contained wine labels. I closed the box and came away with little achieved, except that I had begun to recognise the size of the Gilbey empire. By 1914 it had covered 20 acres in Camden Town alone.

The Engraving of Camden Goods Yard from the north, 1889

The steel engraving opposite and the one on pages 68 & 69, come from 'W. & G. Gilbey, A Complete List of Wines, Spirits and Liquers, with names of 2,510 Agents in the U.K', show the extent of Gilbey's buildings at Camden Town alone. The book was printed and published by Gilbey's in 1896, at their printing works in Poland Street.

This engraving looks from Chalk Farm Road, with the enormous block of Gilbey's 'A' Shed in the distance, on the other side of the Canal. The picture was drawn at the end of the nineteenth century, when Gilbey's already owned much of the site, but were yet to develop the Oval Road area. 'A' Shed stands between Oval Road Bridge (now Pirates' Bridge) and the Southampton Road Railway Bridge. The barges are probably delivering barrels of wine from France or Spain.

The original drawing must have been made over several days, probably from the top of the piano factory in Ferdinand Street, or perhaps from the roof of The Lock public house, in Chalk Farm Road.

In the foreground, the high yellow buttress wall ran unbroken from the railway bridge by Camden Lock Place to the Roundhouse. Today it has been breached to make way for the new road under the North London Railway line, to Safeways and for the petrol station, while all the goods lines have disappeared. The W. A. Gilbey's Bonded Store parallel to the road is now part of the Stables Market, but the triangular Bottle Store was destroyed by fire in October 1981. The modern Interchange building had not been built when this engraving was made. Instead, there is the earlier single-storey railway transfer building, with its pitched roof and open sides. The wharf basin below cannot be seen, but it had been cut long before. Indeed the wharf was shown on the 1834 Parish Map. Goods would have been transferred from canal to rail and vice-versa from the earliest times, but the storage of goods was in separate warehouses. Bringing transfer and storage together in the one building must have been a great saving of time and space.

Horses and carts are seen on the site. Most would have pulled Gilbey's, Pickfords, or L&NW Railway vans, moving goods to and from the railway wagons. All these firms competed in the horse shows. Gilbey's in particular were famous for their horses, breeding prize-winning Shires and winning many prizes. Indeed the horses dictated the site design for years. For example, the semicircular windows in the wall along Chalk Farm Road are stable windows built above the mangers inside.

Mr L. King, now an elderly man, wrote to me saying :-

"As young lads we used to go up to the railway stables and the carters would give us rubbing brushes. After a day's work those horses would be tethered, watered and fed and we made their coats shine. Or we went to the Barracks in Albany Road. We got in there too. The sentries let us in and sometimes we used to be lucky when the horses came back. They used to do ceremonial guards at Buckingham Palace

(continued p.66)

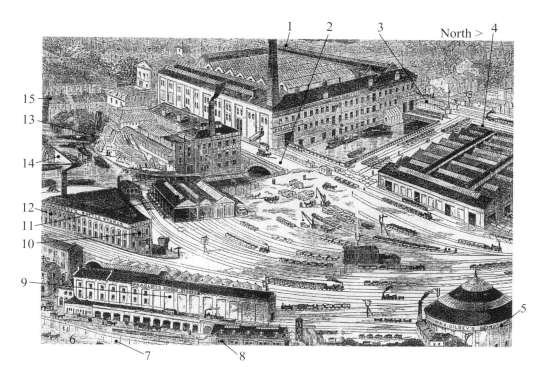

Camden Town Goods Yard from the north, 1889.

This view of the marshalling yards comes from the same book of wines. It was probably drawn over several days from the top of the piano factory which still stands behind Kent House, in Ferdinand Street, or from the roof of The Lock public house in Chalk Farm Road.

I. Gilbey's 'A' Shed in Oval Road with four floors, each of about two acres.

2 Oval Road Canal Bridge (by Pirates' Bridge)

3 Southampton Railway Bridge

4 London & North Western Railway Shed

5 The Roundhouse

6 Chalk Farm Road

7 Unbroken brick wall from Camden Lock Place to the Roundhouse

8 Existing Stables Market building built as the Horse Hospital, 1885, with its curved ramp.

9 Gilbey's No 2 Bond, built 1885

10 Bonded Store in Camden Lock Place, destroyed by fire in 1985

11 Single storey goods shed on the site of the present Interchange building

12 Site of Dingwall's

13 Timber Yard on the site of the 1997 Gilbey House

14 Ice Wharf in Jamestown Road, with the ice well at the canal edge.

and all that sort of place. The soldiers came back and dismounted and again they let us help to clean the horses and feed them and give them their nosebags. We did work hard. They were really well treated, those horses. It was VIP treatment for them.

The Horse Tunnel

At first horses and trains were on the same level, moving almost at random on the site. Indeed it was so dangerous and so many horses were killed or injured by moving trains, that the railway company built a horse passage through the catacombs, below the railway tracks. It can still be found It is the narrow cross passage at the end of some of the vaults which are now used as shops in the Stables Market. It used to run from the end of vault 15 and the tunnel under the Canal, through all the vaults, to the Horse Hospital and stables. In this way horses were able to reach their stables safely and unattended, day after day. (Vault 15 is on the Stables Market map on page 168).

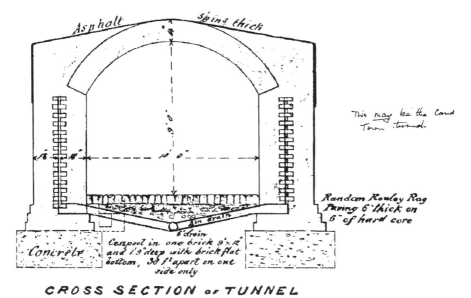

CROSS SECTION of TUNNEL

This may be the section of the main tunnel which ran from Oval Road to Gilbey's bonded warehouses in Stables Market. If not, it is similar. The elaborate cess pit system would have extended the full length of the tunnel.

To return to the engraving on page 65,

Immediately above the Roundhouse are the eight bays of L&NW Goods Shed, with their ridge and furrow roofs and Samuel Allsopp & Sons' Beer Store in the brick arches below. Beyond the canal are Gilbey's former Oval Road buildings, lying between the canal and Jamestown Road. Bewley Cliff Wharf has not yet been filled in and there is a timber yard behind the Gilbey buildings. Later Gilbey's will acquire the complete block, fill in Bewley Wharf and William Huck will build his new Bottle Store in Jamestown Road. This engraving is two complete building periods into the past. We will discuss these later in the book.

The Underground Structures at Camden Lock

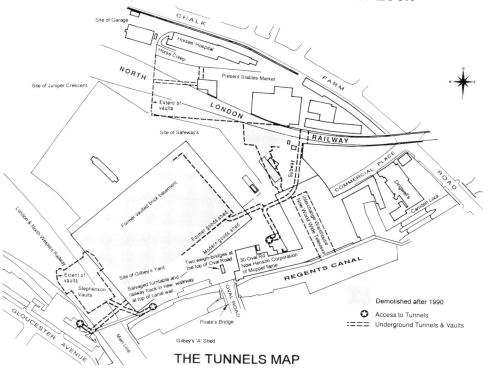

THE TUNNELS MAP

Compiled from the Greater London Industrial Archaeological Society
plan of Eastern Stables and British Rail Structural Survey Maps.
London Borough of Camden, 1990. Updated 1997

The plan of the underground structures at Camden Lock was made by the Greater London Industrial Archaeological Group (GLIAS) and shows the position in 1990. The plan was modified later when the developers demolished the western branch of the horse tunnel, from the T junction to the former goods shed (all shaded).

They also demolished the vaults on the southern side of the North London Railway,

A photograph of the Camden Town horse-tunnel, showing the lighting openings in the roof.

although the parts of the vaults to the north of the railway remain and now form part of Stables Market.[1] The vaulted brick basement below the London North Western Railway Goods Shed was also filled in and Gilbey's Yard houses built on it. Areas demolished have been tinted.

The Stationary Condensing Engine vaults under the canal remain as shown. Many of the other buildings on the map, such as the Horse Hospital, are referred to in the text.

---
[1] Ruth Blum. Camden Planning Department

67

The Bottle Store in Jamestown Road, 1894.

In 1894, Gilbey's Bottle Warehouse was built by William Hucks. He was a natural engineer who submitted no estimates and built as he went along. The building was one of the first examples of ferro-concrete and, according to the legend, was reinforced with old iron bedsteads. If so, they were good ones because the building is immensely strong. Soon it housed two steam engines, the engineering shop and the carpenters' department which made crates for the enormous export trade.

Round House (Gilbey's Bonded Store No 1)
W.A.Gilbey's Bonded Store No 2.

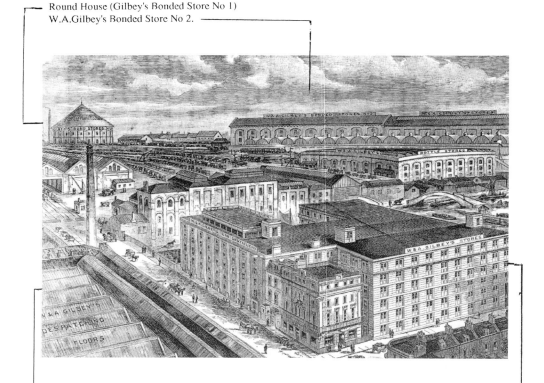

The pub at the corner of Oval Road and Jamestown Road, with the Stanhope Wharf behind. The Stanhope Arms was demolished in the 1930s to make way for Chermeyeff's new Gilbey House, now called Academic House.

Bottle Warehouse built by W.Hucks (converted into flats in 1995).

'A' Shed, W.A.Gilbey's Dispatch Department, connected by a tunnel to the Bottle Store in Jamestown Road, the Interchange Building and Stables Market.

Gilbey's Buildings at Camden Town from the south, 1896

In this engraving of 1889, the Stanhope Arms stands at the corner of Oval Road and Jamestown Road. In 1937 Chermeyeff will build the new Gilbey House on the Stanhope Arms site. When, in 1960, Gilbey's have left Camden Town and moved to Harlow, in 1960, the building will stand empty. Then Gilbey House will be renamed Academic House and the media, including Classic FM, will move in. In 1996, a century after it was built, William Huck's Bottle Store will be converted into flats and called 'Gilbey House'. Thus the name 'Gilbey House' will move along the road. These stories and others are told later in the book.

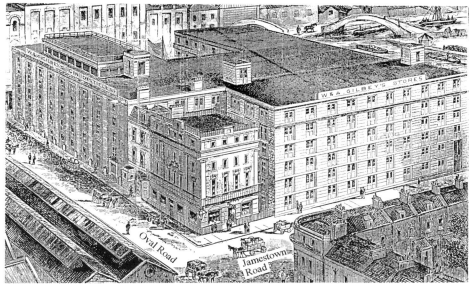

Oval Road and Jamestown Road, with the Stanhope Arms at the corner.

Gilbey House, 1927, which replaced
the Stanhope Arms and now
called Academic House

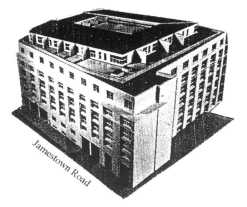

The Bottle Store in 1997,
(now the new Gilbey House)

Booth Maps [1] [2]

Between the 1880s and the turn of the century, Camden Town became poorer and more overcrowded. The proof of this comes from an unexpected quarter, the comparison of the Booth survey in the 1880s, which had culminated in his Descriptive Map of London Poverty, of 1889, and the later Booth survey in 1902-3 made for the report on the work of local churches. Charles Booth, not to be confused with General Booth of the Salvation Army, was a Victorian businessman who refused to believe that a million Londoners lived in 'great poverty', as radical politicians claimed. He started a long survey which took seventeen years to complete, to find in the end that the position was even worse than he had been told. It was the first really careful survey of housing need and led eventually to great changes.

Booth divided people into eight groups H - A, but coloured in his maps in seven colours ranging from Wealthy' to 'The Lowest Class' as follows:-

YELLOW [H] Wealthy (three or more servants: houses rated at £100 or more). Regent's Park was yellow, but there were very few such houses in Camden Town.

 RED [G] Well to do (one or two servants)

 PINK [F] Supervisors with a life condition altogether different from that of the poor. Working Class Comfort. 'The non-commissioned officers of the industrial army'

 PURPLE [E] Better paid labourers and artisans, small shopkeepers; enjoying regular, standard earnings, consistently above the poverty line

 PINK and PURPLE represent the working class with raised ideals; those we would call today 'the upward striving'.

LIGHT BLUE. [C and D] Poor, but not in want. Life is an unending struggle. Intermittent employment or small regular earnings, their means were insufficient for a decent life.

DARK BLUE [B] Incapable of looking after themselves and dragging down C & D.

BLACK [A] 'Semi-criminals'. 'A small and declining percentage'. 'A horde of barbarians'

NON-RESIDENTIAL

The colours ranged symbolically from yellow and red, the colours off wealth and warmth, to blue and black, the colours of cold and outer darkness.

Thus B and A formed an 'Under class', caught in a poverty trap from which they had no hope of escaping by their own efforts.

There were few 'Wealthy, with three or more servants', in Camden Town. These lived in Regent's Park and the West End. The main streets of Camden Town were lined with shops, often with the shopkeepers living above. These were considered Red,

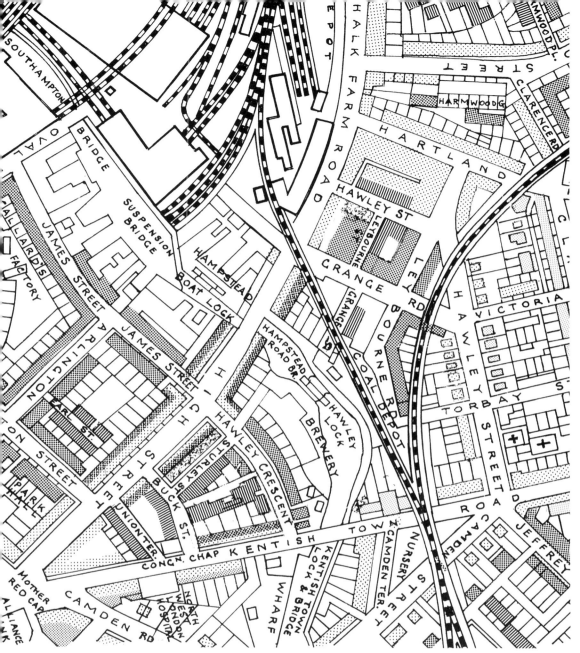

A small section of the Booth Survey of Poverty Map of 1889.

For the purpose of this book I have enlarged a portion of the map and replaced the

A small part of the 1889 Booth 'Poverty' map, enlarged and
redrawn with architectural tints instead of colours.

By the time the Church Survey was being carried out, about ten or twelve years later,
most houses in Camden Town had slipped down a peg or two. As a result, many
houses were printed in darker colours in the 1902-3 Survey than in the one above.

71

Pink, or Pink and Purple. Many would have had quite flourishing businesses, though some may have struggled on occasion. Often, behind the main roads were poorer houses. Hawley Street is purple, indicating 'better paid artisans, etc.' while Buck Street is in light blue, showing that life was 'a perpetual struggle'. Just outside the edges of this map, in Ferdinand Street and off Arlington Road, at what is now the rear entrance to Marks & Spencer's, were patches of dark blue and even black. This agrees with the police reports which are mentioned later.

The 1889 Booth Poverty Map had a profound impact on public opinion, partly for humanitarian reasons, but also because the black and dark blue areas of the very poor, were scattered among the red and pink houses of the better off. People may not have known the full details about the mechanics of microbiological infection, but they knew that filthy conditions might affect their own health. Enlightened self interest often informed their charity.

This was before Lloyd George's Old Age Act of 1906, and there was no Unemployment Insurance. Most charity was organised through the churches, so it was natural for the Poverty Map to be followed by a survey of the work done by the churches to relieve the situation. After the Poverty Map had been published in 1889, local clergy were interviewed and the reports, most written on the spot, in long-hand, are preserved at the London School of Economics, carefully filed in districts. These formed the basis of the later reports and printed maps.

Some interviewers are not above commenting on the clergy. 'Mr Arnold, the curate, is not helped by self-deception. A godly young man – offensive – pious – and self-sufficient – at bottom a hypocrite.' Apparently another Mr Slope.

The reports, in different handwritings, describe the work done by the churches in providing help during illness and free school meals to children, made without distinction as to creed. There is an earthy realism among some of the clergy. 'No change in drink unless for the worse. Mothers attending the Mothers' Meeting would go from a temperance meeting to the public house.' But the churches are patient. 'At first the people come for what they can get, but when they are responsive they can be very good.'

The churches differ, having been set up by different denominations and in different areas, yet all tell similar stories. Park Chapel, for example, had been established about 1850 and became the most fashionable resort for non-conformists. It was always crowded and still retained, in 1902, a large congregation 'coming from a distance' This distance was 'up to a mile', which shows the local nature of most church congregations when everyone walked to church. The clergyman at Park Chapel had begun his ministry there as a young man twenty-seven years before, left and returned after sixteen years, so he was very conscious of the changes in the area..

'Camden Town is becoming a business place. Now nearly every house has a lodger and servants are rare.' In the sixteen years he had been away the houses had come down in the world. When the investigators went round in 1902-3 they were able to compare the present conditions with those on the old map of 1889. Time and again there are comments on the housing. The worst area was Somers Town, where King's Cross, St Pancras, and Euston Stations had all blighted the area. Much of the district was owned by the railways and the land might be needed by them at short notice. This prevented improvement or redevelopment, so the area decayed.

St Mary's Church, Somers Town, included Ampthill Square (near Mornington Crescent) and extended down to the railway stations. It was, 'Full of problems – bad property rather than bad people – leasehold system working badly - transferred again and again – actual landlords, small rack-renting people. A wholesale clearance would be desirable.' Old photographs show Dickensian houses, literally Dickensian for he knew the houses well and described them.

This clearance and rebuilding finally came about, so that the blocks of flats around Charlton Street are almost identical with those world famous ones put up after the First World War in Berlin and Vienna. It was indeed a splendid transformation, but thirty years and a world war after the Booth Church Survey.

As conditions in Somers Town worsened, people crowded into Camden Town. This, and the concentration of industry in Camden Town, packed more and more people into the area. The report on Albany Street reads:-

'A parish of many landlords - much overcrowding - unwholesome conditions. Population of Albany Street working class - respectable, steady people with a few rough characters in Little Albany Street and Little Edward Street. Albany Street is steadily going down and downward tendency is due to the character of Somers Town.'

'Park Village West is perfectly respectable, but is notorious for kept women. Few houses otherwise occupied. Quite decent and respectable outwardly - nothing illegal, but church workers not welcomed.'

Albert Road is described as 'East of Gloucester Crescent but very much west of Park Village (which was still an area with several servants per household). Both 'yellow and red' houses on the 1889 map were now being let as tenements and furnished apartments.

The police too were consulted. Their viewpoint was different, although their comments were often similar. Inspector Wait, who had a 'gorged, unhealthy, appearance, but was intelligent and discreet', knew the area intimately.

'Delancey Street provided, as did so many, good clean lodgings.' 'All in Arlington Road were 'comfortable' (Pink). Stanhope Place, a tiny court near Parkway housed 'costers and labourers - hard-working, decent people.' Chapel Yard nearby was 'a dirty, squalid place with broken windows, in long houses without backs – mostly costers – a rough lot – any amount of drink.' Pleasant Row Mews was the same, with rough costers who boozed heavily. They had market stalls in the High Street. The tradesmen in Wellington Street drove them off, but their own trade fell as a result, so they were glad to have the market stalls back.'

Near Chalk Farm Station there was a downward tendency in 1902-3, so that the non-conformist Church was known as 'the poor church'. There were then about 700 'poor' in the district. At the same time the district round St Saviour's Church was still well-to-do but going down. It had not yet reached the stage of letting apartments, but the inhabitants were of a 'poorer class and impecunious'. New rents were half what they had been twenty years before.

Fleet Road was 'what it had been since the Fever Hospital had been built' [on the site of the present Royal Free Hospital]. The houses had been built for the middle class but were given over to the poor, including many railway, bus and tram men. Out of a population of 6000, one third were working class. However, Fleet Road had been going down before ever the Fever Hospital was built. Many of the people displaced in Somers Town by the coming of the railways had moved directly to Fleet Road, which was conveniently on the end of the tram route and thus easy to reach.

In Chalk Farm the main roads were lined with red houses, indicating 'wealthy', although this often concealed worry. Behind, were rows of streets coloured the light blue of poverty. Ferdinand Place, [which ran parallel to Ferdinand Street and has now been demolished in favour of blocks of flats] was much improved. There were still a number of loose women about but no ragged children. In Haverstock Street, one of the cul-de-cacs which then ran off Ferdinand Street, they saw the first bare-footed lad. Hethersett Street, a similar cul-de-sac, was the worst and drink, not poverty was to blame. There were no convictions for serious crime, only 'snatching youngsters'.

To move forward a couple of generations, these rows of small terraces, let in rooms and floors, persisted until the whole area from the back of the bus garage to Crogsland Road was cleared to build working class flats. After the First World War, memorial plaques had been erected in Heathersett Street and other local roads listing the dead. General Haig had said that those who worked together and joined up together could fight together. This 'pals' system created great loyalty and camaraderie, but it meant that men from the same street also died together. The same names appeared time after time on the same plaques, where whole families of men had died. Where are the plaques now?

In Queen's Crescent, Wellersley Road was 'much improved' and Kentish Town was 'nothing like so rough as it had been ten years before'. Streets were changing from purple to pink, as they attracted supervisors in place of artisans. Areas went up and down all the time.

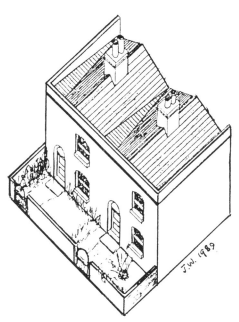

Harmood Street,
Pink: the houses of foremen
and clerks in 1889

Camden Housing in the 1890s

A beautiful stucco house by the Regent's Park Road canal bridge, which Booth would have classed as yellow.

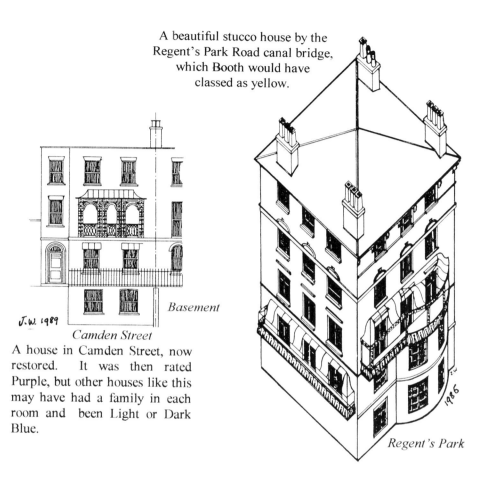

Basement

Camden Street

A house in Camden Street, now restored. It was then rated Purple, but other houses like this may have had a family in each room and been Light or Dark Blue.

Regent's Park

Agar Town, the typical slum, Dark Blue and Black.

Municipal Housing in Camden

The results of the Booth Poverty Survey can be seen all round us, in the blocks of municipal flats. Their history is too vast to be dealt with here, but it was a long, hard-fought struggle. When, at the start of the century, the London County Council and local borough councils finally won the right to build and let at economic rents, municipal housing took off. Goldington Buildings, opened at the lower end of Great College Street in 1904, was the first of many in the borough, but the problem of providing good housing at low rents was phenomenal. In 1921, 11,000 people in St Pancras (the area from Camden Town to King's Cross) lived more than three to a room. Nearly 4,000 lived four to a room. In 1922 there were 10,000 unemployed in St Pancras. The story goes on and on. 'Five per cent philanthropic housing' (the private attempt to solve the problem of low-rent housing); council housing; overcrowding; slum clearance; bomb damage repairs; tower blocks compared with low-rise housing; flat roofs versus pitched; New Towns built on 'green-field' sites, or the rehabilitation of old inner-city 'brown field' ones. They have been the subject of hundreds of books. In London, the Booth Surveys laid the ground for all of this endeavour, which is why the original hand-written reports, with their sometimes acid comments, are strangely moving. They, and other reports in later years, led to a century of building. It is a record of which any borough could be proud.

A small swathe of the Municipal Housing just north of Camden Lock

1 Lawn Road
2 Malden Road
3 Denton Tower, Prince of Wales Road
4 Barrington Court, Lamble Street Estate
5 Fleet Road
6 Malden Road
7 Lismore Circus
8 Southfleet, Malden Road
9 Off Malden Road
10 South End Green
11 Kent House, Ferdinand Street. Built 1935, these were years before their time. (Ref: Architect & Building News 20 Dec 1935)
12 Mansfield Road
13 Southampton Road
14 West Kentish Town Estate, between Malden Road and Grafton Road. This estate was built of re-cast concrete slabs for walls and roofs. When these failed, the flats were insulated with 50 mm of mineral wool and red hanging tiles and the flat roofs replaced with 'upside down' roofs.
15 Tottenhall, Ferdinand Street. It was in Ferdinand Street that in 1890 the Booth Survey researcher saw 'the first barefoot boy'.
16 Behind Queen's Crescent
17 Mansfield Road.

To these can be added the Arlington Road and Camden Gardens flats(pp.182-193) built for the Community Housing Association and hundreds of others erected over the years. Camden streets are lined with them, and all stemming originally from the Booth Survey.

---

[1] The Booth notebooks at London School of Economics
[2] The Booth Poverty Map of 1889, reprinted by London Topographical Society

Moy's of Bayham Street

Ernest F. Moy's were general engineers in Camden Town for about seventy years. It was a very local enterprise, started by young men who had been brought up in the area.[1] They were especially interested in electricity and photography, but were prepared to make anything that was offered.

In 1895, three young men, Moy, Bastie and Fox, had opened a small workshop at 9 Pratt Mews, Camden Town, where they started with literally one man and a boy. Over the years they took out patent after patent, branching out in any direction which seemed to suggest new advances and the hope of further development. They moved to No 3 Greenland Place nearby and, in the 1930s, took possession of a brand new factory at 16-34 Bayham Street. Thus the firm never moved more than a few hundred yards from its starting point.

They were always fascinated with cameras and the application of electricity to them. They formed their Cinematograph Company Ltd and made films on the flat roof of their Greenland Road factory, with the help of no less a person than William Friese-Greene. Born in 1855 in Bristol, Friese-Greene was a pioneer of the motion picture. His gravestone in Highgate cemetery calls him the inventor of the Kinematograph (Patent 10301). In 1889, while living in 136 Edgware Road, in Maida Vale, he first succeeded in projecting a moving picture. He was so excited that he rushed out into the street and dragged in the first person he could find to view it. This happened to be a policeman walking past. Completely bewildered, he became the first cinema audience in the world. This oft-told tale was incorporated in the film 'The Magic Box', in which Robert Donat played Friese-Greene and the policeman was Laurence Olivier.

Friese-Greene's claims to have shown the very first moving picture are contested by others in other countries, notably by the Lumiere Brothers in France. Freise-Greene never made any money from his invention, and died penniless in 1921, but he was certainly among the leaders. Other countries would have turned his house into a film museum, or a cinema school, but in 1997 Camden Council gave permission for the house to be demolished.

'The Policeman's Drink',
with Moy, Beastie, Fox
and Harrison, in Greenland
Place, Camden Town.

136 Maida Vale, where Friese-Greene lived from 1888-92.
The blue plaque is hidden in the shadow of the bay window.
Photograph : Edmond Terakopian, 1997

The frames on the previous page are from an 1897 film called, 'The Policeman's Drink'. They show the founders of the company, Fox, Moy and Beastie, with another man called Bert Harrison, acting on the roof of the Greenland Place factory. There is also in the records a contract for a twenty-to-thirty minute film to be shown in a circus at Bedford, for a showman with the resounding name of M. J. Zaro. Immediately after the photograph above was taken, the 1954 blue plaque was cut out of the wall and English Heritage promised to find a new home for it. Camden Town is now a centre for the media. If the wording of the plaque allows it, perhaps English Heritage should re-site the plaque in Greenland Place, where we know Friese-Greene made films? If the wording does not fit – if, for example, it says 'Friese-Greene lived here' – let us have a new one.

Photoplay Reproductions Ltd., one of our modern Camden Town film companies, specialises in documentaries about film history. Perhaps some day they may find and restore one of Moy's films.

To return to Moy's engineering work. In 1900, Moy and Bastie launched their kine camera which was very successful. It was taken on Captain Scott's penultimate Antarctic Expedition of 1905, and was used in the trenches of the First World War. At the same time, the firm's bread and butter work was still fuse boxes, circuit breakers, and other routine electrical equipment. They made electrical switch gear, patented a film feeding mechanism for kinematograph cameras and a film cartridge, which they called a 'dark box', to allow daylight loading.

In 1911 Moy's invented the Moy Gyroscopic camera, which opened up the field of aviation photography. A hand-held kinematograph camera contained two independent electric motors, one to drive the gyroscope and the other to drive the operating mechanism. The camera, held steady by the gyroscope, allowed aviators to photograph from moving aircraft. Incidentally, in 1997 the same thing was hailed as a new invention when it was applied to a hand-held video recorder.

Moy cameras, similar to the ones used in the First World War and in the Antarctic.[1]

King George V inspecting the trenches in the first World War.
The camera is a Moy.

In the 1920s the firm patented many improvements to film cameras, but times were hard. Only the arrival of sound in the cinema saved the firm when Gaumont British asked them to make sound heads for their existing projectors. This injected new life into the firm, so that in the Depression of the 1930s, Moy's were paying the highest wages in the area. A top-rated skilled man got 3 pounds 16 shillings and four pence ha'penny a week. This was when a labourer was earning about two pounds a week.

By late 1930s the firm was in the position to open a brand new factory in Bayham Street, now occupied by Getty Images. They were toolmakers, turners, founders and enamellers. A photograph shows long rows of machines driven by belts, so they seem to have taken their old machinery with them to the new building. The modern machines with individual electric motors, which were already being installed in the new factories along the Great West Road, seem light years away. During the Second World War the firm made radar equipment. After 1945 they made household appliances and anything else that would pay the wages.

In the mid-1950s Leonard Cheesman, one of Moy's designers, produced a camera capable of recording every three of four frames shown on a television screen. This allowed a film record to be made of a live TV show. Marconi-EMI and High Definition Films collaborated, but the technique has been superseded by video recording. This was the firm's last venture into the film business. In place of film equipment, Moy's began to manufacture Braille transcribers for the Royal National Institute for the Blind. In fact the whole history of the Moy's illustrates the speed of change in inventions, the very small number of patents which make any money, and the pure doggedness needed to keep a firm in business over a period of seventy years.

Moy's was typical of dozens which crowded the streets and mews buildings of Camden Town. Cardboard box makers, motor body builders, timber merchants, glass merchants, paint makers, wire-workers and general smiths, air-conditioning firms which made sheet metal ducting, manufacturing opticians, and the Ace Studios in 73-75 Albany Street which would make you a short advertising film for ten pounds. The St Pancras Chamber of Commerce listed page after page of firms, small and large, all offering employment. Much of it was highly skilled and specialist. Most was semi-skilled. All these jobs and traditional crafts were under threat as British industry collapsed in the nineteen sixties. Camden Town would never be the same.

The old belt-driven machines in the Bayham Street factory which, by the 1960s, could not compete with modern ones. Today the building is part of the Getty Picture Library.

After Moys left the building it was occupied by Anello & Davide, the famous theatrical footwear company. This is their attractive logo in the shape of a shoe.

The Getty/Hulton, Tony Stone logos.

---

[1] The Story of Moy, Eyepiece (Journal of the Guild of British Camera Technicians) July/August 1986.

The Interchange Building

The Interchange

Left – the building with its two side screening walls and the off-set canal wharf

Right – A section showing the five levels:- water, rail, and warehousing. It also shows the cranes and one of the slopes which allowed goods to be hauled from the barges direct to the railway platform above, for loading into wagons. There are two 7 foot wide narrow boats and one 14 foot wide barge in the dock. B, was one of Gilbey's bonded warehouses.

This huge building in red brick framed with blue engineering brick, dominates the north side of the Lock. It is a Victorian/Edwardian building, designed as a fortress, immensely strong and secure. Now listed grade II, it was designed to bring together canal, rail and road transport in one covered building, with three floors of storage above. Some people have called it the Brunel Building although this cannot be correct since the younger Brunel died in 1859. When Isambard Kingdom Brunel was dying, they laid him on a flat railway wagon and pulled it across the new Saltash Bridge so that he could see his noble trusses soaring high above. This was perhaps fifty years before the modern Interchange was erected. The present building does not appear on the 1894 Ordnance Survey map, but is on the 1912 one. In 1905 the Wharves and Warehouse Committee of the Institute of Surveyors reported that the building had been surveyed. This settles the date and proves that Brunel can have had nothing to do with it. [1] [2, 3]

Much earlier, on the site of the present Interchange warehouse, there was a single-storey exchange building. This had been created above the old wharf shown in the 1834 Parish Map, page 28. The Goad Fire Insurance plans (which record the materials used in each individual building) show that it was mainly in wood and was clearly the main place for transferring general goods between canal, road and rail. It is shown in the engraving of the Camden Town Goods Yard (page 65). The present brick Interchange Building was a later reincarnation of this single-storey building.

For years Thames lighters had brought their cargoes to Camden Town where they were transferred to rail, road, or to the narrow boats which took them up the canal to Oxford, Birmingham and beyond. Narrow boats are not suitable for sailing on the waters of the tidal Thames, as was shown when some of them did it during the Second World War. In 'Ramblin' Rose: the Boatwoman's Story',[4] Sheila Stewart describes hazardous journeys to London by narrow boat during the height of the Blitz. Thames lighters, on the other hand, were strong, sea-going craft, so they were used to bring cargoes as far as Camden Town, where they were transferred to narrow boats.

It was normal for lighters and narrow boats to work in pairs. For example, six pairs of boats took cocoa beans from Camden Town to the Cadbury factory at Bourneville and returned with waste products, presumably to be transferred in turn to lighters and jettisoned in the North Sea. Similar regular traffic used rail, road and canal, with Camden Town as the exchange post. Daily traffic was immense. Look at the deep grooves in the iron handrail of the Roving (Diagonal) Bridge across the canal, cut by the chafing of innumerable tow ropes. Consider how many barges must have been warped across each day, against the pressure of the water flowing into the lock to do that damage. Look at the polish on the granite cobbles, made by the iron shoes of huge shire horses. In Camden Town, industrial archaeology is all around us.

The checking of each consignment and onward distribution to its correct destination must have been a major task, but it probably helped to check 'losses'. For canal boatmen had a reputation for pilfering. A cabbage, or some potatoes from a farmer's field, or a partridge brought down by a catapult, were the usual wayside takings. It was not unknown for a man going through game preserves to take orders for birds before he started, while their lurchers were skilled at running down rabbits. Cargoes too could be targeted. Lime, clay, steel ingots, horse manure, were safe enough, but coal could be sold by the bucketful at canal-side cottages and lock pubs. Consignments of bottles of wine or spirits were particularly at risk. If by accident a case happened to drop and a bottle broke, there was often a bowl below to catch the contents. Some boatmen carrying barrels, went armed with fine drills in case the bungs were sealed. Loosening a bung was easier, but if this was not possible, they drilled the barrel and resealed it. Wines and spirits were so vulnerable that eventually Gilbey's ceased to import barrels by water and transferred instead to rail.

Silk, a particularly valuable cargo, was transported inside protective canvas covers, carefully sewn, so the experts extracted the silk with fine wire hooks, a small bunch at a time. Some gravel slipped in to make up the weight, the hole pushed together and covered with bird droppings, made the theft difficult to detect. Barges were sometimes used to secrete stolen goods and spirit them out of the area. In 'Bricks and Brickies' the writer describes how the police descended on a barge carrying household rubbish on its way to fuel the brick kilns in the Thames Estuary. There had been a robbery in the West End and this was the suspected get-away vehicle.[1]

The Structure of the Interchange

The Interchange Building was designed to mechanise the whole process of goods transfer between canal, rail and road. The Pickford building on the other bank, which later became Gilbey's 'A' Shed, had been designed for the same purpose. The Interchange building also included three storeys of warehousing above the railway level. Inside the building were hydraulic lifts which carried the goods to the correct level for road or rail transport, or for storage. The opening in the floor through which the goods used to be lifted from the barges in the wharf below, up to the railway level, can still be seen. Beside it is the original crane, but now bolted still and freshly painted. The hole in the floor has been filled in with glass tiles. so that today it is an elegant glass floor, clean and cleared as if for Fred Astaire and Ginger Rogers to dance a spectacular number. Then, it was a grimy pit, open to the water below and swept by winds above.

The walls which have been built round what was the open station level are inside the old octagonal stanchions. Thus the architect has preserved the stanchions and we can still imagine what it used to be like when everything was open. The old platform buildings, in red brick, where the clerical work was done and the railway men made their tea, have been preserved too, and can be seen in the main entrance hall.

The whole railway level was an open station, with platforms, railway lines and piled goods. It was a place of heavy work, day and night, without walls and standing on massive octagonal pillars. The pillars were built of four 'I shaped' girders, wrapped round with octagonal plates and riveted in place. These sets of stanchions, consisting of one large I girder and two small ones (A) or four small ones (B) are quite common in Victorian work. Most are riveted together with narrow wrought iron bands (C) but the Interchange ones are encased completely with bent iron plates (D). Riveting must have presented problems as one cannot get inside to hammer over the rivets. Presumably the rivets were hit from the outside against some sort of long-arm anvil.

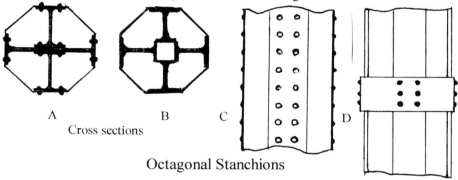

A   B   C   D

Cross sections

Octagonal Stanchions

The massive octagonal pillars were necessary to support the three floors of heavy storage above. At the top is a roof built of very heavy joists indeed. These are no ordinary roof joists, but huge balks designed to support heavy lifting gear. The warehouse floors too are most unusual, with 12 inch by 3 inch timbers laid **touching each other**. Thus the floors consist of solid wood and a square foot of floor space is made of a **cubic** foot of timber. Clearly, floors like this were constructed to bear enormous weights.

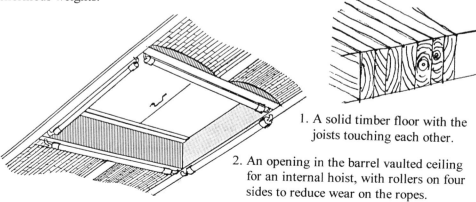

1. A solid timber floor with the joists touching each other.

2. An opening in the barrel vaulted ceiling for an internal hoist, with rollers on four sides to reduce wear on the ropes.

85

At intervals throughout the building were hydraulic hoists which lifted goods to the correct level for road or rail transport, or for storage. At each floor were trap doors, now closed and braced against accidental opening. Each trap measures about 9 feet by 6 feet, and had steel rollers on all four sides which turned with the hoisting ropes, to reduce friction and wear. The hoists hung from the heavy roof beams high above.

By 1948, the Goad Fire Insurance map shows an electric travelling crane beside the railway, but this is long gone.

Besides the internal hoists, there are four columns of external warehouse hoists, now painted a wine colour. From the inside the top halves open as double doors, while the bottom halves drop down on chains to form loading platforms. Above each column of doors was a heavy pulley on a projecting arm for raising and lowering goods.

Railway access to the Interchange Basin

Below the railway level was the Interchange Basin, with vaults on either side. All the vaults were used by Gilbey's to store wine and spirits and, wrapped round one side of the building, was the horse tunnel linking Oval Road with Stables Market.

The vaults of the bonded warehouse are immensely strong, as they had to support the weight of the trains and storage above. From below, one sees low vaults on either side, where the trains ran, and higher vaults in between them where the platforms stood. Originally all this was supported on two rows of octagonal iron pillars, similar to the octagonal pillars surrounding the railway level and now built into the outside wall of Worldwide Television.

The Basin

The Interchange Basin is 210 feet long and 44 feet wide, with a row of pillars down the centre. This gave room for three barges in length and room for one 14 foot wide barge and one 7 foot wide narrow boat, or three narrow boats, on each side of the pillars. Thus the dock could hold up to six barges and six narrow boats, or eighteen narrow boats, at any one time.

In the roof of the vaults were trap doors and long, hinged, wooden ramps. The trap doors were in the railway platform above, so that when the traps were opened and a ramps lowered to a barge below, the goods could be hauled direct from the barge to the station platform, ready for loading into the railway wagons.

Water Flow in the Canal

There are no locks between Uxbridge and Camden Town, a stretch of twenty-six miles. The water moves only when the lock gates at Camden Town are opened, so that it flows immensely slowly, but finally, after many years, all the silt and debris finishes up at Camden Town. As a result, the Interchange dock is the final resting place and has gained the name of Dead Dog Hole. On one occasion a dead body was found, old, bloated and repulsive. When a policeman from Kentish Town Police Station was called, he recoiled.

"I don't want to deal with that," he said, and towed the body over to the opposite bank. Then he rang the Albany Street Police, who are responsible for the south bank, to report the find.

Gilbey's Bonded Warehouse

To the east of the Basin was Gilbey's Bonded Warehouse, now empty. The structure is massive, providing formidable security for the valuable wines and spirit in store and considerable security against fire. Four small openings, each only about three feet wide, led from the Basin. These were protected by heavy iron doors which were self-closing in case of fire. The doors hung on pulleys which rolled on sloping iron runners. Each door was held open by a cable and weight, with a fusible metal link in the cable. In the event of a fire, the metal link would melt, allowing the door to slide down and clang shut.

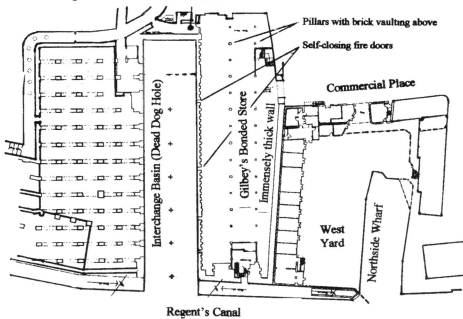

The Basement of the Interchange Building and West Yard
Gilbey's Bonded Warehouse below the Interchange Building

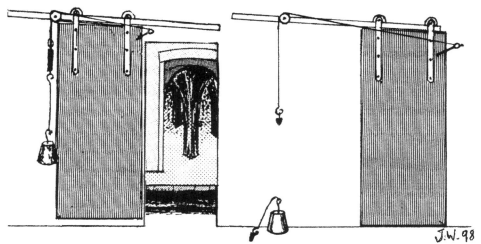

Steel door held open   The Interchange Wharf   The fusible link melted   The door closed by gravity

Security doors between Gilbey's bonded store and the Interchange basin

87

fire. The doors hung on pulleys which rolled on sloping iron runners. Each door was held open by a cable and weight, with a fusible metal link in the cable. In the event of a fire, the metal link would melt, allowing the door to slide down and clang shut.

The only other access to the bonded warehouse was down a short staircase in the north-west corner and through a small door leading to the horse tunnel. This tunnel linked the different factory buildings on both sides of the canal to the bonded. warehouse.

The vaulting and doors of the west side of the basin are more conventional, as they were used solely for storage of ordinary goods.

The Interchange reveals Camden's past better than any other local building. It shows that Camden Town was once a major manufacturing and transit centre, full of industry, with goods from both this country and abroad on the move day and night. The railway level was lifted above the local street level on a vast subterranean world of brick arches and horse tunnels, which stretched under the Main Line, under the Canal, up to the Roundhouse and as far as Primrose Hill Goods Yard. Only Dingwall's Yard and the present Stables Market area were at street level. The arches were used as stables, workshops, and above all for the storage of goods; fodder, potatoes and wines and spirits in bond.

All this involved tight security. Today we wander at will through the 'catacombs'– the mass of brick tunnels and arches containing stalls and cafes, bands and exciting gloom – but when this was a working goods yard, the public was kept out. A high wall extended unbroken from the Railway Bridge over Chalk Farm Road right up to the Roundhouse. One solitary gate was used for the multitude of carts and vans which served the yard. The Interchange Building was part of this security system. It was a fortress with strong walls, where the small-paned windows acted as safety grilles.

Interchange
in 1998
A satellite dish
and modern
vans block the
old warehouse
doors.

World Wide Television and the Nineteen Nineties.

The Interchange building is now, in the 1990s, occupied by World Wide Telvision. Today it is clean, warm and protected from the elements, but we can still imagine what it used to be like. There were no protecting walls at this railway level, so that the wind blew through. Four rows of octagonal pillars, railway lines and raised platforms, with the names of different towns displayed above. Below each were the goods brought by road and canal, piled ready to be loaded into the small railway goods wagons for dispatch. The old platform buildings, in red brick, where the clerical work was done and the railwaymen brewed their tea, have been preserved. The sunken tracks on either side where the trains used to run, have been filled in level with the platforms to form the flat floor of the reception area. The water in the wharf below can be glimpsed through the thick glass floor. The canal crane is still there, the roof still barrel-vaulted, with one of the hoist openings and its rope rollers still in place and the octagonal pillars are painted blood red. Only one pillar has been removed, that in the centre of the reception desk. The fact that it could be removed safely, apparently with no extra strengthening, suggests that the whole building is even stronger than was required. The Victorians always over-engineered, making their buildings heavier that was necessary, and this is an example.

The Logo of World Wide Television

World Television News has been providing news twenty-four hours a day for almost fifty years. The Company has a presence in over a hundred countries, making and transmitting programmes day and night. It also has the international distribution rights of the BBC and the ABC television service of the United States. It has large libraries on film and tape to draw on at a moment's notice. This is a big player who needed a big home in Britain.

Interchange, built a century ago for the storage and transmission of goods, has found a new user doing a similar type of work. Now its railway platforms have become a clean, silent reception area. Its high ceilings provide room for studio lighting gantries, while its station yards hold satellite dishes and television vans. Electronic signals have taken the place of raw materials and manufactured goods. The transformation is almost symbolic of what has happened to Camden Town in its search for a new future.

Scientific Instrument Making

Modern factories can be silent temples, with part-made goods being transported from machine to machine by robot trolleys, guided from afar by computers. No humans appear to be involved. This is a very recent development indeed. When Camden Town was a buzzing centre of manufacture, things were different. A heaving mass of men and women appeared at the factory gate each day. Arrived, they waited to the last moment before going in, men leaning against the walls pulling at the ends of their cigarettes. Women had to run the gauntlet of all these male eyes, the comments and whistles. Young girls in particular found this difficult. Carefully dressed in the latest fashion, they could be devastated by a rude comment. A few could brazen it out, but often it was a difficult start to the day.

At the last moment, dignified gentlemen, who were town councillors, and even at one time the mayor of a south London borough, could be seen running for their lives to reach the factory gate before the clock struck eight, breathless to be on time. A minute late and they would be shut out and lose a quarter of an hour's pay. Inside was an assistant foreman who enjoyed his petty tyranny. He went up to any group of young boys or girls and hissed, "Time and tide wait for no Jimmy," and they would scatter. The more dignified men, those with gravitas, were not imposed on by such a small power. They had run only in response to the clock and money.

Inside the gate they proceeded in a more decorous manner. They walked soberly to their familiar benches, changed into overalls, looked over their work and began the eternal battle of wits with the foreman. In highly skilled trades like instrument making, or tool making, everything was made on piecework. An instrument consisted of a number of separate parts, each calling for a particular skill and made on a particular machine, each priced and haggled over separately. The foreman would bargain for perhaps a hundred of a particular part, made to fixed tolerances, finished to a certain quality. The craftsman would protest at the price and finally they would agree.

From then the foreman played no part in the actual production. He had the right to buy, but he had no right to dictate how the work was done. Manufacture was the jealously defended right of the craftsman and, if the foreman approached, a cloth was ostentatiously thrown over the bench so that he could not see the methods being used. This was craft small-batch production at its most secretive.

This method of production can be traced back to the medieval guilds, where apprentices entered a 'mystery'. They had to swear to keep secret the special knowledge that the guild would teach them, defending it if necessary with their lives. John H. Harvey tells a shocking story from the thirteenth century of a young apprentice who let out a secret. Masons building a cathedral were encountering difficulties with water. A stream was affecting the stonework and damp was creeping up the wall. The boy's father, the master of the freemason's lodge, had described how they were going to solve the problem, passing on information which might lead some day to his son himself becoming a master. The young lad, in his innocence and enthusiasm, described the solution to the bishop. The bishop was paying for the work, but had no right to know how it would be carried out. When the father heard the story, his honour as master and father required him to prevent the secret from being lost.

The only way was to silence the bishop. The man stabbed his bishop to death and was duly hanged for it. The secret was kept.

Instrument makers did not go that far, but they kept their secrets close. Men thought out ingenious methods of making parts more quickly, or with less effort, and so increase their weekly money. Men watched each other, puzzled at a man who apparently started the job from the wrong end. Each one was anxious to pick up yet another tip which could be stored up at the back of the mind for later use. No craftsmen let out his secrets easily for they were his bread and butter. One often heard the phrase, 'learning by sitting next to Nellie'. This was how craftsmen did learn, but Nellie was not always willing to help.

These small groups of skilled craftsmen were trapped in each other's company like rowers chained to the same galley oar. They could not get away from each other without leaving the firm and in the next, they must join a similar group. To be held in the same workshop, with large machines and room to move about, was one thing. A bench of jewellers could be far worse. A line of small benches in some back room in a converted house could be a life sentence.

Some of them might be clever men. All would be skilled, but conversation could be acid. Banter could have its cutting edge, or a provoking insistence, so that some would become silent and morose. Tiny incidents, revealed in a moment of confidence, were recalled for years. The same jokes, homilies and prejudices, were aired day after day, making life a misery for the victim. Religion, politics, gambling, football – conversation varied from group to group. One dominant man could change the whole tone.

In the midst of this was the overriding concern with prices. Firms needed to reduce labour costs in a competitive market. The price of an article was argued to the farthing, so that each batch of work was a separate calculation – a separate tussle with the foreman. This gave a unity to the group. Everyone had to combine against the foreman. In the words of the workshop, the foreman and the workers 'were right daggers.'

The antagonism between the foreman and the trades union representative was natural. They met and negotiated, fighting closely over fractions of a penny, but it was the lesser lights who earned the dislike. One assistant foreman was particularly irritating. He was in the meeting but had no proper role, merely reiterating what the foreman had just said. No sooner had the foreman stated his position than the

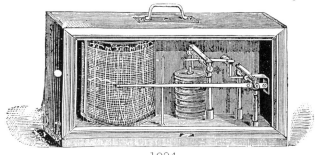

1094

1094 Self-recording Aneroid Barometer ... £5 5 0

91

assistant jumped up and repeated his words. He added nothing, put things in a more confused way and sat down well pleased with himself. After about the third time the trades union representative began to look under the table in a puzzled way. Each time the man stood up the trade unionist bent down and peered under the table, completely ignoring what the man was saying. Soon the foreman started looking under the table too. At last he said:-

"What's wrong? What are you looking for?"

"I'm looking for the string?"

"What string?"

"The string you are working this puppet by".

The second struggle was against the dilution of the trade. Outsiders had to be kept out by a strictly controlled apprenticeship system. The key to both of these was craftsmanship. Work could always be done less accurately, or finished more carelessly, and so prices reduced. This struggle for standards was at the heart of the matter. Craftsmanship was a thing of intense pride. Poor workmanship was despised and rejected by good firms which had built their reputations at the top end of the market. Work was always done to a high degree of polish. Steel parts were blued to exactly the right colour.. No sheet stampings were left with edges torn from the machine. All had to be 'draw-filed' to a high polish, time consuming but the sign of high-class work. This quality of workmanship separated the craftsman from the jobber, the Johnny-come-lately who had served no apprenticeship, who would skimp the finish and cut the price.

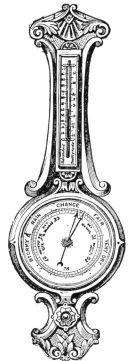

Often the 'finish' would not improve the function of the final instrument at all, but it was beyond the skill of ordinary people and a guarantee the craftsman would have a secure job, at a higher wage than others. A classic example of this protectionist thought came in the Second World War. A newly launched battleship was torpedoed just outside its home port. A new ship, including all its instrumentation, was ordered immediately. At this period, with the Germans at the gates of Moscow, the Russians were boring the barrels of their guns but leaving the outsides rough and unturned. The bores, not the outsides, were killing Germans. The English instrument makers, fearful of reducing standards and their own wages after the War, insisted on draw-filing the spokes of all their wheels. Draw-filing would not shorten the war by a second. It was an unnecessary frippery which could have been dispensed with, but if the instrument makers had given up this craft embellishment they believed it would never have been used again and their wages would have suffered after the war.

———————

Barometer, Aneroid, Pendant form, 8 silvered dial,   £4 . 4 . 0
bevelled plate glass front, enamelled thermometer,
mounted on carved solid oak carved frame.

Eccentrics

Factories had their share of eccentrics, tolerated and ignored. One man, perfectly normal in other ways, went from workshop to workshop with a small board under his arm, to follow up jobs and see how they were progressing. He came inside the door, placed the board on the ground and did a little tap dance. Nobody took any notice, but he had announced his presence and he then proceeded to move from one machine to the next checking progress. Another man, when his work was not going smoothly would stop suddenly, raise his hands and face to some unseen god above and cry, "Be fair. Be fair." After a minute he would go on with his work and be quiet for a period. This was taken as a matter of course and hardly mentioned.

Another, completely bald, wore a smart bowler hat to work and all the way to his work bench. Suddenly he removed the bowler and put on a cap, but so quickly that nobody ever saw his bald head. They took bets on it, tried to divert him at the crucial moment, but never succeeded.

A man with a good baritone voice sang the typical Peter Dawson songs of the period about rolling roads and the open air. By the end of two verses of 'I am a Vagabond,' sung at the top of his voice, there were shouts telling him what road to take and threatening to set the dogs on him as a poultry thief. This was accompanied by a hail of screwed up paper balls and small pieces of wood until he had to stop.

In the middle of the afternoon, when the air was hot and people were bored, someone would shout,

"I'm going on holiday.

"Holiday? Where are you going."

"Brighton. I'm going to Brighton."

"I'm going to Yarmouth - fishing"

"Folkestone."

Everyone took up the chorus. In a moment the air was full of shouts and train noises.

"Take your seats."

"Come on you kids. Get in the corner and keep the other people out. No you can't go to the lavatory. We'll miss the train."

"Brighton train. Brighton train"

"Hurry up. Find a seat. There behind the fat man."

There were the sounds of whistles.

"We're off. Hurry up Mabel."

Men up and down the workshop pulled out the drawers in their benches and slammed them shut to make the sound of train doors closing.

"You've got my head stuck in the door."

"Never mind. The first tunnel will deal with that."

People started stamping in unison to imitate the engine starting up slowly and gradually getting faster and faster and softer and softer as the train disappeared in the distance.

After five minutes of shouting and play acting, the foreman put his head out of the office without saying anything. Slowly the workshop returned to its usual calm. Men and women settled down to the final quarter of the day like children in from play.

Some of the work was very specialized . In the 1930s one skilled instrument maker was the only man who could repair a Wheatstone. Not a Wheatstone Bridge, but a precursor of the teleprinters, which have themselves been obsolete now for many years. There was only one Wheatstone machine in the country and that was at Rugby. When it went wrong it was rushed up to London and he had to stop everything, working overtime if necessary, to get the machine back to Rugby as quickly as possible.

Most of the time however, most of the work was real grind. During both world wars many Camden factories worked twelve hour shifts and more, making instruments. Some were secret – pieces of unknown machines to be assembled elsewhere, for purposes unknown. Sensitive work which was not to be spoken about. Other pieces were obvious. Hundreds and hundreds of clinometers were made - spirit levels on brackets for giving the angles on field guns and aeroplane wings. They were set up on a special piece of equipment in the factory and painted green before being fitted to 3.7 and 4.5 anti-aircraft guns. The same firm made specially sensitive anemometers for weather prediction. Three revolving cups weighing less than an eggshell, were joined to arms with some gentle rivetting and attached to a specially adapted stopwatch. Carried aloft by a balloon, they were floated down to earth. As the air got heavier, the anemometer revolved faster. The quality of this workmanship was quite outstanding. Merely waving the hand in front of the anemometer made it revolve.

Marvels of precision were made in tumble-down factories. In 1945, with the world to rebuild, one could sell anything. It appeared that Camden factories would produce goods for ever, but the machines were worn out, production methods obsolete, prices too high.

Apprenticeships

One instrument maker I knew was apprenticed in the 1930s in Camden Town. The firm went bankrupt a couple of years later. This was one firm which had collapsed, a tragedy for people employed and for the creditors, but a normal industrial hazard. The lad was able to continue in another firm and finally became highly qualified. The story was different in the 1960s. Then Camden Town firms were disappearing all round, so that there were no other places to go to.

I was a housemaster in a large London comprehensive school, very concerned about finding jobs for my school leavers. At this time children could leave at the Easter if they had reached fifteen years of age. Traditionally the factories, and in particular those like the printers, controlled by craft unions, favoured the children of existing members. When Dad had a word with the foreman and the union, a place was found. Sometimes this was a safe niche for a lad, but I could see the world was changing. Some boys were very clever and would have done well in their exams, but they were leaving school too early. These were the potential managers who would be helped in their careers by a broader education, leading to further qualifications. Most unions and employers rejected all my letters, even when I could persuade the parents to allow the boy to stay on. Tradition demanded that boys should leave at the minimum age and their training would then take its normal trade course - leave later and they would never get into the industry.

When the school leaving age was raised to sixteen, I had a better case: some engineering firms were willing to allow boys to stay on the extra term to take their exams, but many still refused. In one case I had a letter from the managing director agreeing to defer entry until the end of the O Level exams, but the boy was withdrawn at Easter and I never saw him again. Someone lower down the ladder had intervened.

Slowly we persuaded employers to accept apprentices at a later age. Boys took their exams before signing apprenticeship papers - we appeared to be winning, but a few years later many of these apprenticeships failed. As I was busy persuading more firms to delay apprenticeship entry, other firms throughout Britain were collapsing.

Several factors combined in the 1960s to destroy Camden Town industry. Road transport instead of canal and rail; competition from new factories on green-field sites and abroad, were common to all British industry, but instrument making and fine engineering faced an extra hazard. New computer controlled machinery threatened the old craft skills. Machines could now be programmed to work automatically.

Always up to then engineers had been able to make machines which repeated actions time and time again. A crankshaft rotated, a piston moved up and down, but each part of the machine moved in some well known geometrical path. In a circle, forward in a straight line and back again, or in more sophisticated paths such as cycloids and epicycloids, but never in erratic paths. No machine was ever able, for example, to imitate the path of a firefly. Everything was regular as clockwork. Familiar movements were repeated time and again. Then, in the sixties, came computer control.

Suddenly any path, however unpredictable, could be repeated exactly by a computer. A man spraying a machine part with a spray gun, moves his hand in a completely irregular way, but let him spray it just once and the computer can record every movement of the spray nozzle in three directions. When the next similar component moves into the spray booth, the machine can repeat every action and there is no more need for the sprayer. A modern car production line with its rows of attendant robots, is a display of computer-controlled machines working in four dimensions – up, down, sideways and in time.

Alternatively, a typist can key in a series of processes, precise measurements and a self-checking programme, into a modern machine so that it will work automatically, and with an accuracy which it used to take a man seven years and more to learn. The tape can play for twenty-four hours a day on a machine manufactured abroad. One skilled man can supervise a dozen machines, while labourers collect the finished articles from the buckets below. A revolution indeed.

In addition, in the 1960s the goal-posts were being moved. The micro-miniaturizat-ion of modern electronic components is several orders of magnitude beyond the power of the human hand. This is work solely for robots. As result, industry needed a complete new capitalization – new machines, new transport, new training, new working practices.

For years robots had been resisted in Britain and elsewhere. Japan, with a large man-power shortage and bulging order books, introduced them and, as a result, thousands of old craft skills disappeared all over the world. Japan's success contributed to our local unemployment and the decay of Camden Town industry. My carefully planned apprenticeships for a forgotten world, faded away like mist. Since the nineteen sixties we have seen the biggest industrial revolution since the steam engine, so the workshop stories recorded here reveal a completely different society – one of apprenticeships; long-term employment using traditional production skills; in a world which changed only slowly. Our modern technical upheavals were unknown.

Camden Town in the 1920s

After the First World War life in Camden Town was hard. For most peole work was scarce, hours long and pay small. Many families lived in a few rooms lopped out of old houses and bought their food locally every day because they had no fridges or insect-free larders. Gas stoves were perched on landings, while W.C.s were shared with other families in the house. Very few houses had baths. Instead, most people went to Rowton House, in Arlington Road, or to the public baths in the Prince of Wales Road. One man remembers:-

"Park Street, which we now call Parkway, was full of shops instead of architects' offices and estate agents as it is now. By eight in the morning the shop boy was busy cleaning the windows and polishing the outside brasses, sweeping and burnishing inside ready to open at nine and close twelve hours later, for seven shillings and

sixpence a week. Shops were graded. Fenn's, the grocers at the corner of Delancey Street and Park Street, was a cut above the others, wrapping all purchases in brown paper, while most used newspaper."

"As a young boy of six, and I am now an elderly man, I roamed from Mornington Crescent to the Roundhouse, a wide sweep, congested and alive".

"When Dad was in and out of work, I used to go to the baker at the corner of Arlington Road and Park Street every morning to get two pennyworth of stale bread. If you went there a bit late you didn't get your bread and that used to upset Mum. Dad was out of work a lot. He was a painter and decorator, so there wasn't any work in the winter. Very seasonal was painting and decorating."

"Lidstone's the butcher was there. Mr. Lidstone used to buy his cattle at the old cattle market in Brecknock Road and drive them down the Camden Road hill to his shop. All home killed. He used to slaughter there, of course. We took it all for granted.

"There was a fish shop in Wellington Street, always well patronized. Palmer's Pet Shop, which is still there in Parkway, had a special attraction. Mr. Palmer's daughter used to sit outside the shop with a large snake coiled around her. She was only about eight or nine years old and everyone else was frightened to touch the snake. We couldn't understand how she could dare to do it and her such a little girl. It was quite an attraction and Mr. Palmer did a good business in little mice and rabbits. Everybody had a few chickens in the back yard, so people used to buy day-old chicks from Palmer's for a penny each.

"The dairy shop gave me a job doing a morning milk round, serving all the best districts. Park Village East and West and down Park Street and Arlington Road in a moving float. A horse in front and a low back step almost touching the ground. You could step off with your galvanized jug and you poured it into the customer's container, closed the lid and put it back in the doorstep. But not the ordinary people of course. Ordinary folk in Camden Town didn't have milk. We had condensed milk. Goat brand I think it was called - thick and sweet. It wasn't like ordinary milk. You could keep it open for days. I suppose the sugar kept it from going sour. Too sweet really. I got the after-taste from a biscuit a few weeks ago. Sweet, clinging. I suppose tastes change."

"I remember The Jersey Cow Company started a refinery in Park Street Camden Town in the 1920s and they used to sell off their skimmed milk. You had to be there between six and seven in the morning and you could buy a pennyworth. That was quite a treat and my Mum used to ask me to go for it. That and the stale bread, so I had two calls to make, one for milk and the other for bread. I had quite a hectic time of it before school and I was only about seven I suppose."

"There was no pocket money in those days. Youngsters had to think for themselves Use their initiative. Today pocket money is in pounds, but my first pocket money, especially when my Dad was out of work, would be selling a bucket of manure for a ha'penny. That was my sweet money. When Mum bought a pair of rabbits, which was a matter of ten pence or eleven pence, they were never skinned. When she had skinned them, my sister and I were of an age to use this pocket money and we used to fight for the skins. We got a ha'penny a skin."

"At the bottom of Albert Street and Delancey Street there was an old coal and wood yard. The man there bought everything. He took rags, he sold wood and he gave us a ha'penny for those rabbit skins. If you had two it was a penny and for a penny you could have a bike ride, once round the block. That would be Delancey Street and into Albert Street. He used to sit on a stool outside and for a penny you could have two or three rides."

"He made it very exciting. He drew his watch out of his pocket like a real time-keeper. Your life was really on the line when he looked at you under his eyebrows. He frowned down on his big turnip watch and barked out, "Start". Away you went round the course as fast as the bike would go and it never occurred to us that if you went slower you would have a longer time on the bike. Never occurred to us because he made it into a game. He was a sly one and those old boneshakers earned him a lot of rabbit skins."

"The streets were full of children in those days. Little gangs. So many kids, they were everywhere. It was quite common to see fifty or sixty children playing in the street. The streets were cobbled, polished by the hooves of horses and in icy weather many horses slipped. It was pitiful to see them. Great, proud shire horses with horseshoes the size of dinner plates and long fringes of hair above their ankles. A lot of them broke their legs when they fell and had to be destroyed. They used to shoot them there in the street. They never put screens around, or tried to hide it, with a great crowd of children watching in dead silence."

"Then came the great day when they went in for tar blocks. Workmen took up the cobbles and put down tar wood. They had the squat iron vehicle with the hot tar, to put on the blocks to make the joints secure. It had a chimney with a fire under it, boiling the stuff. Great clouds of fumes. Our mothers used to get all the children round and we all had to stand round this vehicle and breathe heavily. "Breathe in deep," they said. This was not a cure but it was supposed to do your colds and coughs good. And another thing: we used to chew pieces of tar for our teeth."

"Our Mums were really walking chemists. The number of pills people take today is appalling. And if they were only to get themselves a little book on homeopathic medicines and read some of the old books of our Mums – the way they sorted out all these troubles – they would find that they were a lot better off. They had the answer to everything. There was senna pods if you were constipated; there was olive oil if you had an earache. You name it - they had it. I know from experience because I started in the chemists as an errand boy and from there I worked up to being an assistant. The mothers used to come in with little bottles and jars for a penn'oth of this and a penn'oth of that My mother was one of them and she knew all the answers."

"Of course it was hard to live. Most people shopped off the stalls, or in the market. The stalls were still in Camden High Street then, but the costers were not allowed to stand still, so they slowly nudged their barrows along the road as they continued to sell. A man could start at Mornington Crescent and finish up in Kilburn before night fell. There was a little market off Chalk Farm Road, called Inverness Street now. There used to be a butcher's shop on the corner called Page's specializing in pork meat and sausages. Outside the window of Page's there was a big woman, stout woman, sitting in a little hut. She controlled the money in the greengrocery and fruit stalls there. They called out how much for her to take. None of the staff ever got at the money."

"And in those days they daren't give anyone specked apples, or pears, or anything like that. They used to throw the specks under the grass cover of the stalls and on a

Saturday night we used to go down there with a bag. The stallholders knew what we were standing about for and at last they would say, "All right lads. Help yourselves." We'd all dive under there and pick up the specked apples and oranges and what have you, put them in a bag and take them home. Dear old Mum would cut out the damage and that was our week-end treat. That was how we lived in them days. You were poor but you got through somehow."

"The pawnshops were open at eight o'clock on a Monday morning and there was always a queue with their bits and pieces, blankets, or the flat iron, and the old man's suit. Anything to pawn. Put them in Monday and take them out on Saturday. You never got paid on a Thursday or Friday in those days. Always late Saturday. You worked till you dropped and they paid you as you hit the ground."

"My first job was from eight o'clock in the morning to eight o'clock in the evening , six days a week. He never paid me until the Saturday night when the last customers were out of the shop, usually about ten at night. I never got any overtime. I was thirteen and a half. I should have stayed at school until I was fourteen but I didn't. My mother had a bad patch with money and I thought I could be earning a bit, so I took this job on."

"I had to be in the shop at eight to take down the shutters and store them inside. Then wash the windows on a short pair of steps; Brasso the door fittings and sweep out the shop and pavement right down to the kerb. Go over the centre strip of carpet with a Bissell sweeper and polish the glass display cabinets, ready for the doors opening at nine. He wanted a smart shop and he made sure he got it. He had been in the First World War and stood up stiff like Kitchener. He could always find something for you to do, or something that was not quite right. You were hard up in the collar all day."

"People slogged hard in those days but they were a lot closer together. People help-ed each other. There were a lot of bailiffs coming in and distraining and putting people out because they could not pay the rent. The neighbours would all join in and take the kids in for the night and they would find a tarpaulin tent for them in the street and someone would make them a cup of cocoa and perhaps some broth and all that sort of thing."

"Firms were ruthless in those days. The posh landlords and those times have come back today, but that's another story too. In those days you had furnishing companies and I can recall some of them. No names. One was a big company and they came with their vans on a Monday morning. If you hadn't paid the instalment by the Saturday they took all the furniture back. I think it was a man called Geddes, somewhere about 1933, who got an Act passed in the House that stopped all that. It became law that no company could distrain on all the goods. They could only take back furniture to the value of the outstanding amount. But in those days they could take back the lot and got very rich on it. They were the kind of things that happened in those days and they've come back, with loan sharks battening on people trying to put on a show for Christmas and people who thought they owned their houses losing them."

"There used to be trams along the Hampstead Road. They ran in the middle of the road up to the Adam and Eve. That was their stopping place. They used to go from Aldgate to Camden Town. In those days you could get a sixpenny evening ticket, or a shilling all day. Of course that was a lot of money in those days. You could go all over

London, from one tram to the next. Sometimes as a lad I used to get sixpence by my own efforts and I used to buy myself a sixpenny evening ticket."

"Go down to the High Street and pick up a tram and change to other trams. One of my favourite rides was under the old Holborn Viaduct. It went under Kingsway, out on the Embankment and over Westminster Bridge. Backwards and forwards I would go and, if they were playing late cricket at the Oval, you could go round the Oval on the tram and watch the cricket. Get off at the Oval Station and double back over the other side to to get the the tram back to Vauxhall. Back and forth on the top of the tram all the summer evening until they drew the stumps. All on the same ticket. We used to plot how we could stop the tram outside the ground and watch the game. Have the driver arrested and nobody qualified to drive the tram. Cut off the electricity and make the conductor walk all the way back to the terminus to put another coin in the meter. Any daft idea, and of course we never managed it. We didn't see much of the cricket, but at least you could say you had been to a test match without having to pay."

Smugglers

There is another Camden story of the nineteen-twenties worth recording. Slowly, as gin began to be used in cocktails, it became a more respectable drink. Then, with Prohibition in America, came a strange expansion of Camden Town's industry. Mrs Moore, who worked at Gilbey's, remembers sitting in a room full of women, sewing bottles of gin and whiskey into sacks. Each sack had to have two long ears. Anonymous men had arrived at the Pantheon offices with pockets full of dollar notes. They wanted sets of six bottles in canvas sacks, for some unexplained reason. The sacks were to be shipped to Amsterdam, or some other port, where they disappeared. A few weeks later the sacks would be handed down from a large boat by one 'ear' and taken by the other 'ear' into a smaller boat. Rowed into shore at St Pierre, or anywhere along the United States coastline, the bottles were deposited in shallow water ready for spiriting away when the tide went out. Sewing these 'smugglers' was well paid, so that on Friday night Mrs Moore was able to dress up and go to a Camden Town cinema, to see perhaps a gangster film about speak-easies.

As the gangsters and police had moved in and Prohibition became a racket, other methods were used. Huge distilleries were established on Canadian soil. Contraband was run daily in powerful motorboats, with double the horsepower that the police could afford for their boats. A hosepipe was run along the bottom of the lake from Canada to USA and the spirit pumped through, but the gunny sack with two ears was the basic technology, trusted and tried.

Prohibition was so profitable that soon there were illicit stills in every state. Bathtub gin was sold in counterfeit bottles, with forged Gilbey labels. To protect their reputation the firm set up a special department to verify labels sent in by dissatisfied drinkers. Eventually, they invented the characteristic square gin bottle, still to be seen in Gilbey advertisements, sand-blasted on three sides and with the label printed on either side so that it can be read through the bottle. Before this too could be copied, Prohibition was ended and Gilbey's were able to export legally to the USA.

MADE IN
CAMDEN TOWN

Mornington Crescent

Mornington Crescent was built as a sweep of houses with gardens and tennis courts in front. Tenants paid a garden tax each year for the right to use the gardens, which were railed off and maintained as a private space for key holders only. At the beginning of the twentieth century the area, with large rooms suitable for studios, became popular with artists. Sickert lived at No 6, while Gore had lodgings in the Crescent and Gilman, another of the Camden Town Group, lived nearby in Cumberland Market.

When Walter Sickert came back to London in 1905, after seven years abroad, mostly based in Dieppe, he became the doyen of a group of young painters. 'They took their inspiration from the dingy streets and lodgings houses of Camden Town'.[1] Indeed one of Sickert's most famous paintings is 'The Camden Town Murder', a sordid, but pitiful affair. It was not the only one. Ford Madox Ford tells the story of 'The Euston Square Murder'.[2] Borschitzky, his violin teacher, 'came home late at night and found his landlady murdered in the kitchen. Being nearly blind he fell over the body, got himself covered in blood and as a foreigner and a musician was at once arrested by the police.' He was acquitted but the publicity caused Euston Square to be renamed as Endsleigh Gardens, a name we shall hear again later.

The Camden Town artists painted the streets, the cafes, the gardens behind their lodgings, the public parks and the music halls. The Bedford Music Hall, in its worn Victorian red and gilt, was a favourite subject, especially of Sickert. Over the years, Sickert ran several painting schools in the area, which drew in other artists. There were links with the Bloomsbury Group through Vanessa Bell and Duncan Grant, who both painted with them. The artists varied in their subjects and palettes, but they exhibited together and became a very influential group. Mornington Crescent Gardens was the subject of several paintings and drawings.

Mornington Crescent Gardens, 1913-14, by Gilman [3]

When first laying out their estates in the eighteenth and nineteenth centuries, ground landlords had realised that houses with gardens behind and private squares in front, would be more attractive than dense rows of terraced streets. To attract a 'good quality' of tenant and to continue to hold them, landlords laid down the maximum number of houses to be built per acre, the value of the properties to be erected, insisted on householders repainting the properties at regular intervals and made annual maintenance inspections. In addition many landlords laid out private gardens in squares, crescents or circles to give fresh air and green spaces near the houses. Householders paid a Garden Tax and were given a key to the private, railed garden in front of their houses. Purchasers valued the healthy living conditions, the open sky and the attractive trees. By the time that house building slowed down at the start of the First World War, there were said to be 40,000 'squares' in Greater London, of all shapes and sizes.

As Camden Town went down, houses were let in floors and rooms, often with cooking facilities on landings. Tenants and sub-tenants moved in and out frequently, making the garden tax difficult to collect. The gardens were no longer maintained, tennis courts fell into disrepair and the Crescent became a wasteland. One man remembers as a young boy, walking across this rough ground from his home in Delancey Street to the Tolmer Cinema, at the corner of Euston Road and Hampstead Road, where the Tolmer Estate now stands, to see Tom Mix or Rin Tin for a penny. Sometimes a small fair was held in the Gardens, or a travelling circus appeared. It became a village green, untended but friendly. After some years the site was boarded all round with poster hoardings. Slowly the news filtered out that the land, long regarded as public open space, had been bought by some unknown developer. This caused a great public outcry and linked Mornington Crescent Gardens to the far wider campaign for public open spaces.

Building operations at Endsleigh Gardens, Euston Road, c. 1928.
St Pancras Church can be seen in the distance.[4]

Mornington Crescent was only one of the many squares and crescents under threat by developers in the 1920s. Another was Endsleigh Gardens, opposite Euston Station. It had been an open space full of trees, but was now lost to the public. This is the block which now contains the Friends' Meeting House. Coram Fields and many other green lungs were under similar threat.

In April 1928, 'New Health', a periodical which fought for open spaces in cities and the health which they could bring, was up in arms about the planned loss of Mornington Crescent Gardens. Fresh air was the sole known cure for killer diseases such as tuberculosis. Streptomycin, which emptied our TB hospitals in the early sixties, was thirty years away. New Health contrasted the trees and open space with the effects of a new factory on the area.

Captions from 'New Health'

"Look at this picture which shows the gardens at Mornington Crescent some years ago, when trees and shrubs and grass brightened the surroundings of this North London district."

"And on this, after the builder has fallen upon the ground and work has commenced for the erection of a great factory."

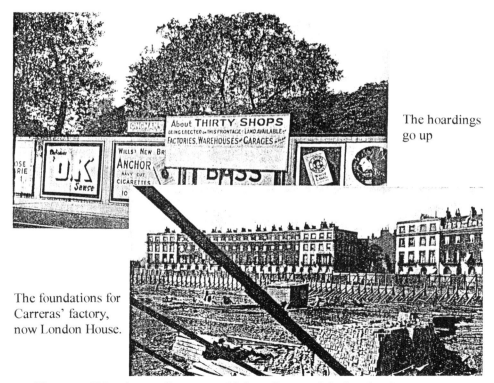

The hoardings go up

The foundations for Carreras' factory, now London House.

Pictures of Mornington Crescent, with hoardings and during development

OPEN SPACES for PUBLIC HEALTH

SOME OBSERVATIONS ON THE DESTRUCTION OF OPEN SPACES
IN LONDON AND ITS SUBURBS.

By SIR WILLIAM SIMPSON, C.M.G., M.D., F.R.C.P., D.P.H.

The New Health article went on to demand that all new factory building should be outside London as there was plenty of room in the countryside and London needed its open spaces to give the population fresh air and health. It was partly this thinking which would begin to empty Camden Town of manufacture thirty years later, well after Mornington Crescent Gardens had been built over and, incidentally, just when streptomycin was beginning to solve the tuberculosis problem

The Carreras 'Black Cat' Factory

In 1927, when the factory was being designed, interest in Egyptian history was widespread. Lord Carnarvon had discovered the tomb of Tutankhamun a few years earlier and a number of 'Egyptian' buildings were being erected at this time, including the Hoover factory on the A40 into London and a cinema in Essex Road. The association with Black Cat cigarettes, then a popular brand, related to an earlier period in the Company history. A Spanish nobleman by the name of Carreras, banished from his country, set up in London's Wardour Street and began trading as a tobacconist/herbalist. He had a black cat which, on sunny days, sat in the window of his shop. Londoners wishing to buy tobacco used to ask cab drivers to take them to the tobacconist's shop in Wardour Street with the black cat in the window, because the name Carreras was difficult to pronounce. Thus the Black Cat name became famous. The combination of the Egyptian theme and the Black Cat, led to the Egyptian Cat Goddess, Bast, and helped decide the system of decoration. Local people still call the building the Black Cat Factory.

The new factory was to be enormous – the largest reinforced-concrete factory in the country. Five floors would completely fill the gardens. Not an inch was to be left and everything green would disappear.

Five deep light wells were to penetrate the building, bringing light and air to the interior, while the top floor was to have north-facing lights, so that heat would not build up in strong sunshine. Pictures of the building under construction show three tall steel towers, the forerunners of our modern tower cranes, and huge walls of wooden shuttering for the concrete. Trams and buses with outside staircases pass along Hampstead Road.

When built, the whole of the exterior (except the coloured parts) were rendered in white cement and sand to give a warm stone-coloured finish. The brilliant Egyptian decorations were produced by mixing ground glass with cement and grinding off. Thus the colours were permanent and, when dirty, could be washed.

The huge factory built over the valuable garden space of Mornington Crescent, Camden Town, N. London. Note, on left, the original houses overshadowed by its bulk.

APRIL, 1928.   N E W   H E A L T H

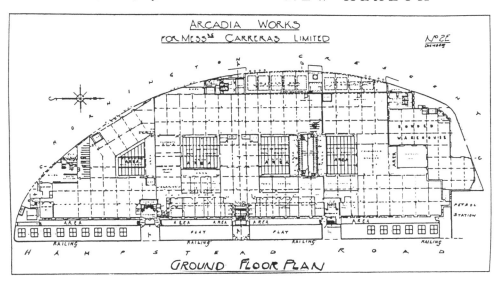

New Factory for Messrs, Carreras Ltd., Hampstead Road NW1
Architects, M.E. and O.H. Collins.   Contractors, Sir Robert Mc Alpine & Sons.

The First Reactions

In 1928, the reviewer in 'Building' was very doubtful about the design of the factory. The idea of dressing up a modern factory as an Egyptian temple was disturbing. An inward slope, or batter (which is imperative in a wall made of sun-dried bricks) is very rare in reinforced-concrete work, expensive and unnecessary. However, he closed his eyes to the decoration and looked at the building beneath. The mass of the building, its form and general composition, were unexpectedly beauiful. The 'sense of beauty' given by the gentle inward slope of the walls, typical of Egyptian building, was particularly satisfying. Of course, the inside walls are vertical, as with Egyptian mud-brick building, but from the outside they slope inwards, gradually tapering in thickness to the top. This is the way we were to see the building in the 1960s, when the decoration had been removed and it had become Greater London House. In the 1990s, with the decoration back, we are again in the position of the first reviewer.

He was also very impressed with the beauty of the vast concrete interiors, 'unplastered and straight from the shuttering (just stoned down and white-washed over).' It was modern work at its best, simple and unadorned.

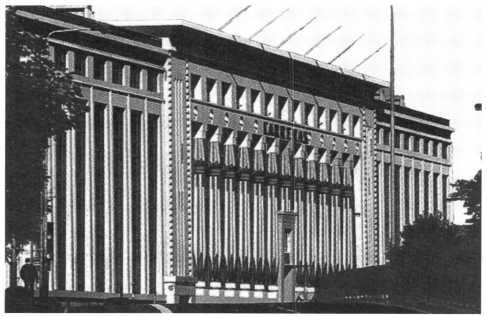

The new Carreras factory about 1929, in all its Egyptian finery

The History of the Rothman Tobacco Firm

The modern firm of Rothman had been founded by Bernhard Baron, who had come to England from Kiev, via the United States. There is an old news film about the opening of the Carreras factory which seems to be from another age. It records the opening ceremony and shows Baron being greeted by a vast crowd. Apparently almost all the 3,000 workers, mostly women, are waving at him. Other pictures show them crowding into the main doors on a working day in such numbers that the scene looks like Wembley five minutes before the kick off.

The original silver nitrate film has been transferred to video, silent and jerky. Short panels of text say:-

| 1 | '800 men built the House of Carreras, the largest reinforced concrete building under one roof in Great Britain, in 18 months.' |

2	'The modern factory designed after the Egyptian goddess Bast, the Cat Goddess, is guarded by two bronze cats of ancient Bubastis ten feet in height.'

3	'The flanking pillars, 47 feet high, with brilliant and handsome colourings ground from glass, to outlast the centuries; with the winged orbs of Rah, the sun God above.'

4	'2.800 tons of steel rods and 77,500 tons of concrete were used in the building of Britain's largest factory.'

5	'Nine acres of floor space were covered with 400.000 square feet of Canadian maple.'

Our modern reaction to the film is very different from the impression it must have made on its first audiences, because we have the advantage of hindsight. In the nineteen-thirties we regarded cigarettes as a source of harmless pleasure. We watched Hollywood films and copied the way the stars lit their cigarettes. Whenever an actor on the stage needed some 'business' to cover a pause, or hoped to take the audiences' mind off the quality of the dialogue, he flourished a cigarette case. Every theatre programme used to carry the acknowledgement, 'Cigarettes by Abdulla', because Abdulla gave free cigarettes for use on the stage.

Thus, when Carreras moved to Camden Town here was pleasure and relief at the prospect of employment. Hundreds of people would have the chance to work in a modern factory which had the latest air conditioning. The film opens with pictures of the park at Mornington Crescent, full of small trees, almost as Ginner and other artists in the Camden Town Group had drawn it before the First World War.

It then traces the making of cigarettes in their millions. Women open bales of tobacco leaves and rapidly strip out the hard central vein, with the dust of broken tobacco leaves rising in their faces for eight hours a day. This was passive smoking, but nobody knew. Smoking cigarettes was glamorous, not stupid. Reading the laudatory film captions about the new factory, we are shocked. Not until the computer death figures began to appear nearly forty years later, did we realise the danger of cigarette smoking, while the risk to passive smokers like these took us even longer to recognise. We look on now helpless, unable to warn them of their likely fate.

All methods of advertising were used to keep up sales. 'Club brand', made at the Mornington Crescent 'Arcadia Works', was the first to give coupons which could be exchanged for goods of all type. In that realistic 1930 world, some of the most popular 'prizes' were boots and shoes. Smokers came to the main entrance, collected their footwear and changed into the new ones at once. So many left their old boots and shoes on the doorstep that one boy had the special job of collecting them every few hours to keep the place tidy. Mr King remembers going up the splendid 'marble' staircase and handing in the coupons. His brother got his first ever overcoat with coupons. What the coupons cost compared to the value of the overcoat, is difficult to calculate.

Every street in Camden Town provided workers for the factory and, since it was the policy to employ families wherever possible, whole households worked there together. This made for a more stable workforce and created a more subtle type of discipline. If a younger member of the family was not behaving well, a word to an older relation often settled the matter. This policy of employing families was pursued by Gilbey's and other local factories until the 1960s, when the patterns of employment and the early breaking up of families into separate households, often living far apart, made it impracticable.

On Christmas Eve the family party often started in the factory. Any musicians were encouraged to bring their instruments. At about 3 o'clock, the band started at the top floor and formed a conga chain, dancing through the factory, floor by floor, until it emerged at the main entrance as an excited throng and held up the traffic in the Hampstead Road.

Camouflaging the Factory

In 1939 the factory was camouflaged in broad patches, which appeared to make it even more gaudy and conspicuous than ever, but it looked different from the air. After the War the camouflage was removed and the Egyptian decorations were restored. However, the proud boast of 'outlasting centuries' seemed unlkely to come about, for in 1958-60 the Carreras factory was relocated to Basildon, Essex. Some workers went with the firm to the new town, and its new houses, while others had to find what other London work they could. Rothman's were to move again from Basildon to Aylesbury, but that factory too is now closed. One of the famous cats was in store and the other is at the Rothman factory in Jamaica.

Modernising the building – Greater London House

When Rothmans had left, the factory stood idle. The building was refurbished. Windows were replaced. All the glass-decorated pilasters were built in as square columns; the winged orbs of the Rah the sun god above the entrance were removed; the building was given a plain colour wash, and the factory could be seen at last as a modern building. With the Egyptian decorations removed, many 'Egyptian ' features remained. There were still the 'battered' walls, sloping in gently towards the top; the cavetto mouldings at the roof; the Egyptian shape of the building, the tall, narrow window openings, used by the Egyptians; a row of circular patches along the front

THOMSON

The logo of Thomson Travel

The Thomson Travel Company has been located in London House for many years.

facade which were part of the original Carreras decoration; and the iron railings with their hieroglyphic motifs. Despite these traces of the past, it became the modern building with its simple inwards 'batter', just as the critic in 'Building' had visualised it forty years earlier, in his report of September 1928.

The building, which had been a factory, was transformed into an enormous office complex, with large floor areas and excellent natural light.

The 1997 Changes

In March 1997 the building changed hands. The new Taiwan-based owners submitted plans to restore the building to its former 'Egyptian' style, replace all windows to match the 1920s originals and reintroduce the 12 foot high black cats at the entrance. In converting the original building into Greater London House, the original columns, with their glass decorations had been destroyed. Now, in the 1990s, new ones have been built over the top of the old and painted to the original colours. An 'Egyptian' building has become a post-modernist Egyptian one.

It was always a very well designed building, with lofty ceilings and large open floors. Today it will become an ideal office for a computer-run world. Modern offices bear little relation to the traditional office of high desks and coal fires. Dickens, who went to school just by Mornington Crescent, and Bob Cratchet, his clerk in The Christmas Carol, are both long dead. Instead of ledgers and dusty files stored in attics and tied with tape, each person has a computer. This can be plugged into any socket in any office, or even be worked by batteries. Today many office workers are 'nomads', travelling around from site to site, customer to customer, and have no need for a permanent space. They have a cubic metre of drawer space in a steel filing cabinet, a lap-top computer and a car which doubles as an office. They can use any convenient empty desk and call up their client files on lap-tops.

Thus many modern offices need only a reception area; rooms for meetings; some small office cubicles where one can work quietly for an hour; a place where people can meet casually; and a kettle for making tea. Architects will need a drawing board and a computer, but even these may sometimes be shared. Solicitors still require a permanent room where the door can be shut and confidential matters discussed in private. Most work however is not very secret. It is routine and can be conducted in open offices.

This is the new pattern for Greater London House. A number of flexible office spaces capable of being used in many different ways, with good communications, minimal overheads and a newly refurbished Mornington Crescent Station on the other side of the road.[5]

---

[1] Walter Sickert and the Camden Town Group, by Maureen Connett, David & Charles, 1992

[2] 'Memories and Impressions', by Ford Maddox Ford, Penguin, pp. 86-7

[3] University of Leeds Collection

[4] New Health, April 1928

[5] Information from the Mr Wadwha and the architects.

Gilbey House (now Academic House)

In 1937 Chermeyeff built Gilbey House at the corner of Jamestown and Oval Roads, as the new administrative building. Today it is called Academic House. Chermeyeff (1900-1996) was a colourful character. Russian born, he had been sent to England by his parents at the age of ten to acquire an English education. He went to Harrow but at the age of seventeen, had to forego a place at Trinity College, Cambridge, when the Russian Revolution broke out. Far from going to college, he had to survive as best he could. He took a menial job at the Amalgamated Press. Without formal training he relied on his charms, becoming a gigolo at the Berkeley and Savoy Hotels and opening a dance hall in Buenos Aires. He became a British citizen in 1928.

With no formal design or architectural qualifications, but a natural flair, he was put in charge of the Waring and Gillow modern art department. There he created Art Deco designs which, in that rather staid setting, burst on a surprised public. He was a decorator with a love of new materials and effects. In 1930 he designed the interior of the Cambridge Theatre in Art Deco style. It was completely different from any British theatre of the time.

In 1933 Erich Mendelsohn, who had designed original cinemas and other buildings in Berlin,[1] fled from Hitler's Germany. He left the keys to his flat in the door so that the Nazis, who he knew were coming to arrest him, should not have to break it open, and took the first train out of Germany. That same year he formed a partnership with Chermeyeff and, in 1935, they built the De La Warr Pavilion in Bexhill-on-Sea, Sussex, It was the first public building in Britain in the international modernist style, very famous and used frequently today as a TV or film set. Thus by the time Chermeyeff came to design Gilbey House, he had been involved with a very successful building.

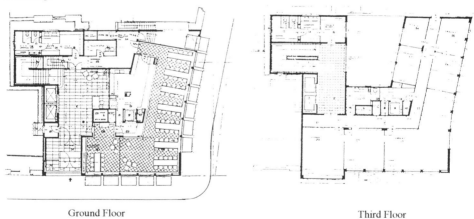

Ground Floor   Third Floor

Plans of Gilbey House (now Academic House)[2]

The heavy black lines around the cross hatched office section is the vertical cork insulation.

Gilbey House presented some interesting technical problems. The old Stanhope Arms at the corner of Jamestown Road, popular with both railway and brewery men for years, had been demolished. In the middle of a noisy industrial area, with trains in the marshalling yard, iron shod wagon wheels day and night and the din of a bottling plant next door, Chermeyeff had to create an administrative building as a place of calm and quiet, where people could work in peace

Noise would enter the building through the windows. Therefore they were made small, sealed except for cleaning purposes and placed high in the wall to allow filing cabinets to be placed below them. Air inside the building was filtered by a plenum system but, instead of the normal metal ducting, all air pipes were made in reinforced concrete and formed an integral part of the structure. This construction was much more rigid and massive than any metal pipe, so reducing noise to the minimum.

To reduce internal noise further, the building was constructed in three separate parts from foundations to roof. Parts 1 and 2 contained all the services, with their noise and vibration, while part 3 held the quiet offices. The vertical isolation joints between the three buildings were packed with cork to prevent vibration from passing across.

External noise was another problem. However well the building was insulated internally, vibration would enter the building through the ground. Therefore all columns and walls were built on pads of natural cork 10 cms thick and transmitted to large concrete blocks below, to spread the weight. The cork was slowly compressed to 7 cms as the building rose and the weight increased. 'Sprung' buildings of this kind are fairly common today, but most rest on neoprene rubber pads, not cork. They were very rare in 1937. James Gilbey and Alfred Blyth, who had investigated the supply of cork from Spanish forests decades before, would have been pleased to see that a new use had been found for their material. The building was highly praised when built and still gives great pleasure

Chermeyeff was a colourful character. A few years ago I went into a Gothic Revival house in Abbey Road, built about 1840. Stepping through the door, I was back in a Heal's furniture showroom in the 1930s. All cornices in the house had been removed and the walls panelled in Australian Walnut, a very popular veneer at that time. The rooms in Abbey Road were full of fitted furniture, built in thick plywood and veneered in huge flat surfaces. Clean, simple and 'Chermeyeff' – for when I asked, I was told he had lived there and had completely redesigned the interior. The contrast between the inside of the house and the exterior, which Chermeyeff was not free to alter, reveals the ruthlessness of an architect..

Chermeyeff too was a creator who needed new projects every day. With Wells Coates, he designed the round Ecko wireless set, in moulded brown or black Bakelite, which has become an icon of the period. He also designed the famous Pel chair. Catalogues were full of his designs, yet in 1940 there was no work for him in Britain. He tried to enlist, but was rejected. He left bitterly for America, to become Professor of Design at Brooklyn College, in New York. He later moved to Harvard as Professor of Architecture and died in 1996, the flamboyant mentor of Richard Rogers and many other architects.[3] We should have kept him.

---

[1] See The Growth of Muswell Hill, By Jack Whitehead

[2] The Architect and Building News, 30 July, 1927

[3] The Guardian. Obituary, 11 May, 1996.

The Camden Town Bombing Map

Black areas represent serious damage. Damage to railway lines is not shown, but the clusters of damage nearby (and near all other London railway stations) reveal the flight patterns of bombers targetting the marshalling yards.

World War Two

By the end of the Second World War, London had suffered an enormous amount of bomb damage. For many weeks young men, just released from the services, cycled round London recording damaged buildings. Their maps and the incident records kept by each borough, were combined to create the Bomb Damage Map which was to be the basis for the Abercrombie Plan for rebuilding London. This map, now housed at the Greater London History Library, Nottingham Road, EC1, can often explain the reason for later building. An incident recorded in one line on a card, or in a ledger, with its date - address - type of bomb - extent of damage - casualties, etc. may explain why a terrace of houses is broken suddenly by a group of post-war ones. It may reveal, as happened recently, why a developer found his house was sinking and, digging deep, discovered plaster, rubble and complete window frames buried five metres below the surface. A bomb crater had been filled with the debris from the houses which had once covered the site, the ground levelled and everything forgotten.

Camden suffered greatly, as this piece of the bombing map shows. The black patches record bomb damage, some of which could be repaired, but many houses were completely destroyed. The damage to the Railway Goods Yard, the main target of the raids, was quickly made good and is not shown. We can still see bomb damage by the side of Camden Tube Station and in other places in the borough, but most has now been hidden by redevelopment. This wartime history is a subject all on its own which

The Bombing of Camden Town Tube Station

In three days, four London tube stations were bombed: Balham, Trafalgar Square, Bounds Green and Camden Town.[1] On 14 October 1940 Camden Town station was bombed and four people killed or injured.[2] When the station complex is developed at the start of the next millenium, this last relic of World War II will finally disappear, sixty years or more after the event.

has been dealt with extensively elsewhere.[2] There is no room to record it here, but instead it may be interesting for one man to recall his particular experiences. They were different from the next person's, but typical. A young man in his twenties, a skilled instrument maker, exempt from the services and making delicate instruments for aircraft and artillery. After the War he was to move with his firm to Harlow, but that was years away. Just listen to his voice:-

A Young Man's Story

"During the War I did my bit. Apart from my job as an instrument maker, I got dragged into the local Dad's Army. Our unit was on Hampstead Heath Fairground, where we had a battery of rocket projectors, called Z battery. It was manned by soldiers in the Army during the day, but gradually it was taken over by the Home Guard every night. We had to turn up there and man it.

The projectors each fired two rockets which burst in the sky. There were sixty-four of them and each one fired two four-foot-six inch rockets. We set the fuses and they went off like a normal rocket. A normal anti-aircraft shell, rocket propelled.

That was quite interesting but I got brassed off with it, so I applied for another unit and I was transferred to an Infantry unit at Kentish Town. Having spent a week down at Walton on the Naze, on a course for this rocket thing, I had had to do a load of square bashing and I was quite good at it I suppose. I had to get these great big, burly railway men - engine drivers and shunters and carriage and wagon men - I was a young man in my early twenties and they were in their late forties and fifties, too old for military service - and I was bossing them about like nobody's business.

My family were living in Gordon House Road and my girl-friend, as she was then, lived at No 1. Behind the garages opposite our house, was a garden. John Lines, the wallpaper factory, had built some shelters there for their workers. The factory was doing war-work, but it had been built as a wallpaper factory. There were several wallpaper factories in the area. Shand Kydd were in Highgate Road. John Lines was the modern one, half way between Gospel Oak Station and Highgate Road..

The bomb shelter was just a pipe, like a small concrete sewer pipe, half buried in the ground. It was about as safe as a paper bag, if a bomb dropped on it. We had an air-raid shelter in our garden, but we felt the need for companionship. Anyway, we asked John Lines if we could use their air-raid shelter at night. They agreed, so we all went over there.

It was cold and it was wet. We slept on sheets of brown paper, wrapped up in blankets. I used to come home from work and walk up the Highgate Road, because the buses had stopped and the sirens were going, so I walked from Kentish Town Tube. I had no protection. Just carried my little gas mask in a canvas bag. No tin hat until I went into the Home Guard and then I used to carry that around with me. I would get home and my mother would be almost standing on the doorstep. The sirens had gone, the guns were going bang, bang and you could hear the bombs whistling down. "Someone is getting it tonight," we used to say.

She'd be waiting on the doorstep with the bedrolls - bundles of her bedding and mine and a small bag with everything in it - life insurance policies, any valuables, letters, documents, ration books - definitely ration books - and we'd dive across into the shelter. In there was my girl friend, who later became my wife, and her family and all the other people who lived in the road. My father-in-law, as he later came to be, used to stand outside with his next door neighbour. They were chums and they might nip up to the local pub for a quick jar. Anything to get away from the shelter. That shelter was really terrible.

One night it happened. They dropped a bomb in Gordon House Road. Everybody was shaken up and the fire watcher from the factory came into the shelter and he said, "Somebody in the road has got some damage. He didn't say, "It's yours." He said, "Somebody has got some damage."

Slowly we ventured out to see this massive flame. They had dropped a bomb in Gordon House Road, just outside our house, No 11. It wasn't a big bomb, but it was enough. Underneath the road there, along Gordon House Road and Mansfield Road, was a massive gas main. About a 24" cast iron pipe, plus a water main, plus the sewage. Plus the cause of the explosion ignited the gas and the sewage and a great flame shooting sixty feet in the air. No exaggeration! Well above the tops of the houses and nobody could get anywhere near to turn it off.

The front rooms of our house were all blown in and the front door was hanging on one hinge. It was a semi-basement house. Downstairs was our living room, kitchen and scullery, with our bedrooms on the first floor. The basement was awash with water. It wasn't just plain water, it was sewage and it was revolting. And my poor Mum she sat there and she cried. She did cry.

After a while my Dad walked down to the Mansfield Road School which was a special fire station - and said, "Can you come up and pump our house out?" So they pulled their little children's pump up the road and pumped our place out. Although it stank, at least it was something like dry. The place was full of all sorts of horrible muck and we had to get rid of the carpet, which was absolutely sodden. There were stains right up the side of the suite and a tide mark all round the wall.

Gradually the hole in the road got smaller and smaller. Young men were sent by the local authorities to repair it. They'd come into our place on a wet day and my Mother would invite them in to sit by the fire and have their sandwiches. She'd make them a cup of tea. They would be sitting by our fire, drying their wet feet and one of them would say, "Well I shan't be seeing you tomorrow Mum. I've got my calling up papers."

So he went off to War and some other poor lad would be roped in to repair this hole in the road. It took months and months to repair. We suffered that and got on with life again. It was just tough that you had copped it.

Some time later we were having the Blitz rather badly and my father was driving his bus right across London. One night when my Dad happened to be home, not working, he said,

"I tell you what. We won't go across the road to the shelter. Let's go down to the Mansfield Road School. They've got the Fire Station there. They've got a smashing room where it is all sand-bagged up and safe. And we'll get a cup of tea and have a game of darts and a bit of a social evening. And you can lie on the bunks. There's rows and rows of bunks."

It was a shelter of sorts, but I don't remember many people going there. It was for the auxiliary firemen - volunteers, not the regular firemen .

Dad said "Let's go down to the School. It's more interesting down there. Decent beds to lie on instead of lying on the floor", which is fairly logical but I wasn't too keen. We got down as far as the little tunnel part of the railway bridge.

No," I said. "I'm not going. I'm going back to the original. I want to be with Doris." She was my girl friend. So we all turned round, my sister Jean, my Mum, myself and my Dad coming up behind. We all hung together like lemmings. My Dad wasn't really angry. Just a bit peeved that his bright idea had fallen flat. So we went back to the little shelter behind the factory.

We went down about four steps. Less than a metre. The rest of the shelter stuck out, with just a thin layer of earth on top of it. You could have dropped a pencil from a great height and it would have gone right through and stuck us in the eye.

We had just got to these few steps when there was an almighty 'Whoosh!' The entrance to the shelter was a flap that lifted up as a sort of gate. You lifted it up and it flapped down behind you. The flap flew up in the air. My mother and sister were in front and fortunately my father was behind and he had his bundle of rolled up blankets on his shoulder. The flap landed on the side of his head and the blankets took the complete force of the flap as it came down again. We got swept into the entrance on top of all the other people who were sitting there minding their own business, reading the paper, playing draughts, playing chess - whatever took their fancy. We all got tumbled up one end, piled one on top of the other. Nobody was hurt. Just shaken. There was just this one 'whoosh' and then the bang, and it was a bang and a half I can tell you.

What the devil was that?" we all said. Everyone composed themselves but were sitting very shaken, very frightened. We knew something serious had happened. People said, "Its this," and "Its that". Don't forget there was still a big hole outside my house, No 11. We had all experienced that.

Then the Air Raid Warden came in. He asked, "Is everybody all right?"

"Yes. Fine."

"Anybody hurt?"

"No we are all right." OK, but shaken . " What was that?" and "Where was it?"

"A landmine has dropped on the school. Two killed and some injured."

If I hadn't said, "No. I'm going back to be with Doris," there would have been four more possibly that night. I think it saved my life - all our lives.

The school was absolutely blown out – right through the middle. A landmine, which was as big as a pillar-box, came down in a parachute and blew it all out. All the houses in Mansfield Road, about the Gospel Oak area, and in Oak Village. The window frames were blown out and the tiles stripped off. People were cut by showers of glass. I don't know if there were casualties in the houses, but there were certainly among the firemen in the school.

Jean, my sister, got married and I got married soon after. As a result Doris, my wife as she had become, went to work in the John Lines wallpaper factory, in Gordon House Road, where we had been sheltering.

When we were married and because she was married to me and I was at home, Doris was entitled to take a job locally, providing she did work of national importance. They wanted her to be a porter on the railway station, but she did not want to carry heavy baggage. She said, "I'm a tailoress. What can I do to make army equipment?"

They said, "Oh yes. You can go to John Lines, in Gordon House Road. Do you know where that is?" So she said, "I should think so. I live at number 1."

The factory had been turned over to making army equipment, gaiters, backpacks, side packs and so on. Before she got the job there she was unmarried and had been sent all the way to the Enfield Small Arms factory, which is way beyond Enfield, nearer to Waltham Abbey. So she fell out of bed straight into her job. Lovely.

We lived with my parents in 11 Gordon House Road. Then we moved next door into a couple of rooms and then we moved round to Oak Village.

There was Jean, my sister, with one child and another on the way, and Doris with a baby on the way. We hadn't had an air raid for a long time and one night the siren sounded. The planes came over and they gave us stick. They dropped incendiary bombs all over.

My Dad and I were standing by the front door. Bombs were falling and a building round the corner, by the station, was burning fiercely. I said, "Let's get inside, away from the blast." We stood away from the front door because it had a glass panel. We had seen fire bombs land in the street, on the road and on the roofs of houses and naturally we thought we must have copped a couple. I said to my Dad, "Let's look!"

We rushed round the house. I ran upstairs to my Mother' bedroom and there was this glowing phosphorous, burning away in the bed. The bomb had broken off the side of the bed and almost collapsed it. Only the spring had saved us. The bomb was burning away merrily in the bedclothes and the room was full of feathers from the eiderdown. My mother's bedroom was upstairs at the back, with one of those old fashioned steel springs on the bed and the incendiary bomb was trapped in the wire of the mattress. It was about the size of a large canister of spray paint that you can buy at a DIY shop. Imagine the coloured top. Invert it and that would be a solid piece of steel which was quite weighty, so that instead of staying on the roof, it had penetrated into the house.

It had come through the roof and the ceiling and landed in my Mother's bed. If it had gone right through, Doris, my wife, and my sister Jean were sheltering under the table in the living room below and the table top was about as thick as a card table. It would have landed between them and it would have burst. It would have exploded and covered them in inflammable material. They would certainly have been killed. It was the spring in my Mum's bed that saved their lives.

I said to my Dad, "Quick. I'll go and get the dustbin." I rushed downstairs into the garden, grabbed the metal dustbin, shook the rubbish on the ground and rushed into the house with it. We rolled the bedding up carefully in a bundle, tightly, shoved it in the bin, put the lid on it tight. It couldn't burn because the oxygen was taken away. We shut the lid on it and it suffocated.

Very, very, very dangerous. It could have spat at us at any time. Phosphorous don't just burn you, it burns a hole in you. It would take the skin off your face right through to the back of your neck.

In the meantime, my Mum was wandering up the road in my Dad's old carpet slippers, my wife, heavily pregnant, my sister heavily pregnant and with a baby in her arms, rushed up the road to the top of Oak Village, which was Lamble Street and Elaine Grove, and went into a surface shelter. Four walls of brick, with a concrete top. It was blast proof, but there was no safety if a bomb dropped. It would just have collapsed and flattened you. But we survived. Some of us did."

The Bombing of Mansfield Road School

"After the bombing of Mansfield Road School, it was a dangerous structure, so the building was completely removed and they built a bungalow Junior School, but that was later. Immediately after the War it was a ruin. We had a big bonfire to celebrate the victory. I was in my twenties. The big pair of wooden gates had been taken off their hinges and left to one side. I suppose they thought they might one day rebuild the school. The kids broke up the gates and chucked the pieces on the bonfire."

"They were box gates. There was a strong wooden framework with tongue and groove boarding on both sides. The frame was made and boxed in to prevent climbing from both sides. Some boys came up and said,

"Look what we have found." Inside the box gate they had found a piece of paper saying:- "This is the day when the Germans are supposed to invade us. We are repairing this gate and expecting the parachutists to land, but so far we have not seen any sign of them."

We were still doing these mundane things like mending gates in 1940 at the time of Dunkirk, and they had put the note inside the gate as a record."

It is not easy to find the details of the bombing in Camden as the Borough destroyed the records in a fit of vandalism. Haringey has a huge grey book with each incident recorded - type of bomb; damage; casualties. Islington has a set of cards. Each borough had its own method of recording the incidents. After the War the London County Council made careful maps of bomb damage, so that one can go from the map to the borough records and discover a good deal about any particular bombing incident. This is not normally possible in Camden as the records were destroyed as an anti-war gesture. However, John Hook has examined the death certificates and worked back from them to compile details about the deaths in some of the incidents. This painstaking work he has printed as 'Dawn Was Theirs', and has given a copy to Camden Local History Archive. [1] [i]

On the night of Saturday, 16th November, 1940, Mansfield Road School, which was being used as a fire station, was struck by a landmine. From the John Hook records we see that Iris Miller, Alfred James Francis and Clifford Moffatt Leak, were killed and Walter John Hubbard was so seriously injured that he died two days later in the Royal Free Hospital.

This is confirmation of the oral account given by the warden on the night.

In 1998, as this book goes to press, a builder's labourer tearing down a partition in a house in South Hill Park, Hampstead, found an unexploded bomb. Weighing two pounds, with its three fins still intact, it had rested there undetected for over fifty years in a fully occupied house. There are a lot of lucky people about.

To highlight a change which has happened in those fifty years, the builder's labourer who found the bomb was a 25 year old zoology graduate. [3]

[1] Dawn Was Theirs, by John Hook, pp.57-8

[2] Kentish Town Past, by John Richardson, Historical Publications, 1997

[3] Camden New Journal, 19 Dec. 1998

Mansfield Road c. 1900

The photograph shows Gospel Oak railway bridge in the distance, with Mansfield Road School on the left behind impressive railings and brick piers. After being severely damaged by a landmine, the building was demolished. Gospel Oak Primary School, a bungalow building in pre-cast slabs now stands on the site.

The houses on the right have been replaced by modern flats. Instead of expensively carting away the rubble of the old houses, it was built into a defensive bank along the road so that there is now a narrow pavement by the road, a bank with mature trees and a raised path beside the flats. Very imaginative. Perhaps the two girls in the lower picture are the grandchildren, or even great-grandchildren of the two in the earlier photograph.

The same view in 1999.

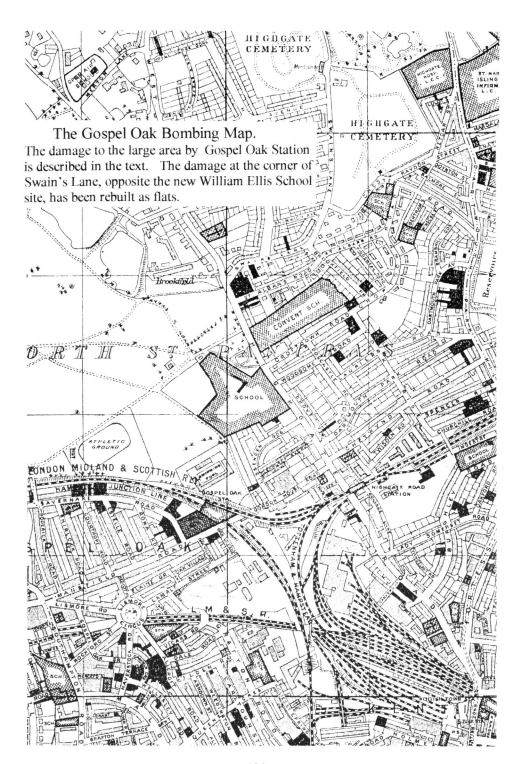

The Gospel Oak Bombing Map.
The damage to the large area by Gospel Oak Station
is described in the text.   The damage at the corner of
Swain's Lane, opposite the new William Ellis School
site, has been rebuilt as flats.

Post-war Camden Town
John Walker at Purfleet Wharf and Canal Transport

Purfleet Wharf before 1945

John Walker, cartage contractor, occupied Purfleet Wharf, now the wharf next to Dingwall's, for twenty years, from 1925 to 1945. From 1937 the firm also had offices at 248 Camden High Street. At the end of the Second World War, the firm ceased to trade and in 1946 T.E. Dingwall took over. They were packing case manufacturers, bringing in timber by barge, converting it into packing cases and shipping them out again by barge. Most of the wood moved only a couple of hundred feet on land.

While the firm found plenty of work in the years immediately after the war, like the rest of Camden Town industry, they faced economic change, but their trade did not change. It simply disappeared. The change was in our manner of transporting goods. Instead of individual packing cases, which would be broken up as firewood when they reached their destination, container ships appeared. Goods were packed in bubble wrap and reuseable plywood cases and then moved in containers. The market for packing cases fell sharply. This change took a number of years, but the disaster was sudden.

The Great Freeze

In the winter of 1962-63 there was a great freeze, with canal boats fixed stationary in the ice for six long weeks. Materials for industry, which had been delivered regularly week after week for decades, failed to arrive. Coal for power stations; goods for export; boats needed to carry away the daily household and factory rubbish; all were immovable. By the 1960s canal transport was already finding it more and more difficult to compete with road and rail, but at the end of this six weeks the canal trade was dead. Firms which had had to wait for vital supplies stuck somewhere in some unknown canal, immediately transferred their custom elsewhere. It is very seldom that one can pinpoint the exact time when an industry collapsed. The sacking of a medieval town could destroy its clock-making trade, but there were other clockmakers in other towns. Most industries peter out and disappear over time. There had been canal freezes before and the canals had survived, but this time there was a predatory road haulage industry ready to pounce. This six weeks of ice killed off canal transport all over the country.

A few individuals working with one or two boats, continued for a few years, but Limehouse Dock was full of empty boats, silent and left to rot. A number were taken to a large lake in the Midlands and sunk.[1] Two were scuttled in the third wharf at Dingwall's and the whole wharf filled in. Its position can be seen by looking across the Lock from the Gothic lock-keeper's cottage. The dock wall changes from old stone to modern concrete.[2] Inside are the two boats, in a sort of Viking funeral, mourning the death of King Canal.

Some barges were adapted as trip boats. Some narrow boats and barges were bought cheaply and converted into house-boats, permanently moored to the banks and now part of local communities. This typifies what happened to the canals as a result of the freeze. Canals became cleaner, emptier, silent: places of relaxation and leisure, instead of industry. Gradually the towpaths, which had been closed to the public like all other industrial sites, were opened up as pedestrian walkways. Now they provide miles of tranquil cross-country walking, away from the traffic. The only interruption may be from cable companies, networking the country with their cables without destroying the streets.

With the collapse of manufacturing along the length of the canal, the destruction of the canal trade, the increased price of timber, and the new methods of transporting goods, there was no market for wooden crates. T.E.Dingwall's sold the end of their lease to Northside Developments. Although it was not apparent at that time, the Camden Lock we know today was being born.

This important story is continued on page 141, but the Gilbey and Roundhouse stories must come first. In a very short period Gilbey's and other firms moved away, terminating a hundred years of industrial history. They emptied the stage, leaving a bare and blank space set with enormous empty buildings, stark and gaunt, ready for a transformation scene which nobody could have imagined.

---

[1] Eric Reynolds
[2] John Dickinson

Gilbeys Desert Camden Town and Move to Harlow

In May 1962 there was a major combination of wines and spirit firms. Gilbey's, Justerini & Brooks, Gilbey Twiss, Twiss & Brownings & Hallowes, Croft, and The Wyvern Property Company, became International Distillers and Vintners (IDV). This brought together J & B Whisky, Hennessey Cognac, Gilbey's Gin, Smirnoff Vodka, and a dozen other names. At the same period, the firm moved to Harlow and the influence of the Gilbey family, which had dominated the firm since the 1850s, was reduced.

In the 1960s there was a major government endeavour to move industry out of London and to zone any industry that remained. Retail Price Maintenance had been abolished a little earlier, so that competition threatened to become more intense. A move to a new site with government help made economic sense to Gilbey's, whatever economic blight it might create in Camden Town. And Gilbey's were not alone. Carreras, with their enormous cigarette factory opposite Mornington Crescent Tube Station, employing hundreds of people, was moving to Basildon. The Aerated Bread Company in Camden Road, on the site of what is now Sainsbury's new store, was losing money as the London tea shops were closing. Moy's, in Banham Street, engineers who seem to have made everything under the sun, including film cameras which were used on the First World War battlefields, were going. Airmed, a specialist engineering firm in Parkway, which made equipment for the RAF and hospitals, was going to Harlow. Suddenly all the large firms were moving away, leaving the mass of small sub-contractors and self-employed craftsmen who depended on them, high and dry. It would take thirty years for Camden Town to revitalize itself and then in a way which nobody could have imagined.

Unlike most other firms which moved to the New Towns, Gilbey's were able to buy a ten acre site in the centre of the town. Others had to be content with one on the town edges. A fine new distillery was built, floodlit at night, while a separate distribution centre was opened, three miles away and capable of handling vast numbers of lorries each day. [1]

By 1964, the new buildings in Harlow were complete and 184 staff and their families moved from Camden. A number of employees felt unable to do so. Some had children settled in local schools, preparing to take exams. Some had dependent relatives rooted in Camden, while others were themselves too near retirement to relish facing the end of their lives in a completely new town. Many regretted having to part from Gilbey's, which had always been a good employer and where they had many friends. The Company had been established in the area longer than anyone could possibly remember. It had become a 'family' firm, where nobody could get a job without someone inside to speak for them. Thus, when Gilbey's moved, it altered many lives.

Harlow was still a building site: a New Town set down in a green field, with families arriving every day to a new, planned town. And planned it was, on the old Ebernezer Howard lines, with housing separated from industry. There were also wide verges to the roads, with sewage, electricity and other services buried on either side. The roads would never have to be dug up, which was a fine concept on paper, but it used up vast amounts of land, created wide verges of grass with small houses in the distance and a sense of isolation. Shops were often a long walk away, with transport scarce, or non-existent. There were disadvantages as well as gains, but most families enjoyed the new life and flourished.

"We had come from the rats, an outside toilet and no bathroom in Gospel Oak, and a right ramshackle place that was I can tell you. If I wanted a bath I had to go down to the Prince of Wales Baths, line up on the stairs and pay about five old pennies for a bath. You took your soap and flannel, towel and a scrubbing brush if you wanted it. You sat in the bath and if you wanted more water you shouted out, or banged on the side of the bath with your brush. "More water please!" They poured it in through a nozzle to the tap at the end of the bath. You couldn't control the taps. If you have not lived in a house without a bath you don't know what it is not to have a bathroom. You really don't. From this in Gospel Oak, we went to Harlow where we had two bedrooms, a bathroom and TWO inside toilets."

"There were about a hundred houses in a block. At first there were no pavements, no street lights, no fences between the houses. It was pioneering really, though the children don't know anything different do they?"

'Gilbeys has been a London-based firm for a century. It is hard to imagine Camden Town without the Oval Road offices and the Camden stores.

Without disrespect, it is like Regent's Park with no Zoo. --- The move to Harlow is now complete. It is a start on a clean sheet with traditions still to be formed for Gilbey's as a member of the IDV Group.'

IDV News, Christmas 1963

Lord Mancroft and Walter Gilbey, having stepped off a helicopter, arrive in Gilbey style for the opening ceremony.

After the Crimean War
GILBEYS AD 1856

→ IDV

1962

Gilbey's and International Distillers and Vintners in the 1990s

To bring the story of Gilbey's up to date, there have been two major changes since 1960 when Gilbey's became part of IDV. In 1972, International Distillers & Vintners, (IDV) combined with the large hotel group Grand Metropolitan, to form an enormous company. The whole group then took the name of Grand Metropolitan. They continued to manufacture in Harlow for only about thirty years, because the site there was land-locked and so did not lend itself to modernisation. What had been a state of the art factory in 1960, did not fit in with the latest 'rationalised' production.

The factory was still modern, but the pattern of distribution and handling had changed dramatically. Grand Metropolitan had decided to give up its retail operations and had sold the Peter Dominic chain of shops. Individual shops were no longer to be the direct responsibility of the firm. Its customers had become the big supermarket groups and brewers who required large, centralised distribution 'drops'. Enormous lorries capable of travelling long distances, dominated everything. Instead of importing in casks and bottling in Britain, bottling moved to the sources, i.e. sherry to Jerez, in Portugal; vermouth to Italy; and whisky to Strathleven, in Scotland. For this international type of distribution, Daventry was a far better centre than Harlow. As result of all these changes, the bottling lines and distribution department at Harlow closed in 1990-91, with the loss of many jobs [1]

At the end of 1997 there was a further change. Grand Metropolitan and Guinness merged to create Diageo, a Branded Goods Company worth £30 billion.[2] Their two distilling and wine sides combined and the name changed to UDV, United Distillers and Vintners. In 1996, when Grand Metropolitan and IDV combined, IDV was selling 85 million cases of wines and spirits, with global annual sales of £3·5 million. Berger King, part of Grand Metropolitan, was the second largest hamberger chain, with 8,700 outlets in some 56 countries. The combined assets were enormous.

The name DIAGEO comes from DIA, Greek for across, and GEO, Greek for the earth. Thus the name summarises the world-wide nature and ambitions of this new partnership. This is the latest piece of the story of Gilbey's, a firm started by two brothers unemployed at the end of the Crimean War, and of the dozens of other food and drink firms which are now part of the Group and must have arisen in similar ways.

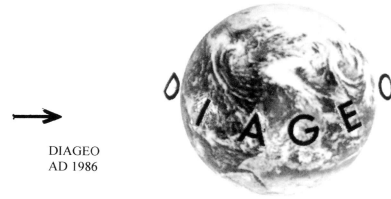

DIAGEO
AD 1986

[1] Information from IDV, 26 Sept. 1995
[2] The Guardian 13 Nov. 1997

Motorway Blight

In the nineteen-sixties, a new motorway was being created to circle London. As a start, Westway was being built from White City to Marylebone. Other stretches would follow. Four special road studies had been carried out covering the whole of London and the proposals published. There would be three ring roads, of which only the A25 was finally built and that not in the place originally planned. The innermost ring would run through Finchley Road, Dalston, Bow, the Isle of Dogs, across the Thames to Denmark Hill and Brixton and so back through West Kensington and Swiss Cottage. This sounds simple in retrospect, but at the time, the turmoil seemed never ending. The lives of thousands and thousands of people was disrupted for years, as huge areas were blighted.

A new six-lane motorway was to run down East Heath Road, on the edge of Hampstead Heath, to an intersection at the bottom of Pond Street, so that people going to the traditional Hampstead Heath fair on bank holidays, would have threaded their way through the piers of a massive overhead road. From there, the road was to meet a massive new road from Swiss Cottage and Belsize Park at the podium of the new Royal Free Hospital. From there to Lismore Circus, where the road was to start to climb. At St Martin's Church, in Savernake Road, a listed building, it would become elevated above the surrounding houses, sweeping away some of Constantine and Savernake Roads and continuing over the top of the North London Railway to Camden Town. At Camden Town there would have been an enormous three-level interchange at a roundabout linked to a Camden Town bypass. There it was to cross the east - west route from the White City and Edgware Road, and continue south over the railway yards at St Pancras and King's Cross, before rejoining the North London Railway at Barnsbury.

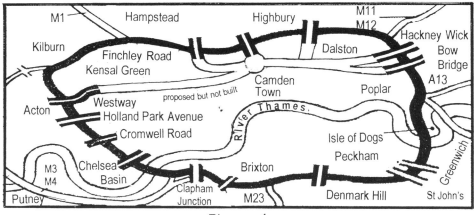

Ringway 1

126

Westway was already a 'high speed link between two traffic lights', one at White City and the next at Edgware Road. It was pouring traffic into Marylebone Road at an uncontrollable rate. Now it would continue straight on from Edgware Road, along Marylebone Road and Hampstead Road, sweep into a cutting behind Mornington Crescent; tunnel under Delancey Street and along Oval Road. From there, the road would travel above the Regent's Canal to meet the roundabout near Camden Road Station.

Because there were several suggested routes and the final one would not be chosen until after a public inquiry, much more land was set aside than would finally be used. Any inquiry would take at least two years, so a pall of blight settled over the area.

For the Planners the timing could not have been worse. Westway had just opened to a barrage of complaints. Residents' lives had been disrupted by compulsory purchase of properties, continual building and traffic diversions over years and the sight of raw cut-off terrace-ends where the motorway had sliced through. Suddenly, when the work was apparently finished, they found themselves in the never-ending roar of traffic. Westway had become the fashionable race track for everyone to try out their cars. The road was attracting more and more vehicles and people's houses were not even sound-proofed. There were demonstration marches and letters in the papers daily. In the middle of this furore, the planners announced the next stretch.

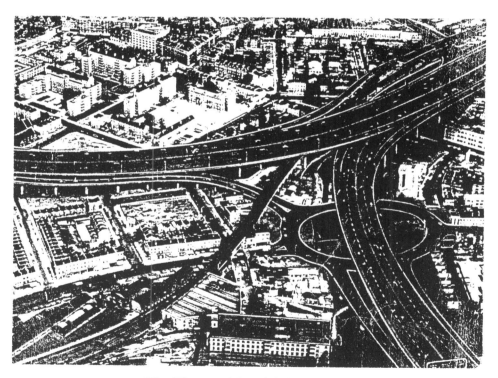

The Planners' Model, looking east.

View of the motorway sweeping in from the left over the North London Railway (hidden), passing Castlehaven Estate (left centre) and with the Camden Town junction at the bottom.

The Threat to Camden

This map shows, better than any words, just what kind of mess the proposed Ringway One and the Camden by-pass will make of the heart of Camden Town. It is to stop this threat that the Camden Motorway Action Group (as part of the London Motorway Action Group) appeals for your support in fighting our case at the forthcoming Public Inquiry.

Camden Town Motorway Action Group

**People of Camden
your own Support
Motorway Action Group**

Thursday 3rd February 1972 at 7 p.m.
At Church House, Dean's Yard, Westminster

First day of the evidence by C.T.M.A.G.

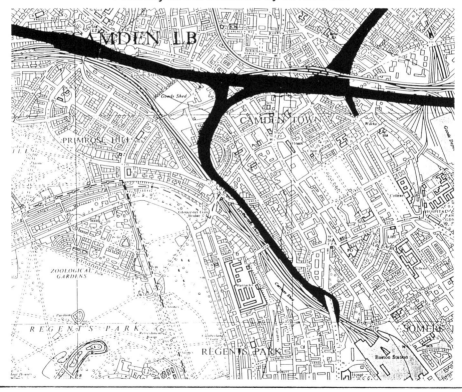

Immediately, there were more protests. Leslie Ginsberg, until recently head of the Post Graduate Planning Department of the Architects Association and soon to become Planning Adviser to the Civic Trust, prepared a case against it. Ably supported by Malcolm MacEwen in Hampstead, and many others, he led a wide public protest. The North Cross Route was not justified and it should not be built until the Greater London Council had produced an integrated traffic study concerned not just with getting cars and freight fast around London, but with public transport as well. The road by itself was idiotic. It would create traffic problems rather than solving them and would devastate the urban fabric immediately along the route.

The road would be impressive, flying and sweeping through the landscape, but it would completely disrupt the local communities and local links. It would be a five-mile barrier wall and, once built, it could not be altered. During the construction period, communities would be destroyed as people moved to avoid the confusion and firms re-located, or went bankrupt. The same population movement had happened to the City of London in the 1860s, when the main line railway stations, the Embankment and four major sewers were being built. The City, which had been full of people, was suddenly emptied as everyone fled to the outskirts.[1] This was the great growth period of, for example, Finsbury Park, Kentish Town and Clapham.

This emptying of an old centre is precisely what happened to Camden Town a century later, in the 1960s, even though the proposed road was not actually built. The motorway blight, combined with the movement of Industry away from Camden Town, ushered in a period of decay. There was no work. Industry had taken many of the young skilled workers and their families to new towns far away. Small businesses collapsed. Shops had no customers. No grants were available for public works, or for house repairs. There seemed no prospect of new industry arriving, no new development was in sight, and there was no hope.

Westway under construction at the White City. Camden Town too
could have looked like this.

[1] The Lost Building World of the 1860s, by John Summerson, Thames & Hudson, 1973.

Decay in the Sixties

During the Second World War the railways had worked at full stretch, carrying goods, troops and other passengers. There were few private cars and little petrol to be had, but by the 1950s the system of transport had begun to change. Army surplus vehicles were cheap. Many more people, trained by the armed services, could now drive and wanted cheap, convenient transport. Local builders had their little vans instead of hand carts. More and more goods traffic was being transferred from rail and canal to the roads. Over short distances, lorries, operating direct from door to door could deliver far more quickly than trains. Rail transport plummeted until only the bulk movement of minerals – coal, china clay, etc. could compete with road transport.

At the same time, the Clean Air Act was passed. After the pea-souper fogs of the nineteen-fifties, coal fires were forbidden in London and Camden Coal Yard became obsolete. Metal-casting, which had been carried out in small factories all over the area, with children peeping in through open doors, became impossible. Many cast iron coal-hole covers, still to be seen in the streets, bear the names of local foundries, but the foundries have all gone. General engineers, like Moy's in Bayham Street, could no longer offer casting, so the machining of castings also stopped. Lathe operators and millers too lost their jobs. The knock-on effect of the Clean Air Act contributed to the decay of what was left of Camden Town industry. Small manufacture was so closely interlocked that, when one firm failed, others suffered and the network collapsed. Today few Camden children have ever seen smoking chimneys, metal casting, or blacksmithing.

Canal transport was dead. About 1945 St Pancras Borough Council had claimed that a million tons of merchandise was passing along the Regent's Canal each year. This traffic, free from road congestion, was seen as a great asset, to be developed and nurtured. A new line of ships called 'The Regent Line' had been established to ply from the Regent's Canal Dock in Commercial Road, London, to the Continent, via Antwerp. The firm already had its own fleet of canal lighters in Europe, so goods traffic would be carried from the Midlands, via sea and canal to cities all over Europe.[1] Unfortunately this environment-friendly scheme, the sort of scheme which may be revived decades from now when fossil fuels become more expensive, collapsed. It was killed not by fuel price, but by the growth of container traffic. The Port of London moved down river to the Tilbury and the big transport ships could take over. Lorries delivered direct to deep-water ports, bypassing the canals. Camden Lock ceased to be a transfer point between rail and canal. As described before, the big canal freeze precipitated matters, but the container traffic did the fundamental damage.

The storage space at the Interchange Warehouse stood empty; Gilbey's had cleared the vaults of wines and spirits, moved their bonded stores to Harlow and severed their links with Camden Town after almost a century. Polished railway lines became rusty; workshop doors were boarded up; goods wagons departed, never to return.

Within a few short years, industry had fled from Camden Town. Not only Gilbey's, but Carreras, Moy's, Airmed and a dozen other firms had left. The splendid Aerated Bread Company building, on the site of the present Sainsbury's store, was empty and derelict. Camden Town was a desert. Young, skilled workers had followed their firms into the country, leaving only the older generation behind. The ones who moved were those with young families, so London schools had empty places. As a result of the post-war baby boom we had been overcrowded – reduced to splitting rooms in half to accommodate all the classes and even to teaching in corridors and playgrounds. Now there were empty rooms.

Some people who had gone to the New Towns could not accept the change. As a housemaster in a large London school, I had a number of families who returned with the mother – always the mother – deeply depressed. Their craving for family and friends left behind in London had been too great to bear. Drawn, desolate faces, hoping that I could find places back in the school for the children But these returnees were far outnumbered by those who left. Each term our school rolls fell.

Then began the slow process of amalgamating schools, painful and disrupting for teachers and pupils alike. When secondary school rolls fall below a certain minimum number, the curriculum does not work. A school must offer a wide range of subjects to suit all pupils and, if the numbers for any particular subject becomes too small, it has to be dropped.. One cannot afford the teacher. The only way to achieve larger class sizes was to amalgamate two or more schools into one new one. Teachers had to apply for their own jobs again. Many retired early, so that a great deal of experience was lost. Others had to move to different schools. It meant unhappiness all round.

At the same time, London house prices rose sharply, so that young teachers with families could not afford to remain in London. Instead, they had to apply for jobs far away, where house prices were lower. Attractive areas like Chester were so inundated with applications for every vacancy, that they could not afford to acknowledge any except the half dozen people they called for interview. Each year the established teaching staffs in London grew older and schools had to rely on peripatetic young teachers from Australia and New Zealand to fill the gaps. Without them, London teaching would have collapsed completely.

With the fall in local purchasing power, shops failed and were boarded up. A building with shop, basement, and two floors above, could be rented for £10 a week. Some shop leases near Camden Town Tube Station were offered rent free for the first two years, in the hope of reviving trade and reducing vandalism.

The Railway Goods Yard Land

A triangular area from the Oval Road to Chalk Farm Road and up to the Roundhouse, which once had been a mass of railway lines, was now empty of work. At one edge of Camden Lock was the Main Line to Euston, while the North London Line ran through the centre, but the goods traffic and the hundreds of horses and vans once employed by The Midland Railway, Gilbey's and Pickford's had disappeared.

The Railway Company removed the rails, leaving a bare, deserted space. This land was to become the centre of protracted disputes and several public inquiries. Developers wanted it for private housing. Camden Council wanted it for low-cost housing to ease their waiting lists. Arguments were polarised and the newspapers were full of letters of protest. Everything was on hold.

Attracting New Industry

At the same time there was the problem of finding more jobs. High-tec manufacturing industries were being established on green-field sites away from large towns, in areas close to motorways. Camden Town was at a disadvantage in this. More than a century earlier the Roundhouse had become redundant and here, in the 1960s, other large buildings were also becoming out of date. History was being repeated as road transport ousted rail. Camden Town, which had been ideal for transport a century earlier, with canal and rail side by side, was suddenly unsuitable for modern distribution.

If industry was to be attracted, it had to be small-scale, small size, and labour intensive. Indeed the only people who have solved the problem of modern transport in Camden Town are the TV Companies, who send out their goods by satellite and cable.

---

[1] 'Water Transport Facilities in St Pancras', circa 1945. Camden Local History Archive.

The Roundhouse from the Eighteen-sixties

By 1860s the Roundhouse had become a shed for corn and potatoes.[1] In 1869 the building was leased to W. & A. Gilbey Ltd. as a bonded warehouse for wines and spirits. The railway tracks within the building were removed and a wooden gallery made of huge timbers, added to carry the vats of maturing whisky and brandy. A loading bay and two double doors were built on the Chalk Farm facade. The building continued as a secure bonded warehouse for nearly a hundred years, until Gilbey's finally gave up its use in 1963.

By this time the building had been listed Grade II*. Therefore a new use had to be found for it without drastically altering its structure. The Roundhouse had survived only by chance. It was useless for its original purpose of turning engines, but its unusual shape and lack of windows had not prevented it from being an efficient bonded store. It was just luck that Gilbey's happened to be on the spot and able to make use of a difficult building. Otherwise it might have been demolished years ago. Pure chance saved a noble building, simple, distinctive and exuding power, like a great dinosaur left stranded in a changed world.

The Roundhouse and Centre 42 in the Nineteen-sixties

When Gilbeys left Camden Town in the early nineteen-sixties, the Roundhouse became empty. The playwright, Arnold Wesker was fired by the idea of using it as a public space, open for any form of public entertainment. Theatre, dance, circus, all would perform there and people would pay what they could afford for entrance. In 1960 the Trades Union Congress passed Resolution 42 which declared that the building should become a centre for the arts, and this gave its name to the Wesker project. From then on it was called Centre 42.

In 1964, the lease of the Roundhouse still had sixteen years to run. When it was bought by Selincourt & Son as part of a larger land deal, their managing director, Louis Mintz, gave it with the remains of its lease, to Centre 42. The Roundhouse Trust was set up in 1965 with Arnold Wesker as artistic director and George Hoskins as administrator, but money was hard to raise. Wesker had set his mind on a fully equipped theatre, with restaurants, film facilities including a dark room and cutting facilities, and ideal working conditions for the actors. All admirable and all expensive.

Converting the building into a theatre would always be difficult because of the central ring of cast iron pillars. The 1837 engraving on page 134, repeated to illustrate the point, shows this perfectly. Remove the three nearest columns and you have a classical theatre shape. Leave them in place and the sight lines are blocked. Thus the fact that the building was listed, meant that it could never become a normal theatre. Secondly, the vast roof dispersed the sound. This was no problem for pop groups with their huge amplifiers, but made intimate dialogue difficult to hear.

The Roundhouse space was ideal for large, spectacular shows. Some highly acclaimed shows were staged and the unusual shape sometimes produced new invention. Peter Brook remembered that after putting on A Midsummer Night's Dream at Stratford, a show which involved a great deal of gadgetry, they arrived at the Roundhouse with nothing. Not even costumes. But the space so inspired the actors that they could forget all their lost sets and create a new, exuberant production on the bare boards. The audience sat on the floor while the actors performed around and among them.[2]

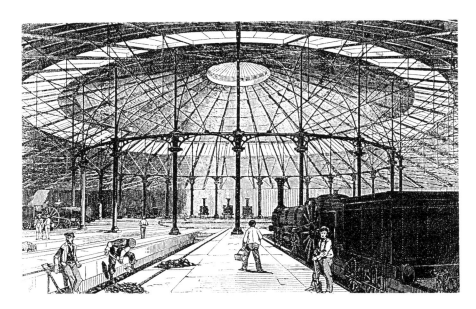

The 1837 engraving of the Roundhouse repeated to illustrate
the problem of the inner ring of pillars. None of these men
would have been able to see a stage at the other side

In 1968, Peter Brook premiered his celebrated production of 'The Tempest'. In the same year Jimi Hendrix, Otis Redding, and The Doors all played to packed houses.

In 1969, Tony Richardson produced his famous 'Hamlet' with Nicol Williamson, and Steve Berkoff his 'Metamorphosis' and 'The Penal Colony'. Pink Floyd, Family, and Fairport Convention, played a benefit concert to help the funds.

1970 saw Jean-Louis Barrault's production of 'Rabelais'; 'Godspell'; and P.J.Proby in 'Catch My Soul'(the rock opera version of Otello written by Braeme Murray and Jack Good).

Wesker had always been concerned that bringing in outside productions would weaken his vision of the Roundhouse as an artistic centre with its own ethos and momentum. Instead it might become a mere theatrical space, let to outsiders. In 1972 he directed and staged his own play, 'The Friends', but so few tickets were sold that the backers wanted to close it after a fortnight. After six weeks they did so and instead brought in 'O Calcutta', the notorious sex show. This so outraged Wesker that he resigned.

George Hoskins then ran the theatre and put on some notable shows, including Arianne Mouchkines' famous Theatre du Soleil production of the play '1789: the story of the French Revolution'. This used the Roundhouse space in a flexible way. It shifted the acting areas from place to place, with several spaces in use at the same time, so that the audience had to move from one stage to the next, craning to find out what was happening, only to realize that they had become part of the action and they themselves were the crowd in the play. This production enjoyed great critical and popular success. People had a good time, but the shows were never financially secure.

In the spring of 1977, Hoskins had to step down due to ill health and Thelma Holt was asked to run the theatre for three months. With the Roundhouse burdened by ever increasing debts and its reputation as a centre of the drug culture, Thelma Holt determined to concentrate on using the building as a theatre. She stopped the rock concerts, which had become a mainstay of the building, and began to mount her own productions. When she was asked to take over as theatre director, she agreed to do so only if the Arts Council grant was increased. As a result, the subsidy rose from £30,000 to £47,500 in the following year.

The major problem was to tackle the acoustic and seating problems. To finance this Thelma Holt brought in prestigious productions, including Helen Mirren and Bob Hoskins in 'The Duchess of Malfi', Vanessa Redgrave in 'The Lady from the Sea', and Max Wall in 'Waiting for Godot'.

Her own first and as it happened her last major production, was an elaborate staging of Bartholomew Fair, in which the whole of the Roundhouse became the fairground. Action took place before and after the actual performance. Genuine fairground equipment was borrowed from the collection at Wookey Hole, in Somerset; booths sold food and there were pens of animals, as if for sale. Pedlars walked among the crowd selling from their packs; there were puppet shows and jugglers, while Shakespeare himself walked among the crowd trying to persuade people to go to his show, which was being performed nearby, instead of this inferior Ben Johnson stuff.

The complication of this production tended to puzzle the audience. The play itself is complicated and rather diffuse, so that wrapping sideshows and animals around it as well, made the whole production bewildering. Academics who knew the play well, praised it. It added yet another dimension to the text and formed part of lectures they were to give for years, but it perplexed most of the audience. As a result, it was not a financial success.

Thelma Holt then set about converting the Roundhouse into a theatre-in-the-round, on the lines of the Manchester Royal Exchange. Like the Roundhouse, this Victorian building had been cavernous and with bad acoustics. Accordingly, Richard Negri, the architect who had so successfully converted the Royal Exchange and D.K.Jones who had solved its sound problems, were invited to tackle the Roundhouse. Negri designed a central acting space with seating inside the columns, on the edges of the old turntable. This reduced the seats from 940 to 600. Lit from above and with a large canvas awning suspended over the central space, the theatre became more intimate, while the sound was contained, instead of disappearing into the roof space.

Auditorium designed by Richard Negri in 1977, similar to his Royal Exchange Theatre in Manchester. The stage is set for Family Reunion, by T. S. Eliot.

135

The Royal Exchange Theatre now had a London venue. The London and Manchester spaces were similar; scenery on this type of stage was minimal; so Manchester productions could be brought down easily. This was seen as a new form of touring. Manchester and theatres from abroad used the venue until 1983, when funding failed.

In 1981, Thelma Holt had persuaded the Greater London Council to subsidize the Roundhouse for £120,000 a year. This was not all she needed and economies had to be made. Thelma Holt had filled the building for six years from 1977, but unexplicably Camden and the Greater London Council refused further funding. They had the money but withheld it. The Arts Council would fund only if the local authority was prepared to match their contribution. When Camden Council refused to support the theatre, the Arts Council withdrew its subsidy and the Round-house had to close, with recriminations all round. All creditors were paid, but in 1983, after eighteen years, the theatre became dark.

Shortly afterwards the Council sunk the money in a Centre for Black Music and Drama but the enterprise collapsed in 1990.[3]

The Camden Goods Yard Site – Public or Private Housing?

At the same time as people searched for a new use for the Roundhouse, the battle about the future of the Goods Yard Site continued. It was owned by the National Freight Corporation. In 1987 there was a five-week Inquiry into their plans to develop the fifteen acre site for expensive housing. Camden wanted instead to compulsorily purchase and develop it for fair-price housing. The old John Nash controversy lived on. In December the Inspector ruled in NFC's favour. A new access road would have to be developed from Ferdinand Street to Oval Road at the cost of several million pounds. This would have been paid for by the Ministry of Transport, so that figure did not come into the equation. Later the proposed demolition of an industrial building in Oval Road was turned down, so that the through road could not be built, but the plan for speculative housing had won the day. However, the slump put paid to that particular scheme almost at once.

In 1990 Hyperion, the property arm of the National Freight Corporation, proposed a multi-million pound scheme to build 437 'yuppie' homes on the site and a large office development. The plans did not include any community housing, leaving Camden with no planning gain at all. Supported by a vigorous local protest campaign, Camden opposed this. The Council, in its turn, planned to reposition the Arlington Road Works Depot and the Jamestown Recycling Centre on the Goods Yard site, thus making way for low-rent housing development on the other side of the canal.

There was a Public Inquiry at the Town Hall, but during the course of it Hyperion went above the head of the Inquiry and appealed direct to the Government.

In October 1990 too, Camden Town Development Trust, a charity, proposed new plans for the Arlington Road site, on the other side of the canal. They proposed to create nearly 700 much-needed jobs and house 207 people on Camden's waiting list by erecting 59 low-rise flats, training workshops and a creche. All this was to be subsidized by shops and offices, together with a cafe or restaurant built alongside the Canal.

The outcome of this story is told in detail on pages 186-8, 189-192 and 194-7.

The First Sign of Economic Revival in Camden Town
Northside Developments Ltd, 1973

Two old school friends, Peter Wheeler (a professional valuation surveyor) and Bill Fullwood, who was a psychiatrist at the Maudsley Hospital, had formed a company called Northside to develop and convert houses on the north side of Clapham Common. In 1971 they became interested in Camden Lock, then a derelict site blighted by the threat of a new road. The road plan aroused such a protest that eventually the extension of Westway was shelved, but it was a near-run thing. Had the plan gone through, Camden Town would now look like Spaghetti Junction.

A long series of protests and enquiries cast a blight over the area for years, so that no long-term planning was possible. In this situation, Northside Developments Ltd bought the last seven years of Dingwall's lease cheaply for £10,000. It consisted of about an acre of derelict buildings and granite cobbles extending from the canal to the private road called Commercial Place (now Camden Lock Place). T.E.Dingwall's had been there from 1946. Before that there had been John Walker and a printer on the site and earlier still it was storage for Anglo-American oil drums. A photograph of Dingwall's about this time shows rather a decrepit yard, but this impression may be pure hindsight. Timber yards are not famous for their beauty or smartness.[1]

Northside reckoned on being able to extend the lease later if they so wished. If and when the motorway scheme was dropped there could be long-term development, but until then short-term use must at least cover the rent and rates. It was this short-term vital energy and the need to develop fast, that launched Camden Lock.

John Dickinson, the architect who worked on Camden Lock from the start and who later designed the new Market Hall, had known Peter Wheeler for years. Before John Dickinson qualified as an architect, he had worked on Peter Wheeler's first development scheme, so they started together. That project was to convert a row of houses on Clapham Common Northside into self-contained flats. Later, by an odd coincidence, they converted a row of houses and a coach house in Muswell Hill, into flats. These were opposite Cranley Gardens, on the site of what was once the market garden of the Woodside Estate. I have dealt with this estate in my book *The Growth of Muswell Hill* and printed the old auction sale plan.[2]

This estate was owned by Frederick Lehmann, the grandfather of Rosalind, Beatrix, and John Lehmann, and father of Rudolph Chambers Lehmann, who was a liberal MP and humorous writer. Frederick and his wife Liza held a literary and musical salon there so that Dickens, Wilkie Collins and many other writers and musicians probably stabled their horses on this site. To add to the coincidence, an estate agent offered to sell me the converted coach house only a few months ago. Irrelevant but odd.

In 1971, Eric Reynolds joined Peter Wheeler and Bill Fullwood, the original pair and each of the three brought his particular skills to the company. Peter Wheeler was the original deal-maker; Bill Fullwood was the consolidator and organiser; while Eric Reynolds became the hands-on promoter and manager of activities. John Dickinson was the architect.

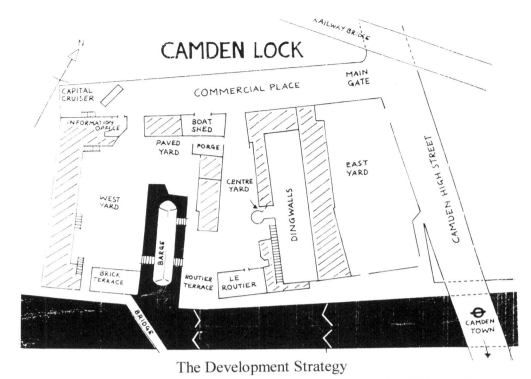

The Development Strategy

The first task was to attract people to the Lock and generate activity. If the Lock was to succeed it had to become the talking point of London, yet all they had was an empty industrial site, a romantic but derelict canal, some old buildings, and three-phase woodworking machines. Being practical people, they used what they had.

All early development had to be very cheap as the lease was for only seven years and everyone expected the motorway to come thundering past on the other side of the canal well within this time.

There were three cobbled yards which could have been used for car parking. Instead, they were packed with covered stalls selling all manner of goods. Stalls were quick and easy to erect and brought in quick cash. Each weekend they were rented out to all manner of people selling anything and everything and on Monday there was cash in the bank. Immediately the market atmosphere generated energy and interest. And there were unusual things to see. It wasn't an ordinary market. There were things you could not get anywhere else. There was rubbish too - 'a real flea market' - but there were craft objects that were unique and also cheap.

The stables in the West Yard, divided naturally into small units suitable for shops, cafes, or craft workshops. Individual craftsmen and students leaving college needed workshops but had no capital, so they were happy to rent workshop areas by the week. Spaces were let rapidly and cash flow began. Thus what was an advantage to the craftsman, was also an advantage to the developers, because at once there was money coming in for small improvements. At the same time, the organisers were selective, choosing people on the basis of what they had to sell, and attractiveness to the public, rather than on pure rent.

Artists and Craftspeople

For young artists the Lock workshops offered a rare opportunity to rent space at a low price and provide a possible outlet for retail sales. Cabinet makers, jewellers, potters, repairers of antique furniture, blacksmiths, glass workers and others, had small bays where they could work and where their customers could see the work being done. This is a rare thing in a modern London, bereft of industry, where goods arrive in plastic bags from remote galaxies.

Several students who had known each other at college, Hornsey School of Art, Camberwell and elsewhere, came together, moving into Camden Lock as a kind of postgraduate annexe. Three potters from Camberwell managed to save enough to buy a kiln. Rents began at £1 a square foot, so that, by combining, it was possible for beginners to start, but over the years rents rose and became a problem.

Some crafts people made a great success, moving off to bigger premises. Some combined their work with teaching, while others failed and moved into completely different fields of work. Whether they succeeded or failed in the end, it was their energy that gave birth to Camden Lock. A vital group of entrepreneurs and artists had suddenly come together and the place began to buzz.

The jeweller, Sarah Jones, who was to become a member of the Goldsmiths' Company, and has had successful shops now for many years, began on a stall at Camden Lock. On her first day she took £16 and could not believe her success. Roger Stone, who began in the same way, still has a popular jewellery shop and workshop in the West Yard.

Jeremy Gane making delicate adjustments to a tiny watch movement
Camden Lock News, Summer 1987

Danny Lane, who later developed an international reputation for his abstract glass furniture and sculptures, came to England in 1975 from his birthplace in the USA. He studied at the Central School and took space at Camden Lock. It was here that he began to create his extraordinary furniture which borders on the bizarre. Some of his tables and chairs are made of thick armoured glass with 'broken' edges, sandblasted, and supported on legs twisted and distorted like unregarded scrap metal. Powerful, dramatic, ephemeral, comfortable it is not. He moved from Camden Lock to a studio in the disused X ray department of a Hackney Hospital.[ii]

Jeremy Gane set up as a clock repairer. Lead & Light (or 'The Glass House') began on a stall in the market and expanded to take over the complete first floor in the centre block.. This was a wooden addition to the old stables, for almost all the early additions were in wood. Wood was cheap and T.E.Dingwell's had left their large woodworking machines on site. Large circular saws and planing machines, all with three-phase motors, were there, available, so it was natural to build in wood.

The market opened only at the weekend, allowing the craftspeople to create work in their workshops during the week and open to customers on Saturday morning. During the week, for example, Eric Reynolds built his 30 foot racing yachts in the wooden shed by the canal and, on Friday nights he winched them up to the ceiling to erect market stalls below, ready for Saturday.

Glass workers, jewellers, furniture makers, wood carvers, musical instrument makers, toy makers, weavers, makers of scented candles, artists and a hundred other creative people appeared. Suddenly, in a derelict area where a year before you could have sat undisturbed in the middle of the road with your newspaper, there was excitement. Something to see. Some new thing each week. Fresh, alive, different. It was the place to be.

The Glass House, Camden Lock.

Early Craftworkers

Food

The crafts would produce things to see, discuss, buy, an ever-changing shop window. Having shopped, people would need food. The Company decided that food could become a great attraction but it must be of a good quality, well above the standard generally expected in street markets. To ensure that the food stalls and restaurants were of a suitable quality and type, Northside set up partnerships with individual managements. Here they were fortunate in finding June Carrol, who opened Mother Huff's on a shoestring and her food set the standard. She has stayed 22 years, in the Lock and in nearby restaurants.

Later came Rose Antoine who has provided vegetarian and organic food, mainly cakes and bread, for twenty years. Later still Do Bighn, who had escaped on a rice boat from Vietnam, provided authentic North American food. All of these had been carefully selected for quality and their success expanded the Lock.

As the Lock opened only at the weekends, these restaurateurs were free to open shops nearby and the influence of the Lock began to spread down the High Street. They kept a foothold on the Lock but its vitality was spreading. Shops up to the Tube station and beyond, which had been let at peppercorn rents a few years before, slowly became desirable. Thus stalls begot restaurants and many local eating places with neat napery began in far more humble circumstances.

Today people remember their first visits with nostalgia. Before Sunday opening laws were changed, the Lock was the only place open and buzzing. To plan what to wear, arrive in your exotic, stylish dressing-up clothes. Mods, Rockers, Skinheads, Goths, Rockabillies –everyone could find their particular fashion. People spent a couple of hours going through the rails of clothes, haggled the price of a jumper down from perhaps fifteen pounds to thirteen and went off well pleased. They looked through the records at Rock On, the shop which stocked the records W.H.Smith banned, and also rare old discs. Tray after tray of 45s and 78s which trace the history of music and pop. They became experts at sliding the record out of the sleeve, holding it against the light to judge the wear, and so hear the damage with their eyes. Rock On stayed until 1996 when rising rent forced it out. At last, feeling hungry, the crowds would move towards the smell of food.

This was served from a long line of covered stalls, with the steam condensing on the tarpaulin roofs and dripping on to the cobbles, or hissing as it hit the hot-plates. The area was a huge meeting place where you could be sure to find friends and acquaintances, swop stories, compare outfits, tell lies about your bargains.

It appeared that anyone could set up a stall and sell their wares, but there have been rules about markets for centuries. Two young girls who had visited Camden Market for several years, decided to set themselves up as cake makers. They stayed up all one night baking rock buns, put them in a bag on wheels and took an early bus to the market. Just after six in the morning they put their names down for a stall and were told to come back later. They wandered up and down the road, returning every half-hour, but were never granted a stall. They met all their friends and by two o'clock had eaten half the stock. The rest they took home. Neither seemed too put out by their failure to sell, putting it down to experience.

A young man's memories of Camden Town

To young people Camden Lock was a magnet. Just listen to one account:-

"Out of Camden Town Tube Station and down the High Street we come to the Electric Ballroom, full of records, clothes, anything. The 'EB' was mainly for the rockers, punks and weirds. Mods like us very seldom went there, except for the occasional 60s record fair, or the odd gig in the evening. Looking in from the street, it was dark even in the daytime. The music always blasted out from the lower main floor, but the entrance and balcony were full of trinkets, badges and dark-looking clothes.

Just beyond the Electric Ballroom were some good shoe and suit stalls which marked the beginning of the First Market, opposite Inverness Street. There were long, close-packed rows of black leather boots and shoes of all types - industrial, army, fifties, sixties, seventies - even forties, thirties and twenties . Often shiny, with the strong smell of boot polish. About 1984, I also bought some good two and three-piece suits from the early sixties and a beautiful black leather box jacket for about £15. I remember, paying not more than £20 each for good trench coats, in black and beige, which lasted at least a couple of years.

There is a popular myth that all the best bargains are found in the back stalls, hidden away from the ugly masses, but these front stalls were some of the most consistently good ones. The rest of the market was a low, deep, ground floor cavern of rusty racks and drug paraphernalia, candles, beads, old watches and lots and lots of records. The best record store in Camden, bar Rhythm Records, but I cannot remember its name. It was always hard to move because everywhere was narrow. When it rained you got wet from the humidity, not the rain. Steamy long-haired middle aged men and women sat in corners reading books .

For anyone who wanted to smoke cannabis this was a good place to come. Pipes, bongs, hubbly-bubblies, gauze and stash boxes, scales, incense holders and incense to disguise the smell, rolling mats and machines, Rizzla cigarette papers, were everywhere in different colours, patterns and sizes. Some looked like currency (American dollars), some rainbow colours, and in all different thicknesses and weights. I saw some called 'Camouflage', with its packet showing a cowboy smoking a huge 'cigarette' in the desert. They looked just like the real thing. I kicked myself for not buying them. The only food stalls here were on the outside, looking on to the street. I can't remember the food, but there were always chips.

I can't remember buying many records from the big right-angled stall which marked the end corner of the market, but it was always very busy. The stallholders were loud and sometimes menacing men in benny hats and thick jackets. They always kept their eyes on their goods and commanded respect from the people around.

The second market had its entrance at the end of a long wall. Huff's food stall ran a long way down the right hand side. It had a tarpaulin roof which was always catching the steam coming up from the urns. Sometimes when it rained the water would drip through the gaps and sizzle on the hot plates. Huff's made the whole market smell of onions and hamburgers, tea and coffee. It always seemed busy and generated a lot of noise. Maybe people had to shout above the cookery noises just to be heard.

This market was full of antiques and things of metal - watches, rings and ear-rings, belts, buckles, drinking flasks, walking sticks with fancy handles, cigarette cases, old maps, stamps, stuffed animals, old fashioned cards, etc. They were stored in large hinged glass cabinets with dark brown wooden frames. You could spent ten minutes looking at just one case. They always seemed full and each was only slightly different from the next.

Going up the side of the cabinets would be brass rubbings, horse shoes, brass buckles and old metal street signs. I even saw glass Underground signs for sale. There must have been sixty stalls in total and each one had its own tarpaulin roof . When it rained the gaps between the stalls would leak water. This made it a constant challenge to stay dry. But as well as the drips, the roofs could take only a so much weight of water, so that if it rained all day the roofs would have to be emptied a few times. Maybe this was a private joke for the stall-holders, but they never seemed to give much warning before they moved the water down the roof by poking the roof with a stick and tipping it over to the ground. The tarpaulins held a lot of water and someone, but never the stall-holder, got wet."

Entertainments

Camden Lock had been opened in 1973 by Jock Stallard, the local MP, with a three-day display of work by craftsmen and a fireworks display on the Monday.

Dances, events, concerts, boat trips, performances, charity events, were organised and widely advertised, especially on local radio. These attracted more and more people and with them the cash to make improvements. The buildings were still gaunt and grimy, but the atmosphere was alive. In 1974 the Evening Standard said,
 'Two years ago Camden Lock boasted only a disused timber yard across the road
  from the Council's rubbish dump and today -----'.

Dingwalls and the Music Scene

A long, narrow building ran down the centre of the old site (see p. 138). It had been a set of double-storey stables, with a horse slope, or creep, along the side so that horses could reach the upper stables.   This has now been converted into the steps by Jongleurs

The fact that the building had very few windows meant that it was an ideal place for making a lot of noise, although its narrow shape was a problem. The stage was at one end and the bar far way at the other end, with dancing in the middle. When you were at the bar it was difficult to know what was going on: if you were near the stage you were gasping for a drink. At one time a TV screen showing the stage was installed, near the bar, but this was still not the same as being part of the action. And action there was.

Opened in 1973, no rent was charged until the dance hall was up and running, but in 1973, Dingwall's was the only venue open in North London, so crowds flocked there. It was the place to be. Of course it was accused of attracting drunks and undesirables, but weathered these standard protests. There is a long, detailed account of the early days of Dingwall's in 'The Rock and Roll Years Guide to Camden', which cannot be bettered here.[3]

The fame of Camden Lock had travelled far from London even in those days. One young man said:-

"Before I came down to London from Doncaster to find work, I had heard of Camden Town because of a film I saw called 'Withnail and I'. It was about two unemployed actors, and it was set in Camden Town, in about 1968. It was reviewed in Face, but that was all I knew. I was struck with the idea that there was a town inside another town, so it was a puzzle and it stuck in my mind.

"When I got to London I heard someone in a bar say, "You don't want to go to the suburbs. Soho and the centre is all right, but steer clear of the suburbs. North London is very dangerous. All those football hooligans. Arsenal and Tottenham. Stay in the centre"

"So North London was far too dangerous for me. But it was Dingwall's that brought me to Camden Town. The thing about Dingwall's was that they had solved the Sunday drinking problem. At that time all the bars closed at three o'clock on a Sunday, but at Dingwall's you could drink from 11 to 11 provided you had a bag of chips. Whenever you liked for a bag of chips, or some other food. When you bought food they gave you a string of raffle tickets and they entitled you to buy drinks when you wanted.

"The music show then was, 'Talking Loud, Saying Something',with the promoter Giles Peterson. Great! It was Giles Peterson and the chips brought me to Camden Town and I found it was just like Blackpool. Full of tourists - people there for the day and gone tomorrow. People you could have a laugh and a drink with and never see again. That's why I went to Dingwell's – lots of people. And then one day there was this girl and we got close and that was that. We met at Dingwall's and that's where it happened.

Hugh Casson

144

Hugh Casson

CAPITAL MUSIC FESTIVAL '83
Five weeks of Live Music for London

24 · 25 · 26 JUNE

Entertainment at Camden Lock

In 1983, ten years after Jock Stallard had opened the Lock, there was a five week Festival of Entertainment. Midsummer Night was celebrated by a three-day weekend packed with shows and events. Orchestras, dance companies, Royal Opera House workshops; an enormous chess game with human pieces; jazz; street performers; Punch and Judy, and fireworks; a musical entertainment based very remotely on Moby Dick, and the programme illustrated by Hugh Casson.

On another occasion there was a Festival of Clocks., designed by Richard Loan. Camden Lock was turned into an enormous water clock, with the gates set to allow water to run out at a steady rate all day. The time was shown by a giant golden key floating in the dock. The key told the time. It sank slowly with the water level in the dock and, as it did so, it passed a series of keyholes marked with the hours.

A Shadow Clock – a 150 foot banner attached to a weather balloon – cast a shadow over North London, with the time marked on the buildings surrounding the Camden Lock, like an enormous suspended sun dial. In addition, for when the sun had set, the Price's Candle Clock – a candle 20 feet high – was calibrated to count the night hours. People danced, listened to the bands and watched the hours melt away.

These were only a few of the stunts and attractions arranged to publicize the Lock.

145

Gerry Cottle, Christmas 1985
Gerry Cottle's Circus performed at Camden Lock Place at Christmas 1985

Gerry Cottle's Circus performed at Camden Lock Place at Christmas 1995 and, in 1997, Webb-Foote Productions brought a Summer Spectacular to Camden Lock. A 17th Century wedding is taking place when a Recruiting Sergeant arrives to enlist the bridegroom. The bride nobly volunteers to go in his place and so does her mother-in-law and so does the pig. Audience participation, a lot of water splashing about, sword fighting, and the Great Cannon being fired – it was the very spirit of Camden Lock.

The old programmes are full of similar details, events, shows and stunts.

As this book goes to press in February 1999, Jerry Cottle's Circus is appearing in Camden Lock yet again, this time at the Roundhouse.

The Recruiting Sergeant
Webb-Foote Productions

The Camden Town Mural

In Spring 1985 there was an enormous mural, 32 feet high and 30 feet across, displayed at the end of Camden Lock Place where it created a sensation. It was shown on Blue Peter by the BBC, but was too large for the studio and had to be shown in pieces. This colourful design incorporated many of the architectural features and styles of familiar Camden Town buildings.

Spring 1985

Regent's Canal
tranquility

147

The Birds

On yet another occasion, The Framework Theatre produced an exotic version of 'The Birds', by Aristophanes. A huge, multi-layered set climbed up over the roofs of West Yard. Twelve main actors, thirty birds and twenty-five extras, performed on four successive days at 9 p.m. and at dawn (3.30 a.m.) on Sunday, June 30th. To sustain the audience in the hours from midnight to dawn, there were showings of Hitchcock's 'The Birds' and Roger Corman's 'The Raven'. As ever at Camden Lock, there was no entrance fee.

The Birds, Midsummer 1985

The Portable Foundry

David Reid, a New Zealander and a skilled foundry man and teacher, set up a portable foundry in half an hour. Using two piles of sand, a few bricks, a cut-down 45 gallon oil drum, a gas cylinder and a few simple tools, he was ready for work. Reid invited members of the public to try their hands at casting. Using the 'lost wax' process', the first-time artists moulded a piece to their own design and carried through the whole process, so that they had a solid bronze sculpture to take home with them the same day.

Phosphor bronze casting in Camden Lock

Model of Camden Lock showing the New Building on Chalk Farm Road

Northside was awarded the Times/Royal Institute of Chartered Surveyors Conservation Award in 1974.

149

The New Market Building

The new building, seen on page 149, was designed to merge with the old Victorian industrial scene. Built in yellow London Stock bricks, edged with blue bull-nosed industrial brick, and large factory-type windows, it could have been built a century or two earlier. Everything is solid and built to last for ever. In the centre, is a large open space, clear to the roof and lit from above. The ceiling is painted match-boarding and the whole supported on semicircular arches which could have come from some Victorian railway station. But look very closely. Things are not as they appear.

The pillars and the capitals on which the semicircular arches rest are not in cast iron, but in steel. The capitals, which one expects to be in some classical design – Corinthian perhaps, or Ionic – are thick pieces of steel welded to the columns. The arches seem to be riveted together, as the Victorians would have made them, but instead are curved I-shaped steel joists, with 'rivet heads' in plastic, glued on. Round the balcony and in the spandrels above the arches are new cast iron panels which are in keeping with the rest. Staircases, outside and in, are copies of Victorian work, very strong, generous in their nature, and good to handle. Floors are in modern ceramic tiles, solid, attractive, hard-wearing and easily cleaned. The building fits in perfectly with the old canal scene, links the existing buildings comfortably with the new and absorbs the thousands of people who pass through each year, easily and safely. Even the outside access staircase is new, but hardly anyone realises this and some will argue fiercely that it has been there as long as the canal.

All this truth did not happen by accident. John Dickinson, the architect, looked round for real Victorian examples of buildings of about the bulk he needed. In West London, where Ladbroke Grove crosses the canal, was a most attractive building which has since been demolished. It was opposite where the new Sainsbury supermarket now stands. The proportions and outside appearance of the old canal building have been echoed in the new Camden Lock building, except that the original had no window in the gable.

The inside of the new Market Hall has been copied from Gas Hall, Birmingham. This was built as a sales department for the Gas Company, but is now a Birmingham art gallery. The Camden Market Hall has the same roof, the same balustrading, and the same filigree spandrels above the arches.

The Chalk Farm Road facade copies the original pillars and heavy cast iron beams of the original building, but the new building is in ferro-concrete, with a brick skin. The pillars and beams are not in cast iron, but in fibre glass. Similarly, the brick arches are not whole bricks, but brick tiles glued to the ferro-concrete beams This accounts for the fact that they are laid like bathroom tiles, with no bonding, as one would find in real brickwork. It seems possible that the building could have been built at the same cost, or even cheaper, using traditional methods and materials. However, this is a time of ferro-concrete building and what we have is a very attractive and efficient pastiche.

Market Hall was opened on 1 August 1991 by Simon Callow, who lives on the Camden Town/Kentish Town border. Lester May, now the Corporate Director of Cable London, had co-ordinated an exhibition called 'Camden Town 200', to celebrate two hundred years of the history of the area – a forerunner of this book – and that exhibition was the first event held in the Market Hall.

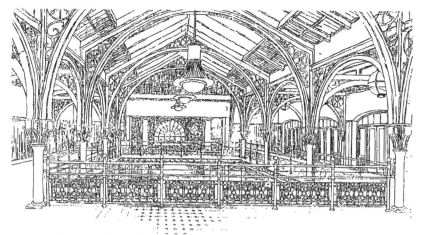

Internal perspective of the Retail Hall, by John Dickinson, derived from
the design of The Gas House, Birmingham.

The Chalk Farm Road facade of the New Building

To allow the market to continue smoothly, the first half of the building (shown above)
was completed and occupied by the traders before the second part was started.,

[1] Camden Town and Primrose Hill Past, by Johm Richardson, Historical Publications, 1991, p. 31
[2] The Growth of Muswell Hill, by Jack Whitehead, p. 100.
[3] Crafts, Mar/April 1986, pub. by the Crafts Council.
[4] The Rock and Roll Guide to Camden, by Ann Scanlon, pp. 64-75.

The Pirates' Club

The Pirates' Club was started in 1966 by Lord St Davis and Paddy Walker, with four youngsters and one barge – a Swallows and Amazons beginning. Soon children were paddling about the canal in canoes, coracles and boats, or else holding up people on the towpath for pirate gold to build up funds.

A child as young as five could become a barge mouse and, if proved reliable and could swim, be promoted. By fourteen he, or she, might be promoted to skipper. Rosedale, a delapidated Regents Canal barge, more rust than steel, was transformed into a club-house, while smaller boats were begged or borrowed. At one time the numbers were to swell from the original four to 1200. The object of the club was to 'satisfy the urge for adventure and useful occupation among London boys and girls by providing facilities on the Regent's Canal for them to learn boating skills, and to develop their physical capabilities so that they can grow to full maturity as individuals and members of society.'

This was Inner London and not free from trouble. The Rosedale was vandalized twice and it was obvious that the club needed a secure storage for all the boats and equipment. Running the club and creating a new building demanded a great deal of money. Fund raising went on all the time, with concerts, a bazaar and donations from charitable trusts, the Inner London Educational Authority, and the public.

Camden Council gave a generous wedge of land on the south of the canal, on the edge of Gilbey's old 'A' Shed site, and the castle was built.[1] Tony Henderson, a senior partner in Seiferts, designed the clubhouse as an impressive castle, the first defensive castle built in Britain since the sixteenth century. This style of building is far from the normal run of tower blocks and huge ferro-concrete hotels built by Seiferts, but was fun to build [11]

Built across the Canal at the end of Oval Road, the Pirates' Pedestrian Bridge is on the site of one of the private bridges which Cubitt built for Pickfords in 1841.

Rosedale, the original Pirates' Barge, with a swarm of pirates starting on a raid.

The 'Castle' is in brick, or rather it is in reinforced-concrete faced with brick, and built on three levels. There is a warden's flat and a small office at the top; a canteen and Club area on the first floor; and a basement boat house which opens on to the canal. With a battlemented top storey, gun slits giving a wide field of fire on the first floor, gun ports in the basement fronting the canal, and a swivel cannon which can fire black footballs at the first sign of an invasion, the 'Castle' is designed to be impregnable.

The building was opened by the Lord Mayor of London, in 1977 It was open for schools use during the day in term time and for members during the holidays, plus two evenings a week throughout the year, besides Saturdays and Sundays. In 1983 there was a daily average attendance of between 50-70 and the Pirates' Club had 35 craft of varying types.

The staff consisted of the Warden, two assistant staff and 2,000 assistant hours. They employed 12 part-time staff. All salary costs were met by the Inner London Educational Authority, but when this body was abolished the club became the responsibilty of Camden Borough Council. Things continued as they were for about a year.

Camden Council now had two water clubs to support within a short distance of each other, the Pirates Club and the Jubilee Waterside Centre. The latter is further down the canal, at Camley Street, just by the King's Cross gasometers. An old railway shed there had been converted into a Youth Centre, with canoeing, mountain bike racing, and a fine inside climbing wall, all as part of Camden's celebration of the Queen's Jubilee.

At the end of 1992 Camden was having to pull its horns in because a loan taken out from a French bank some years before had been forgotten and now had to be repaid immediately. A large sum was due and each council department had to make cuts. In this situation the Youth Service had to make decisions on how to deliver the best service in the coming years. Since the Pirates and Jubilee Clubs overlappd, one had to be preferred.

The Pirates Club had more going on at the time and was attracting more children, but the Jubilee Club had the greater potential. It was a larger building which, unlike

CAMDEN TOWN · LONDON NW1

153

the Pirates Club, had disability access. There was a fine indoor climbing wall, more storage so, while the two clubs had equal access to the canal, the prospects for broader outdoor activities of all kinds was greater at the Jubilee.

In the end Camden withdrew its support from the Pirates Club, concentrating all available funds on the Jubilee Waterside Centre. For a number of years the Pirates Castle, at Camden Town, stood almost empty.

The Jubilee Waterside Centre

Today the Jubilee Club offers canoeing, kayak racing, indoor rock climbing, and runs one-day trips for mountain biking to Epping Forest. It is the centre for the Duke of Edinburgh Award Scheme, an Accredited Centre for mountain leader training for adults and runs British Canoe Union courses for teachers. In addition there is an Urban Bunk House which can sleep 27, offering accommodation at very low prices to young people visiting London.

The Jubilee is considering applying for a National Lottery Award to improve, among other things, their climbing wall. Only a very tall wall would be considered, so tall that it would go through the roof. However, there is a deep cellar below the floor which used to house engines. By starting the climb in the cellar, there might be room.

Access to the bottom of this new wall would be by stairs, or a ladder, but they could add to the fun by creating a series of narrow tunnels and larger caves around the cellar, leading eventually to the base of the climb. While there would be emergency lighting inside the tunnel system, it would normally be negotiated by scrambling and crawling on hands and knees in darkness, lit only by a torch held in a miner's helmet.

The Pirates Club

In 1995 the Pirates Club was revived, with Giles Higgitt as the only paid employee, helped by a number of volunteers. The club has two narrow boats, The Pirate Princess, which was named by Prince Charles in 1982, and The Pirate Viscount, named after Viscount St David who founded the club. The Pirate Viscount is hired for day trips by youth clubs, pensioners, Prince's Trust volunteers and many other groups. The Pirate Princess is hired by groups for longer periods as a holiday boat.

These narrow boats provide income which supports other club activities. There are rowing boats, three coracles, open Canadian canoes and the club is hoping to attract volunteers qualified to teach the use of kayaks and other covered boats. With the influx of families with young children into the new housing nearby, there is need for a local club and it is hoped that Pirates Club will be able to expand to something like its previous importance. At present there are about thirty members, but the number is limited by the number of volunteers ready to teach them. Increased funding support is important if the club is to prosper. Perhaps it is something which should be examined seriously by any new Mayor of London. In the meantime, it is hoped that visitors faced with fund-raising pirates demanding their treasure, will hand it over with a good grace.

[1] Waterways News No 9, 1976, Camden Archive.
[11] Ibid.

Gilbey's No. 2 Bottle Store

The Gilbey Bottle Store in Commercial Place was a handsome industrial building with brick outside walls and a slate roof. The Goad Fire Insurance plan of 1891 shows that it occupied the triangle between Camden Lock Place and the two railway lines. It shows 'Bottle washing' on the first floor, 'Bottles in crates' on the second, 'Packing case makers' on the third and 'Bottles and packing cases' on the fourth. The 1948 plan is identical, but also shows sprinklers throughout. Inside were huge uncluttered floors built on metal joists supported by cast iron pillars.

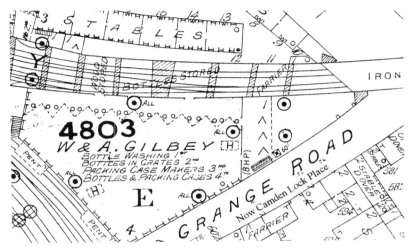

Goad Fire Insurance Map, 1891

When Gilbey's left Camden Town, the building was used to store furniture and to forward it in crates by rail and road. The site was crammed with wood and the large open floors meant that, when fire struck in October 1980, it spread rapidly. The sprinkler system was not in working order, so that fire raced through the building unchecked. Firemen, unable to get inside, were reduced to spraying the fire from outside and dowsing all the neighbouring buildings to prevent the flames from spreading.

The roof collapsed first, turning the building into a huge chimney and, as the floors and furniture burnt, the heat was concentrated on the cast iron pillars and joists. These expanded, pushing out the walls, collapsing the building in a mass of bricks and distorted iron work.

Eric Reynolds, was in his Northside office on the other side of Camden Lock Place, watched the fire start, but was without a camera. The firemen (concentrating on closing the road, turning off the gas mains and spraying the buildings) did not notice when he went out of the building and slipped back again with a camera to take the pictures on the following pages. The fire smouldered for days. Later the site was cleared and was to lie derelict for years.

No. 2 Bottle Store

Interchange

The Bottle Store after Gilbeys left. The Interchange Warehouse is seen behind.[1]

Firemen in Camden Lock Place spraying the area to contain the fire and prevent
it from spreading to other buildings. Bricks from the fallen walls cover the road
The Interchange Warehouse is obscured by smoke and flames.[2] .

The mass of steel joists and cast iron pillars a couple of days after the fire[2]

There was great controversy about the cause of the fire People talked of arson by a maniac and also of deliberate destruction of the building for financial reasons. What these reasons could be in an area of such decay was not clear. The fact that the sprinkler system was not working at the time of the fire and that, according to newspaper reports, correspondence with Camden Council about repairing it stretched back for more than two years, added to the complaints. Some individual craftsmen who had workshops in the building, lost everything.

These photographs raise two technical points of great interest to anyone concerned with building history. Firstly, most girders are 'I' shaped, but here the 'I' has been doubled. Clearly the ends of the wooden floor joists were ledged in the top I and floor boards laid on top. Secondly, the moulded capitals at the top of the columns show that they were made of cast iron. The joists too can be seen to be made of cast iron, not steel, because they have remained straight and one of them in the centre of the photograph has broken off. When steel expands in great heat, it bends and twists, whereas cast iron expands and stays straight. It sometimes then fractures. In the centre of the picture is a joist which has broken off short. This shows that the interior of the building was a cast iron structure with cast iron joists, resting on cast iron pillars. Very Victorian. But not all the joists in the picture are 'double I'.

Malcolm Tucker, who surveyed the building a few years before it was burnt down,

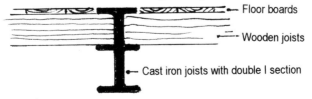

The double I girders on the cast iron pillars.

157

says that it was, 'in the same red brick style as No 2 Bond, but supported on heavy cruciform columns. Long-span timber floors, propped at mid span, as in No 2 Bond, by rolled steel beams, with rolled steel stanchions at ground level but timber stanchions above.' One of these steel beams, with a single I section, can be seen in the foreground and the cast iron ones are higher up in the picture.

Some people may think that the last couple of paragraphs are too technical for a book on local history but others will be fascinated, as I am, by the forensic detail to be teased out of these pictures. The way that this cast iron reacted in the intense heat of the fire, dictated the way that the outside walls were pushed apart and collapsed the building. If they had bent, like mild steel, the walls might have remained standing.

The final demolition with a ball and chain[2]

In 1998, Stables Market have opened new doors at the corner of Chalk Farm Road and Camden Lock Place (the old Grange Road). These lead to the site of the old Gilbey's Bottle Store. There are now lock-up market kiosks on the site, but Stables Market is applying to erect a permanent building there. In January 1999 a plan to rebuild has just been rejected as out of spirit with the site and too large, but no doubt something will be agreed before long.

---

[1] Photograph; Malcolm Tucker
[2] Photograph, Eric Reynolds

The Early History of Sainsbury's in Camden

In 1868 John Sainsbury, dairyman, opened his first shop at 173 Drury Lane, with a possibly apocryphal one hundred pounds of capital. He had just married Mary Anne Staples and in 1872, on the birth of their second son, the family moved to 159 Queen's Crescent, to enjoy the better air.[1] This was the second shop in the chain. By 1881, Sainsbury's had no fewer than three shops in Queen's Crescent, besides several elsewhere. The 1881 census shows that the accommodation above one of them, No. 94, was used as a hostel for the six young men, aged fourteen to eighteen, who worked as shopmen in the various Sainsbury shops along the Crescent. By this time too, John Sainsbury's family had grown to four sons and two daughters.[2] As the business expanded and the bulk buying demanded large warehouse space, John Sainsbury set up his first wholesale depot at 90 Allcroft Road, Kentish Town, near his three Queen's Crescent shops. [2]

Picture of the
Kentish Town depot

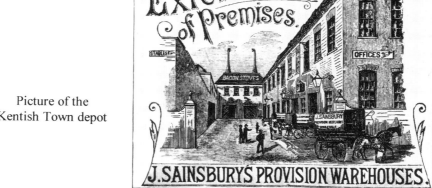

Betty Scott, with her greengrocery stall outside 159 Queen's Crescent in 1914.[4]

The stalls outside the shops in Queen's Crescent were all part of the same busy market scene. Betty Scott's daughter remembers going into Sainsbury's each day to buy a farthing's worth of milk for her mother's tea, while her brother used to deliver vegetables to the housekeeper of the shop where the Sainsbury employees lived.

Since there was hardly any competition from other firms in Queen's Crescent, the three managers competed against each other, especially during the Second World War. They watched each other's deliveries carefully and if one received a crate of rabbits and the others did not, the phones to the depot became incandescent.

The manager and assistants at 98 Queen's Crescent, 1939[3]

A tiled floor, circa 1900.

The Aerated Bread Company

By the 1960s great changes were taking place in the way we lived. The traditional London tea shops were disappearing, public manners were changing, and supermarkets were arriving. Up until then every London shopping parade had a Joe Lyons tea shop, an ABC, or Express Dairy tea shop. Many districts had all three. They were clean, with waitress service, and highly popular. The imposing red brick ABC building in Camden Road supplied bread and cakes to dozens of tea shops, bakeries and grocers all over London and the suburbs.

A young lad left school at fourteen with one ambition, to work at the ABC. The smell of fresh bread which filled the neighbourhood, had been a lure for as long as he could remember. There were no immediate vacancies for van boys, so he started at Dingwall's, which was then a wood factory, at one pound six shillings and sixpence a week. A few months later he was offered an opening at the ABC, at a slightly higher wage.

At the end of each day the delivery vans were all backed into their positions at the loading bay, ready for an early start. Each van delivered to four or five shops in different parts of London and the suburbs. He quickly learned how to swing up the metal trays of bread or cakes, carry them on his head and slide the trays into the greased runners in the vans. Vegetables, sweets and cigarettes completed the load. This was to be his life for years.

By the 1950s, snack bars were starting up in small premises, with lower rents and no room to sit comfortably, or linger. The old tea shops in spacious surroundings, with leisurely tables where people could sit for hours, play chess, or read their papers, began to close. People too began to eat in the streets, a thing unheard of before 1939. It was simply not done. No respectable middle-class person ate in the street, yet today smart

The ABC building at the corner of Camden Street and Camden Road

business executives can be seen queuing for sandwiches at a street window and eating them while walking through major streets, on their way back to work. The leisurely lunch has gone. People eat at their desks and if, under the new 'hot desk-ing' system, they have no personal desk, but merely plug in their lap-top in some convenient socket, they perch where they can.

In this atmosphere, with old-fashioned tea shops closing, the Aerated Bread Company began to fail. In the days of fast food, their customers had gone. In 1976, the firm made 800 people redundant and set up instead a smaller and leaner firm called Allied Bakeries. This was to supply shops of any sort, but succeeded in making a small profit in only one of the next six years.

One employee said, "If we can make the Mini Metro, you would think we could make a few sausage rolls", but the building and machines were antiquated, unable to meet modern production targets. Other firms were offering lower prices in a vicious discount war. On 19 March 1982 the factory closed completely, with another 200 redundancies. The workers received three months pay, tax free, but most did not expect to get a new job easily. Because of their age, some might never work again and prospects looked bleak. [3]

The ABC building was imposing, in red brick with white facings; the smell of new baked bread had wafted from it for decades, but now it was empty. Despite a vigorous local campaign the Department of the Environment refused to spot-list it and so preserve it from demolition. Within months the building had disappeared.

The New Sainsbury Building

The site at the corner of two busy roads, which had been filled as long as anyone could remember with the familair red and white ABC building, was now a eyesore on a derelict stretch of canal. Then came a new lease of life..

Sainsbury's proposed to build a new supermarket on the ABC site, with 32,000 square feet of sales area and room below for 427 cars. Supermarket buildings need to be flexible, easily adapted spaces, so that racks of goods can be placed in the most convenient positions and repositioned easily. Fixed pillars can hinder this, so Nicholas Grimshaw, the architect of Waterloo Station and many other major buildings, designed an enormous market hall, completely free of pillars. A light-weight steel roof hangs from two rows of cantilevered steel girders, with no centre poles. It is like an enormous tent, held up by outside guy ropes. It would cost ten per cent more than a traditional building, but Sainsbury's thought the extra flexibility worth the price.

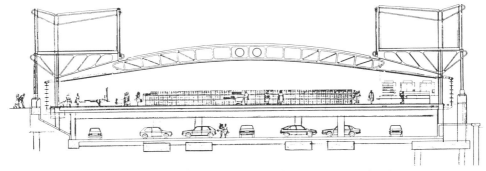

Sectional view showing the market hall, with car parking below.

162

The Sainsbury Building by William Grimshaw

The Sainsbury Market Hall lies along Camden Road and all the bus routes, while customers' cars and all delivery lorries are confined to the back of the store. The building is a vast and efficient machine for moving and displaying consumer goods of all kinds. The quantities involved and the number of people who pass through the doors are staggering. Efficiency is the watchword.

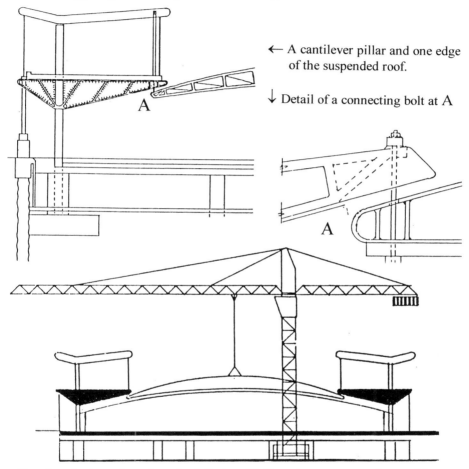

← A cantilever pillar and one edge of the suspended roof.

↓ Detail of a connecting bolt at A

A

A

Sectional view showing the Market Hall under construction, with car parking below.

In the diagram above the supporting structures are in place on either side and a tower crane is lifting one of the curved roof beams into position. Before the roof beams were in place, the site looked like an empty shipyard, with two rows of cranes along the outside edges.

When the roof was in position, a false ceiling was added, so that the construction cannot now be seen from inside the Market Hall, but the cantilevers dominate the building from the outside.

Contrasting Past and Present

About 1960 a small grocery shop in Kingsland Road, Hackney, closed down. Nobody would buy the business, so the shop re-opened for some different trade. Before the shop fitters cleared it out, they offered any historically interesting pieces to a local primary school which happened to be involved in local history and had a small museum. The school collected the shop scales, its brass weights, a few tiles and other memorabilia, including two strange pieces of wood. Nobody knew what they were.

One block was made of 3 inch by 2 inch softwood and about eight inches long, with a shaped handle at one end. The second was of 4 inch x 2 inch timber with a 3 x 2 inch hole through it. Clearly one fitted loosely into the other and they showed signs of long wear, but their purpose was a mystery. Then a television programme showed similar blocks and I remembered having seen them in use in the distant past. With my head reaching just above the counter, I remembered a grocer's assistant towering above me. A pile of pieces of blue sugar paper, each about eight inches square, was stacked by the scales. When a customer bought half a pound of currants, sultanas, or some other dry goods, the assistant wrapped a square of paper round the end of the longer block, folding the corners neatly. He then up-ended the block with its paper covering, put them in the hole in the second block and removed the first. The man had started to make a paper bag. He poured the currants from the scale into the paper tube, folded over the top tightly and tied the packet across in two directions with string. All this for half a pound of currants. A home-made Christmas pudding contained currants, raisins, sultanas, candied peel, almonds, sugar, flour, and half a dozen other things, most of which would need wrapping. No wonder that the queues stretched the length of the shop.

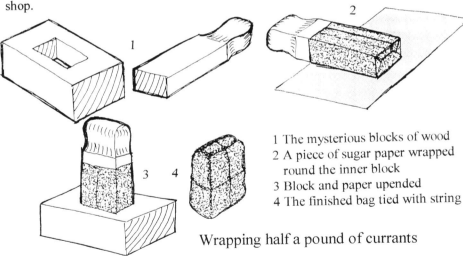

1 The mysterious blocks of wood
2 A piece of sugar paper wrapped round the inner block
3 Block and paper upended
4 The finished bag tied with string

Wrapping half a pound of currants

Today the supermarkets have solved all this. We do our own fetching and carrying. Everything is ready weighed and pre-packaged. We select, carry, load on to a conveyor belt, pay and then pack the goods into plastic bags. This method of selling has spawned a multi-billion pound packaging industry and some say that the packaging is even tastier then the food.

Delivering groceries with a covered handcart and by modern methods
The two pictures have been reduced to the same scale

A Final Note
Reactions to the new Sainsbury building

Some critics welcomed the innovative building. In the Guardian, Martin Pawley hailed it as, 'the most extraordinary piece of take-no-prisoners architecture since the Lloyds building.' The Financial Times praised it as 'an unremittingly sophisticated structure - - - - as grey as a battleship and structurally expressive as an oil platform.' Many of the general public disliked it intensely, repelled by its alien frontage, extraordinary structure, and forbidding colour. However, it must be said that some of its most vocal critics at the start, can be seen shopping there each week.

---

[1] The Best Butter in the World, by Bridget Williams, 1994, p.14
[2] Ibid p. 26
[3] Ibid p. 26
[4] Photo Mrs. Sophie Jones and Sainsbury's.
[5] Sainsbury's.
[3] Ham & High, 19 March, 1982

Stables Market and the Stanley Sidings

During the 1920s, the modern Stables Market was part of the much larger Stanley Sidings, which ran unbroken from the corner of Commercial Place, right up to the Roundhouse. The present main entrance to Stables Market was then the only entrance and was a security point. Behind the yellow wall were immense stocks of wines and spirits, coal and goods of all kinds in transit, so the public was not admitted.

The unbroken Chalk Farm site stretching right up to the Roundhouse, before the Horse Hospital was built. This engraving must be imaginary as the stretch between the end of the vaults and the Roundhouse is missing, and the ground levels are wrong.[1]

Memories of the Stanley Sidings in the Nineteen Twenties

The elderly man who described his childhood earlier (p. 102) remembers that he roamed with his friends from the Tolmer Cinema, at the corner of Euston Road, past Delancey Street where he lived, over the Hampstead Road canal bridge, to the Roundhouse. It was an area heaving with activity, with something to watch at every corner. Some medieval manuscripts are decorated with elaborate drawings of scrolls and curlicues. Out of the scrolls appear strange, mythical creatures, surprising and diverting. The railway arches at Camden Town were inhabited scrolls, full of unexpected, mysterious life. Stables with great shire horses, hay stores, farriers and blacksmiths, car repairers, paint sprayers, sheet-metal workers, furniture restorers, furriers, rag and bone men, washers of old bottles and a hundred different trades – each and every arch was occupied.

His passion at that time was for horses and the place to watch them was at the entrance to Stanley Sidings, but the gate was guarded fiercely by a giant. Beyond were the forbidden railway arches, the coal yards, the North Western Railway goods yard, Gilbey's bonded stores, and the Roundhouse, all in one huge sweep. By making friends with the carters, a couple of lads could sometimes worm their way in as far as the stables. There they would be given a curry comb and a stiff brush to help rub down the huge shire horses. Having spent hours doing this, feeding, watering and mucking out, they finally returned home reeking of horses.

On some lucky day they might see a horse suspended from a hook in the roof of the vault, its belly held in a broad canvas sling and feet barely touching the ground. The horse would have fallen and its leg was being rested. It might be in the Horse Hospital, but in the 1855 stables along the Chalk Farm Road as well, there are still sling hooks to be seen in the roof of the vaults. No child could be bored among all that activity.

The Accident Box with Horse Slung

Picture of a horse with a damaged leg[2]

This drawing comes from an article about the Royal Veterinary College in Great College Street, but similar sights were familiar in the Horse Hospital and some other stables

Gilbey's Bonded Store and Dispatch Yard

Opposite the main gateway were the sixteen bays of Gilbey's No 2 Bonded Store, though only three of them are still standing. These three are now called The Gin Store, which is presumably the vernacular for a bonded warehouse. The rest of the buildings shown in the early engraving were demolished Only the vaults were left and the front ends of these were cut back. Earlier a row of coal drops had been built at the Chalk Farm Road end of the vaults but, with the Clean Air Act, these quickly became redundant and were removed. Today the vaults are let out to various firms selling furniture, metalwork, antiques, etc.

At a much earlier period, when the goods yard was in full swing, the dozens of horses on the site knew their own way back to their stables. At first this involved crossing railway lines and many were maimed or killed by moving trains. A narrow tunnel was then built below ground, parallel to Chalk Farm Road, through the existing railway arches so that horses could walk safely back to their stables. Remains of this horse tunnel can still be seen at the ends of some of the vaults, but a large central portion has been destroyed. Originally the horse tunnel led from Oval Road, under the canal and what is now Safeway's car park, through No. 15 vault (shown on the plan on page 168) and then through the long line of vaults and up to the Horse Hospital. At the Hospital there was the present slope (or horse creep) to the first floor level. At the top it turned, as it does today, into the upper level of stables, but then there was a manure heap in the curve.

Thirty years ago the horse tunnel was much taller than it is today. It used to be high enough for a large shire horse, but today the roof is much lower. Someone has lifted the floor by about two feet and built steps up, so that some of the vaults have raised ends. This may have been to get rid of spoil from the rebuilding, but it seems far too expensive a method. The real purpose remains a puzzle.

. When British Rail prepared the Goods Yard site for building, before handing it over to Safeways and the Community Housing Association, they built up the western ends of the vaults with rough walls made of concrete blocks. They then filled in the vaults on other side of the North London Railway to make a sound foundation for Safeway's car park.. The detail of this can be seen on the Tunnels map on page 67, while No 15 vault is shown on the Stables Market map below. Most of the horse tunnel remains, but the entrance is in Oval Road and not open to the public.

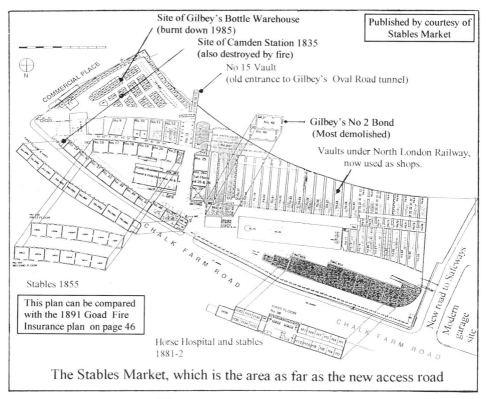

Site of Gilbey's Bottle Warehouse (burnt down 1985)

Site of Camden Station 1835 (also destroyed by fire)

No 15 Vault (old entrance to Gilbey's Oval Road tunnel)

Published by courtesy of Stables Market

Gilbey's No 2 Bond (Most demolished)

Vaults under North London Railway, now used as shops.

Stables 1855

This plan can be compared with the 1891 Goad Fire Insurance plan on page 46

Horse Hospital and stables 1881-2

The Stables Market, which is the area as far as the new access road

The Present Stables Market

The present Stables Market is a triangle bordered by Commercial Place and Chalk Farm Road, up only as far as the new road leading to Safeways. The main entrance is still as it has been since 1835, but recently the end of the site has been opened up by building new double doors through the Chalk Farm Road wall. These new doors, below the railway bridge, give access to the section of market in the Northern Line stable vaults and the nearby lockable wooden stalls. This was once the entrance to Camden Station, built in 1835 and shown on the 1848 map, but destroyed by fire soon afterwards. It was never rebuilt. Instead, a complex of stables was built and these have now been converted into shops and workshops. On the site of Gilbey's Bottle Store, which was also destroyed by fire (October 1980[1]) there are lockable wooden stalls, a great improvement on the open stalls which had to be re-erected each day. Paving has been improved, with the addition of curved pathways in broken red tile and some patches of mosaic. Lastly, the site has been opened to the new access road at the far end, opposite the garage. Instead of one entrance, there are now three.

Stables Market entrance about 1970

Future Plans

In 1895, Gilbeys built their No. 2 Bond Warehouse over vaults of the North London Railway. These vaults, each almost twenty feet high, are now used as shops. They were then stables for the dray horses of Benskins Beers. The present Stables Market company hope to rebuild the rest of the sixteen bays of Gilbey's Bond as a new building, with a conference hall, events centres, restaurants, etc. and on the site of the triangular Bottle Store. The old Horse Hospital, which is listed, will remain as it is today, with the horse stalls used as shops, while the small end section will be a café.

The Company has improved the area steadily over the past few years. Large new doors built on the ends of the vaults give greater security. Behind are enormous 'shops' full of furniture, metalware and furnishings, new and old. The spaces are so large that several different companies may share one vault and customers move from one to the other without recognising the boundaries. Today the vaults are well known for their collections, especially of nineteen seventies furniture.

Over the last few years the whole site has been in a state of movement and this looks likely to continue.

THE STABLES MARKET (CAMDEN) LTD
STANLEY SIDINGS
CHALK FARM ROAD

169

Planned Redevelopment for Stables Market, 1998

Plans for the redevelopment of Stables Market were submitted to Camden Council in August 1998. All that follows is tentative, depending on the outcome of the planning application, but it shows how the developers' minds are moving.

The scheme is to revelop the 3½ acre site into an arts and leisure complex with a variety of buildings containing exhibition spaces, shops, bars, restaurants, offices and workshops.

Artist's Impression of the New Development

1. **New building on the site of the former Gilbey's Bottling Store.**
   This will be a glass-fronted building with a curved front and a glass tower, to contain a covered market, leisure space, and offices.
2. **New building behind and beside the three remaining bays of Gilbey's 'Gin Shop'.** This will run over the top of the vaults as Gilbey's bonded store used to do. It will contain market stalls, exhibition space and a roof piazza.
3. **New building adjacent to Safeway's.** More market stalls, offices and studio workshops.

4	Interchange Warehouse	5	Camden Lock buildings
6	Chalk Farm Road	7	Yellow brick wall
8	Sloping road up to old railway level	9	Horse Hospital
10	Horse creep	11	North London Railway line
12	Safeway's car park		

[1] Gilbey's archives at Henrietta Place
[2] Royal Veterinary College

170

Television Comes To Camden Town in 1983

In February 1983 Breakfast Television was launched at new studios built in Hawley Wharf, just below the Hampstead Road canal bridge. Before conversion, the TVam Television Studios were a collection of dilapidated garages. on the canal bank. Terry Farrell, the architect, transformed the site as a post-modernist building and in doing so. breathed new life into Camden Town architecture.

This is a description of the building as it first opened:-

> 'The design brief had called for reception and hospitality areas, two television studios, control rooms, technical facilities and office space for 350 employees. The production facilities are on the ground floor level and the administration on the first floor. Linking these two floors is the central stairway. Sitting in a sea of blue carpet and in the form of a Mesopotamian ziggurat, the central stair at half floor level becomes a platform from which the activities of the first floor can be seen, but more importantly this platform functions as a meeting place, a sort of street corner where employees can interact. Like the great Hollywood musicals of Busby Berkeley, this stair is not just a stair, but also functions as a stage set for the studio's programmes, which since the studio opened in 1983 has been in regular use.'[1]

The building was aggressively modern and jolly, with fibre glass eggs four feet high laid along the parapet. They were bright blue and yellow, to challenge the local decay. A place deserted by industry was trying to make a living in any way it could. Other buildings were still gaunt and bedraggled. Large areas had been demolished, or were empty, covered in weeds and rubbish, like a mass of old bomb sites. Here instead was a building thumbing its nose at decay. Immediately, parts of the architectural press attacked it, forgetting that this was Camden Town. Camden Lock and Dingwall's had been holding street parties here for ten years, so people and even buildings could be encouraged to come in fancy dress.

Breakfast TV arrived in a flurry of media quarrels, with high profile presenters calling each other names. In view of all this, the building was only a part of the controversy. Now it has settled down in the centre of the Camden Town scene. Architectural students visit Hawley Crescent regularly to photograph Terry Farrell's

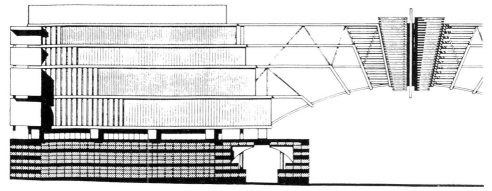

Terry Farrell's Breakfast TV, now MTV, in Hawley Street, NW1

TV building (now MTV) and Nicholas Grimshaw's Sainsbury one, in the same shot.

The photograph on p. 200, showing the new Breakfast TV flanked by a derelict building, sums up the change. Breakfast TV was one of the first signs of revival in the area. With its minimalist gateway in curved tube work and a fascia like a nineteen-thirties cinema, it was a sudden, startling apparition, forecasting the future.

MTV comes to Camden Town in 1988

MTV, the music television, cable and satellite station, was launched in Amsterdam on August 1, 1987 and took over the Breakfast TV building in Camden in February 1988. By June they had launched in Munich and Frankfurt; in July in Antwerp. By August 1988, their first birthday, they had 3.5 million subscribers. Numbers increased rapidly year on year, in country after country. By 1996 they had reached Azerbaijan and the expansion goes on.

180 Oxford Street **London** W1N 0DS

TVAM   Terry Farrell and Partners
Photographer R. Bryant.

At the same time, more and more media firms began to crowd into the Camden area. In 1990, Getty Images established their headquarters in Bayham Street and took over Moy's old engineering factory opposite, as well. Getty Images is a world-wide picture agency with 900 active photographers on its books and offices in all major cities. Their collections include the Hulton/Getty Collection, which includes the Picture Post and other photographs, the BBC Archives in all their variety, Tony Stone Images, and Liaison, who are photo journalists based in New York. People ring in from all over the world for old pictures and photographers send in their new ones every day. Moy, who made films opposite, in Greenland Road and took out dozens of early camera patents, would be delighted.

172

Television in the 1990s

By 1995, the media was very active on the other side of the canal as well. World Wide Television News was in the Interchange Warehouse. Nearby were Henson's, makers of TV monsters. Rush's Motion pictures were there and Classic FM, which had been set up in 1992, was in Chermeyeff's Gilbey building in Oval Road. Classic FM may or may not have known how Chermeyeff insulated his building against outside noise before they moved in, but it was certainly a good choice.

World Wide Television's satellite dishes stand next to the tall columns of warehouse doors in the Interchange building. These loading doors, long shut, are the way goods were transported at the turn of the last century. Heavy crates were winched down to waiting carts or railway trains. At the end of this century, Camden's profitable goods, which are media services and television programmes, are carried in and out invisibly by satellite dish and cable. The media has solved Camden's transport problems. Men with cameras and lighting umbrellas can be seen everywhere, while the battered old warehouse doors are still and silent, painted in designer maroon.

New housing has been built on the railway land and the whole site is transformed. The red Interchange building has been re-roofed and looks new, while the railway buildings, in old London Stock bricks, still appear as gaunt as ever. By the sides of the doorways are curious pottery hemispheres let into the wall. They are the remains of old fashioned door-pulls which visitors to these Dickensian offices must have tugged at long before even electric bells, let alone satellite and cable, were invented.

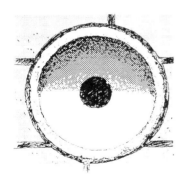

A pottery hemisphere

An old Victorian bell-pull

By 1998 the new housing was occupied and had won awards. Safeway's was open from both the Oval Road and Ferdinand Street ends. The whole area was beginning to settle down after forty years of turmoil. A century earlier the large piano firms attracted to themselves a mass of smaller, specialist firms. In the same way, the large TV companies and media firms have attracted many others, large and small. Their massed logos make an impressive display.

Logos from only some of the many media firms
now in the Camden Town area.

Classic FM plc
(100-102 FM)
24-28 Oval Road
London NW1 7DQ

RED PEPPER
FILM COMPANY

31 Oval Road   Camden   London NW1 7EA

6 Church Studios
Camden Park Road
London NW1 9AY

Chalk Farm Studios
10a Belmont St.
London NW1 8HH

IMAGE DYNAMIC
PRODUCTIONS LTD

HILLTOP PICTURES

Unit 8, Utopia Village,
Chalcot Road, London NW1 8LH

THE
COMPANY

EUROCREW LTD
7-9 Ferdinand Street, London NW1 8ES

werner forman
archive

Anthropology · Archaeology · Architecture · Art · Africa · Americas · Ancient Europe · Asia · Australasia

36 Camden Square London NW1 9XA

BAMBOO
FILM & TELEVISION PRODUCTIONS LT
15 Rochester Square
London NW1 9SA

FIRST FREEDOM PRODUCTIONS LTD
16 Rochester Square London   NW1 9SA

PHOTOPLAY
PRODUCTIONS
LTD

TWENTY
TWENTY
TELEVISION
Suite 2 · 20 Kentish Town Road · London NW1 9NX

aimimage
CAMERA COMPANY

AIMIMAGE LTD. UNIT 5, 63 PRATT STREET,
LONDON NW1 0BY

174

The Camden Town Sculptures

Terry Farrell's Breakfast TV building had yet another effect. The yellow and blue eggs and eggcups gave rise to a new art form. Out of the breakfast eggs were to appear all the fibre-glass figures of men on motorbikes, silver skulls, unicorns, aeroplanes and giant boots which now adorn the shops in Chalk Farm Road.

The plane, which was camouflaged in 1997, seen in its earlier livery.

Some are very dramatic – a new form of pop art, to rank with the painted murals which appeared suddenly, on bridges and house gable ends, in the 1960s. And these fibre-glass figures are always changing, growing, altering. First, a motorbike burst through the front wall of a shop, to the delight of the tourists. Where had it come from? What had happened to the people in the house? What was a motorbike doing at that level, high above their heads? It was photographed again and again. After a few years it was removed, to be followed by a different bike which crashed through sheets of corrugated iron, and, in 1997, a camouflaged tank followed. What will come next is difficult to guess, but I am sure they are working on it.

Other displays are equally startling. Boots the size of boats; pairs of jeans two-storeys high; a chair to fit Goliath. There is no end to the fantasy, but few of these figures have permission to be there, and the Council is split on the subject. The figures add a sense of gaiety to the street. They help trade. The tourists love them, yet the figures should not be allowed to spread too far. While there is a tacit acceptance of them north of the Tube Station, in 1988 the Council refused permission for a display in the conservation area, south of the Tube Station. It is all matter of balance. The huge aeroplane which dive-bombs Chalk

Farm Road is a classic example of Camden Town shop art. According to gossip, Camden Council required it to be removed, but the shopkeeper protested. The plane had been far too expensive to be trashed after only two years. If this rumour is correct, the two sides must have come to some sort of agreement, because the aeroplane is still in place, but now painted in different colours and the shop has changed its name to 'Army & Navy'.

Other shops seem to have a different strategy. Every few months a new figure, or a different boot, or an extra skull appears. Pieces of the display change. New performers come on the stage and old ones are retired. The scenes never stands still.

It is an extremely difficult problem to control and would take money and time, which the Council can seldom afford. Court appearances can be frustrating. When did the display start and when did a particular item first appear? Where is the evidence and which particular figure is in dispute? Is it the individual item, or is the group in question? There are no ends to the games which could be played and the only people who would gain from taking the displays to court would be the lawyers.

Elvis and boots

THE
BootStorE

Timberland   Dr. Air Wair Martens   NO FRONTERA

WALKER   SALE   BootStore Camden Lock   SALE

Duckland   RED WING SHOES Made in USA   Duckland

Georgia   SALE   SANCHO WESTERN BOOTS   SALE Red Wing

Community Housing in Camden Town

At the same time as people searched for a new use for the Roundhouse and for new industry to revive Camden Town, the battle about the future of the Camden Goods Yard site continued. It was owned by the National Freight Corporation, which hoped to develop it for profit. This would be achieved by building expensive houses for sale. Instead. Camden Council wanted to compulsorily purchase the site and develop it as fair-price rented accommodation. Should it be for sale or renting? What sort of people should be able to live there? In 1987 there was a five-week Public Inquiry into National Freight's plan to develop the fifteen acre site for private sale.

In December 1987 the Inspector ruled in NFC's favour. A new access road would have to be built from Ferdinand Road, under the rail line from Camden Road to Primrose Hill, at the cost of several million pounds.   This would be paid for by the Ministry of Transport, so that figure did not come into the housing equation. Later the proposed demolition of an industrial building in Oval Road was turned down, so that the planned through road could not be built, but the scheme for speculative private housing had won the day. However, the slump put paid to that particular scheme almost at once.

In 1990 Hyperion. the property arm of the National Freight Corporation, proposed a multi-million pound scheme to build 437 'yuppie type' homes on the site and a large office development.   This plan did not include any community housing, leaving Camden with no planning gain at all. Supported by a vigorous local protest campaign, Camden opposed this.

At about the same time, the Council planned to reposition the Arlington Road Works Depot and the Jamestown Recycling Centre on the Goods Yard site. This would make room for low-rent housing development in Arlington Road, on the south side of the canal. In October 1990, Camden Town Development Trust, a charity, proposed new plans for the Arlington Road site. They proposed to create nearly 700 much-needed jobs and house 207 people on Camden's waiting list by erecting 59 low-rise flats, training workshops and a creche. This was to be subsidized by shops and offices, together with a cafe or restaurant built alongside the canal.

The stories of the various sites and how they are to be developed will be examined in the rest of the book. It could be a very different Camden Town a few years from now.

Camden Town Conservation Area

In 1986 a Conservation Area was set up to protect some parts of Camden Town from unsuitable development. It included the area north-east of the railway cutting and from Mornington Crescent to Inverness Street. In 1997 it was extended to cover more streets beyond the High Street, including a wedge which started from the Tube Station

On 30th April 1998 the Camden New Journal reported that London Transport was buying up leases   near Camden Town Tube. Plans were still secret, but shops and a church between the station and Buck Street had been approached. Two months earlier the same paper had mentioned an 'aerodynamically designed glass box' which would hold the new station, with an extra entrance in Buck Street.   The liver-coloured Doulton Ware frontage of the station and the Art Deco Midland Bank would go. There would be a large covered shopping mall, but little else was known.

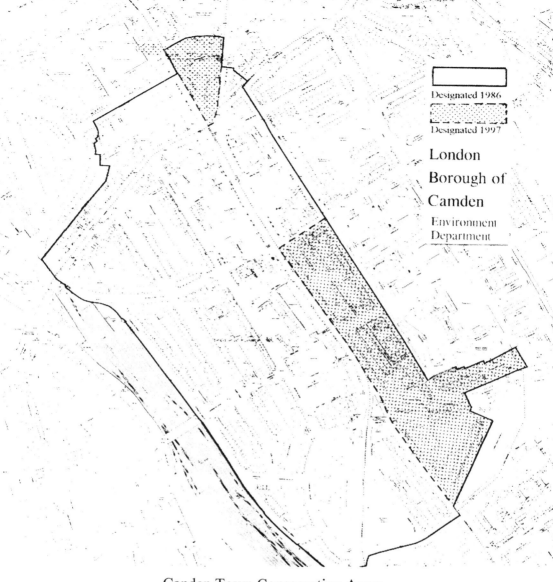

London
Borough of
Camden

Environment
Department

Camden Town Conservation Areas

The market traders opposite Inverness Street are up in arms, calling on Camden Council to protect them. The whole nature of the area could be threatened.

London Transport has given away no details. Let us hope that the heights will be kept down and the mass is not too overpowering. Keeping Camden Town's small-scale market friendliness will be a real design and public relations challenge. Another Bond Street or The Angel type of development will not suit Camden Town.

Camden Goods Yard and the New Access Road

Camden Goods Yard was a notoriously difficult site to develop. It consisted of a large triangle bordered by Chalk Farm Road, the Main Line to Euston, and the canal. At the north was the Roundhouse, while the North London Line cut the site in two. Surrounding the site are a number of listed buildings – the Interchange Warehouse, now occupied by World Wide Television, the Roundhouse, the Stanley Sidings, the Horse Hospital, and the Stationary Engine House vaults. The canal is part of the Nature Conservation and Metropolitan Walk network. Finally, the further part of the triangle was inaccessible, cut off from Chalk Farm Road by the North London Railway line.

Almost the whole site was raised high above Chalk Farm Road, supported by the yellow buttress wall which was discussed earlier and. the southern end was raised by nearly four metres above the towpath. This raised ground was riddled with old tunnels, cellars, and railway workings.

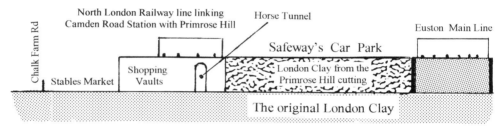

Section through the Stables Market and Safeway's Car Park.

This cross section shows the difference in height between Stables Market, which is at the level of Chalk Farm Road, and Safeway's car park which is built on the old railway yard, raised when the line was first built in the eighteen thirties. The difference of height is made up of the clay from the Primrose Hill cutting. This vast triangle of material was packed between the Main Line and the North London Line, with a high retaining wall at the canal end. There were pockets of ash, but the vast majority was clay from Primrose Hill.

About 1990, Hyperion, the land arm of British Rail, cleared the site for development. The Baldock Quick Partnership, specialists in soil mechanics, made a two-hundred page report on the site[1] before work started. A typical ground section shows:–

1. Layers of Made Ground, mostly coarse sand and flint gravel; 2. Mottled silty clay;
3. Firm black silt; and 4. Reworked London Clay. The last must have been from the Primrose Hill cutting.

When the Goods Yard was in full operation, trains arrived day and night. The vaults under the North London Line were workshops and stores. In front of them there were coal drops, where the private coal companies stored coal for sale to the public

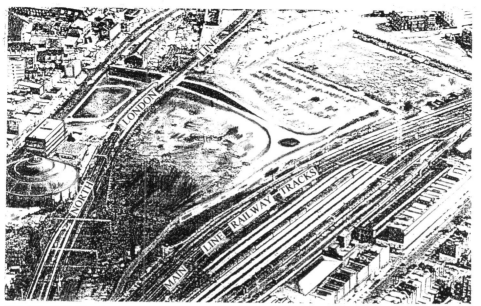

THE SITE CLEARED AND THE ACCESS ROAD BUILT,
c. 1990

These two drawings show how the dead area between the railway lines was transformed from derelict wasteland into housing and a super-store, to create a vibrant community.

THE SITE
REDEVELOPED

Traces of Camden's Past

Railways are notorious carriers of weeds from distant places. Seedlings from the Southern States of the United States have been found all along the railway lines between Liverpool and the cotton mills of Manchester. In the Camden clay and ash there may be pollen brought by the railway from the whole of the North West of England. But the canal too would have brought seeds in goods to be transferred to the railway. Seeds and the spores of ferns must have arrived from Scandinavia with the timber used to make the innumerable packing cases for pianos and other goods. Hardwoods from far afield were carried through Camden Lock. The vaults of the Railway Goods Shed were once a wool store. [2] Fleeces of sheep from Southern England, Australia and New Zealand rested here on their way to the woollen mills in the north and each may have carried seeds. Perhaps there are grape seeds from Gilbey's vineyards in France and Spain, and seeds from the cork forests of Portugal. This patch of Camden Town has been worked and reworked over nearly two centuries, so it would not be like examining a column of undisturbed soil, but pollen is very long lasting and, even if the order is disturbed, a botanist might find some surprising evidence in a vertical core of earth bored out from the goods yard.

Building the Access Road

Before anything could be done, an access road had to be built from Chalk Farm Road, below the North London Railway, without interrupting the train service. A stretch of the yellow brick wall along Chalk Farm Road 113 metres long, was demolished to give accesss to the new road and later a petrol station was built alongside. Beyond, under the bridge were to be the two areas of housing, with Safeways and its car park between them.

Along the edge of the North London Railway Line huge concrete piles were poured deep into the ground and touching each other, to form a massive retaining wall to support the railway. Today it can be seen as a great cliff behind the garage, faced with yellow brick. With this wall built, a tunnel was driven below the railway to the land behind.

Building the Houses

With the ground prepared, and after considerable negotiation, Community Housing Association and Safeways agreed to develop the site together, but each being responsible for its own building. Safeways wanted a large store with a car park which would be accessible to people from both the Chalk Farm and Oval Road ends. Camden Housing Association wanted to provide affordable housing in a densely populated borough. It has wide experience of the area and all the problems involved.

Representing seven housing associations and working closely with Hyperion, CHA successfully steered the way through the complex negotiations with Camden Planning Department in only nine months. A scheme designed by Pollard Thomas & Edwards was granted planning consent in January 1994. This was later transferred to Willmott Dixon. The two directors in charge of the project at PT&E, Peter Mason and Judith Trante, then left with two other PT&E directors to set up their own practice, J.C.M.T.. The scheme was then transferred to J.C.M.T. [3] The final buildings are somewhat different in detail from those in the original application as one would expect.

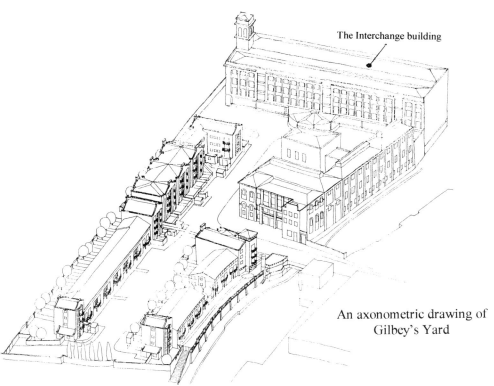

The Interchange building

An axonometric drawing of
Gilbey's Yard

In 1997 Gilbey's Yard, the more visible part of the development, was awarded the Evening Standard Award for the Best New Development by a Housing Association in their New Homes Awards.

The site is in three different parts – Gilbey's Yard to the south, bordering on the canal; Safeways with its car park in the centre, with car access via the new road under the railway on one side and pedestrian access from Oval Road on the other; and Juniper Crescent at the north. The housing development, which was opened on 29 May 1997, took three years to build, with a contract worth £10.5 million.

The buildings are in Smeed Dean Multi London stock bricks with bands of blue engineering bricks and Anglian buffs. These are used to blend and contrast in a variety of ways. Some buildings are in a single colour, yellow or buff; some are banded light on dark, or dark on light, while others are dark, with light attic storeys. Some slate roofs are visible, some hidden by brick pediments.   The whole effect is of unity but with subtle colour changes.

To show their individuality, each of the seven housing associations who nominate tenants, imposes its own colours to the front doors.   There are 202 homes for rent, varying in size from one to four bedrooms, 82 in Gilbey's Yard and 120 in Juniper Crescent.   They include maisonettes and flats (some specially adapted for people with disability and/or mobility problems) communal gardens, parking spaces and a community hall.   Some houses have private gardens, while the flats above have private balconies. The latter have bold horizontal rails, but since these could be dangerous with children, they are carefully screened on the inside with almost invisible wire mesh to prevent climbing.

Gilbey's Yard, at the southern end of the site, stands high above the canal, with a wall nearly four metres high and a warm, sunny terrace. Embedded in the terrace, as a reminder of the old industrial past, are a turntable and the old railway lines which can be seen in the early Goad Fire Insurance maps. Granite cobbles have been retained throughout and, set in the cobbles at the top of Oval Road, are two weigh-bridges made by Pooles of Birmingham which must have checked thousands of vans in and out of the site over the years. It was because of the din of all these vans that Chermeyeff decided to sound proof his Academic House on cork pads. Today the weigh-bridges, their purpose gone, are, concreted in place and almost forgotten.

In Gilbey's Yard all private gardens and main rooms face the canal and the sun, while the windows at the back are small and double glazed. By its position the site is rather cut off. It could never be a through road, one end is isolated by the steep drop of the canal wall, while the north entrance is narrow and leads only to a road which skirts Safeways and can be closed off. The entrance from Oval Road is narrow and protected. The whole site is well overlooked by windows, so that the architects have built security into the site.

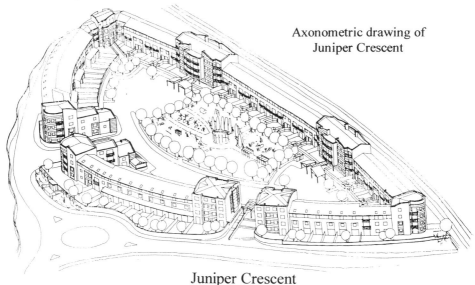

Axonometric drawing of
Juniper Crescent

Juniper Crescent

In the same way, Juniper Crescent is built as an enclosure with only two entrances, so the architects have stolen Nash's clothes. The same principle of restricting the entrances to keep out the unwanted, that John Nash used for his Regent's Park Estate in 1811, has been applied here. The crescent face inwards, with all gardens and balconies inside, so that the central space is under continuous observation and all outside windows are small. The outside walls are fortress walls and, with this public supervision, there has been little crime since the estate was opened. According to an article in the Ham & High in October 1996, in a few months the tenants had formed themselves into a self-protective community with a sense of peace and security.

Juniper Crescent

Safeway's Supermarket

The new store and its car park separate the two housing estates. A spacious building, crowded at the weekends, it is becoming a social centre, with people arriving to shop and staying for long periods in the cafe. Now that the housing is fully occupied and there is access from both Chalk Farm Road and Oval Road, its success seems assured.

[1] To be deposited in Camden History Archive
[2] Stanford map, 1862
[3] Architects' Journal, November 1996

Development Trusts

In the late 1980s, Camden Council proposed moving the Arlington Road Works Depot and the Jamestown Road Recycling Centre from the south of the canal to the Goods Yard site. This was to make room for low-rent housing development in Arlington Road. By this time house building by local councils was frowned on by the Conservative government. Everything had to be privately built and run. In this climate of opinion, Development Trusts were invented.

A Development Trust was defined as "A people's entrepreneurial organization (probably taking the form of a charity owning a trading company) created by the local community to revitalize the surrounding area by rebuilding or renovating the local buildings and so lift the community's spirit." The Grassroots Developers, David Rock.

Similarly, HRH Prince Charles, speaking about Creative Development Trusts, said:–

"Development Trusts represent a third force which will mobilize public, private and voluntary sectors, including business resources, and direct them where most needed in the community."

In 1990, '*Camden Town Trust & Six Wards Trading*' was set up by local people, based on the Carol Street Community Centre and Workshops. The latter had been formed in 1988 to ensure a measure of community control over the future of Camden Town. It had been involved in several local issues; the Bowman's site in Camden High Street, the King's Cross development scheme, job opportunities for over 50's, and played a large part in the 1990 Public Enquiry into the future of the Camden Goods Yard site.

The 1988 Housing Act had introduced a new financial regime for Housing Associations which made it more difficult for Housing Associations to provide affordable housing. As a charity, the Trust would not be under these restrictions.

On this basis, plans were made to develop the four sites shown.

The sites were:–

1. Suffolk Wharf
2 Jamestown Road,
   (the Salt Store).
3 Jamestown Depot
4 Arlington Rd &
   Piano factory.

In the end none of the schemes worked out as planned. Central government and lack of funds ruled otherwise. The following pages describe what happened in fact.

The plan of the four sites [1]

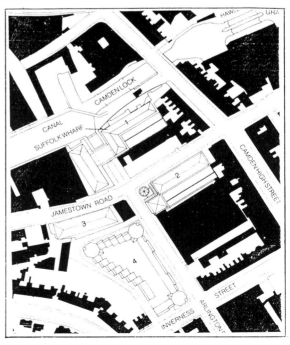

A New Heart for Camden Town
A Development Proposal

In October 1990, Camden Town Development Trust proposed new plans for the sites south of the canal. They would create nearly 700 much-needed jobs and house 207 people on Camden's waiting list by erecting 59 low-rise flats, training workshops, and a crèche. All this was to be subsidized by shops and offices, and a restaurant built alongside the canal.

1. Suffolk Wharf, which was then the Council's waste disposal and recycling centre, was to become an area for shopping, eating and canal-related facilities. The Canalside Walk would be extended to the Suffolk Wharf area. Bewley Wharf, which had long been filled in, was to be re-instated as a public amenity, with a footpath leading from Jamestown Road to the Canalside Walk. Above the shops were to be up to 110,000 sq. ft. of office space on three or four floors, to be let at commercial rents. These would provide the main source of the Trust's income and subsidise the social housing.

2. The north end of Arlington Road, with the Locomotive public house at the corner, would become 45,000 square feet of office space, let to small businesses. There would be a new recycling centre and possibly a meeting hall, or café.

3 and 4. These sites would become community housing, let at affordable rents.

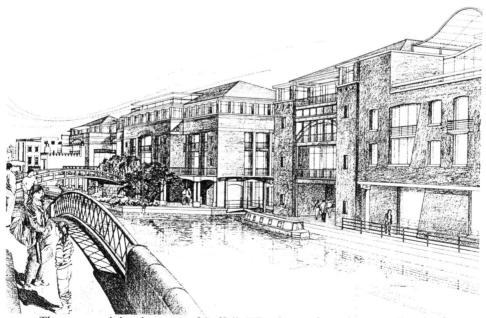

The proposed development of Suffolk Wharf, seen from the towpath opposite.
This may be compared with pages 208-9.

Planned developments which were never built

ARLINGTON ROAD HOUSING ↑

ARLINGTON ROAD OFFICES AND WORKSHOPS
VIEWED FROM JAMESTOWN ROAD ↓

What Happened to Site 4 on page 186?

The Arlington Road Development[1] [2] [3]

In 1993 an area of land on Arlington Road, between Inverness Street and Jamestown Road, (Site 4 on page 186), became available for housing. It had been the Camden Council vehicle testing centre and waste disposal site. Because of an unexpected change in the method of government funding, the building process had to be up and running within three months of the purchase of the site if it was to qualify for government funding under the previous rules. This is a very short planning time indeed but the result of all this intensive work is outstanding.

The Arlington Road development is a city design, showing what can be done with 'brown field' sites when there is a will. Following the clearance of the site, inspection pits, petrol interceptors, storage tanks and disused pipe work were removed. Because of the old obstructions, and the doubtful nature of the site, the buildings were built on piles. These were augured into the soil and reinforced concrete ground beams cast to join their tops. This was expensive compared with normal foundations, adding perhaps ten per cent to the total cost, and this factor should be taken into account whenever the government is encouraging the use of brown-field sites in towns. Without it, builders will still find it cheaper to clamour for permission to build on the Green Belt.

The Arlington Road Scheme
by Jestico - Whiles,
for Community Housing Association

189

The new buildings are designed for city living, echoing many of the traditional principles of the 18th century London square, but uncompromisingly modern in character. The flats are built to high standards of heat efficiency and comfort, while still being cost effective. They are also very secure and private: built in fact not unlike the corner of a Georgian square turned inside out.

The three-storey, L-shaped block has a five-storey corner block and two other raised sections. There is also a four-storey villa block in the further corner of the site. These bold shapes give the buildings the same sort of monumentality found in, for example, Bedford Square. Security, elegance and good proportions, but without the classical architectural details. So different from many other modern buildings, which are square hutches, tiny, with reach-me-down classical nonsense hooked on here and there.

Georgian squares solved the servant problem by putting them down in basements. The houses had sunken front areas leading to basement doors for servants and raised front doors, up flights of steps, for householders and guests. Thus there were no gaps between the houses for an intruder to slip through and the houses were very secure. The backs of the houses and the gardens were private and safe. In 1997, Jestico and Whiles, the architects, no longer had to separate servants from residents by giving them separate entrances and so had no need for sunken areas in front of the house. However, they used the same unbroken terrace construction as part of the inbuilt security. Besides this, all entrance doorways are safely barred to all but tenants.

The scheme provided 48 units comprising 19 one-bed flats, 12 two-bed flats, two two-bed maisonettes, seven three-bed houses and eight four-bed houses – a total of

Part of the Arlington Road elevation, to show the classical proportions and sense of balance which control the design, without the classical pediments and other decorations so often pasted on modern speculative buildings.

100 bedrooms. By building right up to the pavement edge, the architects created a continuous outside wall and found room behind the houses for small private gardens, a landscaped central garden and some car parking, all inside the site and overlooked by dozens of windows.

There are only three entrances, one at the corner and one on each road..[i] The two road entrances lead to small car parks, leaving the central garden area for the residents to enjoy. The exit from the courtyard has been placed exactly opposite the main entrance to Arlington House, with its handsome ceramic transport mural. This gives an unexpected richness to the exit from the courtyard and brings the older building in conjunction with the new.

The Entrance to Arlington House

—————— o ——————

Camden Gardens, at the side of Sainsbury's.

Another Jestico -Whiles scheme

The canal bank opposite Camden Gardens had been empty for years. Several years ago the Gardens themselves were invaded by gypsies, who broke down the frail hedges and set up camp. It took months of legal battle to dislodge them. The gardens were then railed in to prevent further break-ins and replanted.

The canal bank site had been acquired by Camden Council in 1988 for the building of affordable rented housing. The Council split the site in two and asked two housing Associations, Community Housing Association (CHA) and Circle 31, each to develop one half. CHA had been formed in 1972 to develop and manage affordable rented housing for the London boroughs of Camden, Westminster, Islington and Hackney. CHA asked Jestico and Whiles, with whom they had worked before, to design some efficient, imaginative housing which would be comfortable to live in and pleasant to look at.

In Arlington Road, Jestico & Whiles had adopted a terraced style, creating what amounted to a Georgian square turned in on itself, built right up to the pavement and without the basements. In Camden Gardens the architects used another traditional form in a new manner. They built three modern versions of the large Victorian villa, such as one can see in Adelaide Road, with low-pitched roofs and again in yellow brick. Behind them is a simple terrace

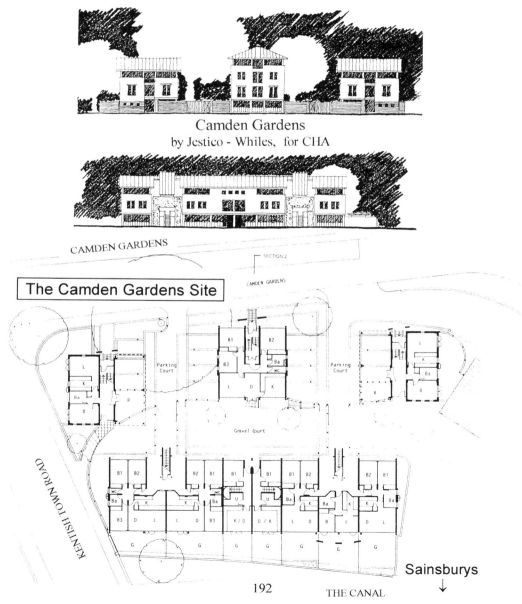

Camden Gardens
by Jestico - Whiles, for CHA

The Camden Gardens Site

Sainsburys
↓

THE CANAL

Solving the Problems of the Site.

It was a difficult site, with a railway viaduct to one side, the canal on another, and a two-metre diameter storm drain which passes immediately below where the proposed houses were to be built. There were three listed trees which would add immeasurably to the maturity and attraction of the site, but presented a problem to both architects and builders during construction.

To bring rents down to reasonable levels, the site had to be developed to a higher density than had been planned originally. This called for very careful use of space. The architects built 27 dwellings, flats, maisonettes and houses, some for people with special needs. The villas face Camden Gardens, while the terrace backs on to the canal.

All the living rooms, kitchens and bedrooms are stacked one above the other. This has advantages in plumbing, aspect, and noise. Incidentally, it is exactly the opposite of the argument used for the 'scissors type' flats designed by Colin Jones, which I described in 'The Growth of Muswell Hill'. There bedrooms and sitting rooms were stacked alternately one above the other, on the theory that they would be used at different times of day and so noise interference would be reduced. In fact, after nearly thirty years use, all the tenants have moved their sitting rooms to the south, facing the sun. So much for theory.

Access to most blocks of flats is dull, with no personality or spirit. In Camden Gardens the architects have built outside staircases with entrance at first floor level, but protected by double-height curved screens. This has turned the entrance spaces into conservatories, with character and personalities of their own. The quality of the building is high, in yellow brick, with a slightly recessed mortar joint. This gives a clean, attractive finish. On the side of the canal, in a most unpromising situation, the architects have enhanced the neighbourhood.

Community Housing Association

CHA, now twenty five years old, has won no fewer than eleven design awards in the past few years. The Arlington Road development won a RIBA housing design award. The Camden Goods Yard estate of 200 homes won a 1997 Evening Standard Award. The Castlehaven Road development won yet another and so the story goes on.

CHA commissions architects to work with the grain of the local neighbourhoods, keeping to local building heights and using sympathetic materials. Their new work blends with the buildings already familiar to everybody and so Camden Town has been almost invisibly improved. The buildings are unmistakably of their own time, modern and efficient, but without any shock of the new. Good manners in architecture is a subtle business. Perhaps the most difficult task was to build modern housing on the old Bedford Music Hall, among the terraces of Albert Street, yet it too was a most successful development.[4]

Recently CHA has been converting redundant public houses into housing Often having been boarded up and vandalized for years, they will be brought back into use once more. Altogether, Camden Town is becoming an exemplar of urban renewal.

The Redevelopment of Suffolk Wharf

Suffolk Wharf, the area between Camden Lock and Jamestown Road, lay derelict after Camden Housing Trust failed to develop it in 1990. In 1998 new plans have been submitted by architects CZWG.

Jamestown Road will be transformed. On the left (west) will be a glass-faced, 132 bedroom hotel; on the east an office/light-industrial building; and restaurant/bar space along the canal. At present Jamestown Road is a nondescript back alley. With Arlington House and the new Camden Pavilions on one side, and the new entrance road curving away in both directions, there will be a clear view to the Diagonal Bridge. Jamestown Road will become visually part of the Lock, with a pedestrian pathway lined with cafes, to draw people to the towpath.

In the High Street will be multi-floor shops. At the canal end, the ground floor level will curve back from the existing building line to give easier access to the towpath. This entrance will be paved with blue engineering stable block pavoirs to mark the transition fron the new glass building to the old industrial canal landscape.

The castellated lock-keeper's cottage, listed grade II, is the oldest canal building at Camden Lock. Today it may appear to have been a folly, built two hundred years ago by some dilettante who wanted to create an elegant entrance to Regent's Park, but it was once a very practical building. A lock keeper recorded the passage of each craft through the lock and charged tolls on the goods carried. Soon it was hemmed in by industrial buildings and later, with the collapse of canal traffic, was abandoned.

The lock keeper's cottage will become a British Waterways information office, with public access from both sides and a small garden. The canal ends of the new building are shaped as a curving ziggurat, stepping back floor after floor. This arrangement will allow light and air to reach the cottage and a widened quay side as it has not done for a century and a half.

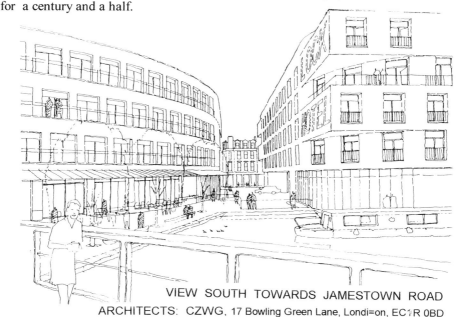

VIEW SOUTH TOWARDS JAMESTOWN ROAD
ARCHITECTS: CZWG, 17 Bowling Green Lane, Londi=on, EC1R 0BD

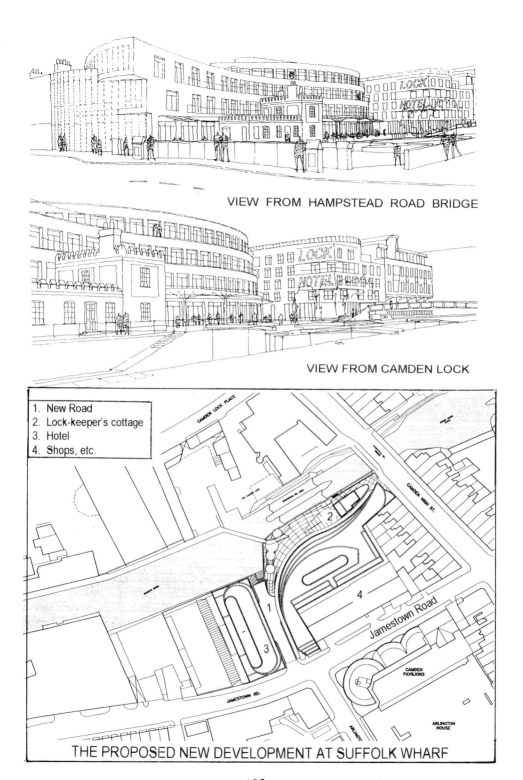

VIEW FROM HAMPSTEAD ROAD BRIDGE

VIEW FROM CAMDEN LOCK

1. New Road
2. Lock-keeper's cottage
3. Hotel
4. Shops, etc.

THE PROPOSED NEW DEVELOPMENT AT SUFFOLK WHARF

The Glass Building in Jamestown Road

This site was the old Camden Council Salt Store (No 2 on page 187) on the corner of Jamestown Road and Arlington Road, adjoining Arlington House. The latter is the huge red brick building in the picture below and in the plan on page 197. It was one of the great acts of Victorian social charity, put up at the end of the last century to house single men who had come to Camden Town to seek work, but had nowhere to live. This vast block of individual rooms, to be let by the week, was built at his private expense by Montague Corry, Disraeli's private secretary. Lord Rowton, as he became, built six such buildings and this is the last one remaining. The mosaic over the doorway, a much later addition, shows the respect and affection in which it was held.[1] The new Glass Building next door will be a contrast in every way.

The design of the new Glass House is based on a series of interlocking drum forms, which create a series of curved bays. Each apartment occupies one 8 metre wide bay. The drums are of varying heights so that from the street outside, some of them are seen as much larger segments of a complete circle, both at street level (by the main entrance) and on the upper floors. The geometry of the bays will make the entrances visible from oblique angles up and down the street.

All facades are of slightly tinted glass set in thin steel frames, creating an effect of lightness. The basement and ground floor cover almost the full site, while the apartments above follow the street frontage in an L shape. Behind the flats, in the corner of the L, is a landscaped garden at first floor level, with Arlington House forming the third side. The garden is an amenity and also provides access to some of the flats, so there will be a certain amount of movement here. The sectional view shows how the garden has been landscaped as a verdant cliff between Arlington House and the new building, dividing their two worlds.

---

[1] Camden Town, by David Thomson, pp.122-6.
   and in 'Lord Rowton and Rowton Houses', Richard Farrant Cornhill Magazine vol 89, pp. 835-44. 1904.

This is what happened to Site 2 on page 186

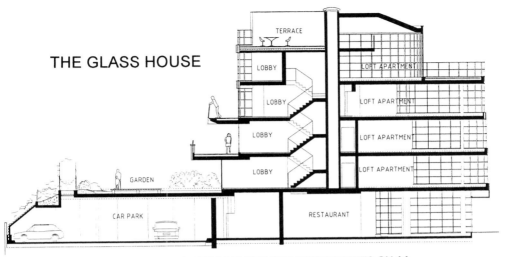

THE GLASS HOUSE

SECTION THROUGH CORNER LOFT APPARTMENTS ON AA

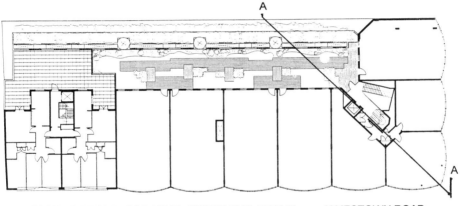

PLAN AT FIRST FLOOR LEVEL SHOWING PLANTING   JAMESTOWN ROAD

THE GLASS HOUSE

ARLINGTON HOUSE

Good Manners in Architecture: the Conversion of 128 Albert Street

Architects CZWG were asked by the developers Linkline to convert and enlarge this building, adding two floors of residential accommodation at the top. Albert Street is in the Camden Town Conservation Area, so the architects were not free to raise the apparent height of the building. All the additional work above the original first storey pediments had to be added invisibly. This problem they solved most ingeniously.

The new design provided a basement and parking for 21 cars, one space for each of the residential flats and one disabled space for commercial use, all served by a new ramp at the south of the building. None of this affected the appearance of the building from the street. Additions above would be more difficult.

Section drawings show that the architects set the new 2nd floor back from the original facade, so that it is less than half the footprint of the building below. This made room for terraces behind the existing parapets on the two street elevations. Thus all that can be seen from street level are the original pediments, leaving the new flats completely hidden.

The third floor flats were placed even further back, to sit out of sight in a sunken bowl. The terraces outside these top flats were each enclosed to about waist height on three sides within the inward-sloping roofs, so that all that could be seen from the street level would be people's heads.

Finally, there was the problem of ensuring that light to the adjacent building was not blocked. The section drawing below shows how carefully this was arranged. The handrail to the second floor terrace was actually bent inwards so as not to interfere with the angles of light.

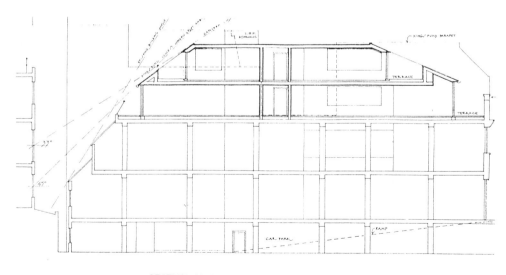

SECTION ON CC PARALLEL TO ALBERT STREET.
This shows the four floors, basement car park and the angles of light to the adjacent building.

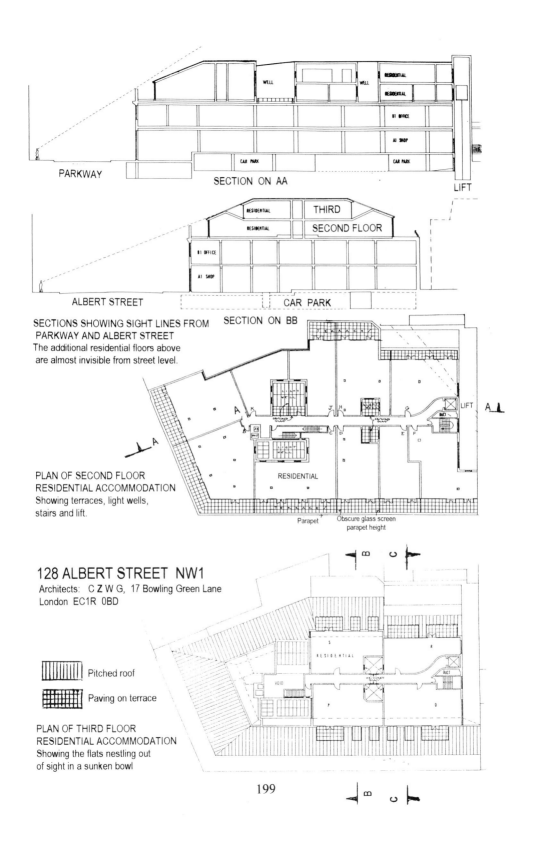

SECTION ON AA

PARKWAY

WELL   WELL   RESIDENTIAL

RESIDENTIAL

B1 OFFICE

A1 SHOP

CAR PARK   CAR PARK   LIFT

RESIDENTIAL   THIRD

RESIDENTIAL   SECOND FLOOR

B1 OFFICE

A1 SHOP

ALBERT STREET   CAR PARK

SECTION ON BB

**SECTIONS SHOWING SIGHT LINES FROM
PARKWAY AND ALBERT STREET**
The additional residential floors above
are almost invisible from street level.

LIFT   A

RESIDENTIAL

**PLAN OF SECOND FLOOR
RESIDENTIAL ACCOMMODATION**
Showing terraces, light wells,
stairs and lift.

Parapet   Obscure glass screen
                parapet height

128 ALBERT STREET NW1
Architects: C Z W G, 17 Bowling Green Lane
London EC1R 0BD

|||||||| Pitched roof

▦ Paving on terrace

RESIDENTIAL

VOID

**PLAN OF THIRD FLOOR
RESIDENTIAL ACCOMMODATION**
Showing the flats nestling out
of sight in a sunken bowl

199

NW1 - A Space Age Restaurant

In 1997 Papaloizu, who are local architects based in Crouch End, converted the old Henley garage at 30 Hawley Crescent into a high-tec restaurant. The first photograph, taken when Breakfast TV (now TVAM) was opened next door, shows the original building. It was a derelict shell, unchanged for half a century. In a few weeks it was converted into an exciting new building like a set for some futuristic film.

The architects retained the old walls, raised them by four feet, and built an external wall in coloured glass blocks. They installed a barrel-vaulted roof/ceiling on curved steel girders and a mezzanine floor to give more space. This extra floor, with a sweeping front edge set well back, opens up the volume rather than reduces it. Instead of a bedraggled old street frontage we have a dramatic double-height wall of structural glass. This reflects the surrounding houses and at the same time reveals the interior of the restaurant, so that one seems to be inside and outside the building at the same time. The sheer glass wall becomes a cinema screen, full of the movement of the local streets.

Henley's Garage, c. 1983, beside TVam

NW1 Restaurant, 1997

Photograph John Donat

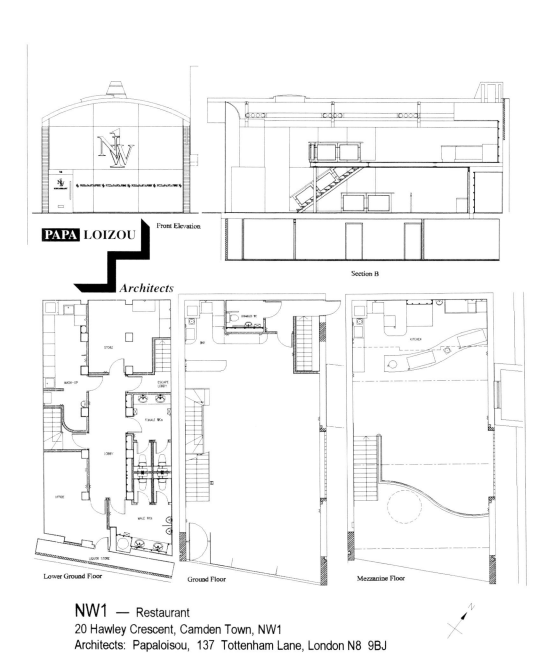

Front Elevation

PAPA LOIZOU

Architects

Section B

Lower Ground Floor

Ground Floor

Mezzanine Floor

NW1 — Restaurant
20 Hawley Crescent, Camden Town, NW1
Architects: Papaloisou, 137 Tottenham Lane, London N8 9BJ

William Huck's Bottling Plant Converted Into Flats

When Chermeyeff rebuilt the corner of Jamestown Road and Oval Road as the new Gilbey House in 1937, he also altered William Huck's Bottling Plant next door. This had a basement and five floors, with 2·6 metre high ceilings. The building was a slightly lozenge-shaped square with 50 metre sides, so the floors were immense. It had a flat roof where timber was stored and where, incidentally, the staff used to play cricket at lunch times. Chermeyeff considered adding two more storeys, set back like a wedding cake, but the foundations could not take the extra weight. Instead, he altered the building slightly, adding back balconies, a few access doors and two new loading bays.

It was a very successful building, but when Gilbey's left in the 1960s it stood almost empty. At one time a part became a dress factory. There were a few other small tenants. It was a grade II building, protected from arbitrary change or demolition. No major industrial use seemed likely for years to come. Then Regalian Properties plc bought the building for conversion into flats. After two year's work there were 78 new apartments, many with direct views over the Canal. The corner flats, with double-aspect windows are particularly impressive and priced at up to £510,000 each. Smaller flats varied from about £150,000 to £350,000 at 1995 prices.

Conversion was a major operation since Huck's building consisted of enormous industrial floors with windows round the outside edges. By law every habitable room must have windows open to the outside light and air. Unaltered, these rooms would have been big enough to hold swimming pools. To create normal sized rooms with proper ventilation and light, Regalian opened a large hole down the middle of the building, supporting the cut edges of the floors by new ferro-concrete pillars. This huge atrium was open to the air above and so introduced light and air to the new inner rooms. It also created an impressive space. Above was added a new sixth floor, slightly recessed into the fifth and set back to give penthouse patios all round the outer edge. The flats are reached by lift and wide access galleries all round the central courtyard, which reaches up to the full height of the building, with a huge

Model of Gilbey House, canal and side elevation, circa 1996
Architects, T.B.Bennett Partnership

protective canopy above. This plastic cover, rather like the new stand at Lord's, has a scalloped edge allowing the free passage of air up and down. Rain falls from the canopy on to a sloping glass rain-shield running all round the inner walls and then drains into gutters below. Thus the courtyard remains dry, but open to the air. It is an impressive conversion of an old industrial building to a new use.

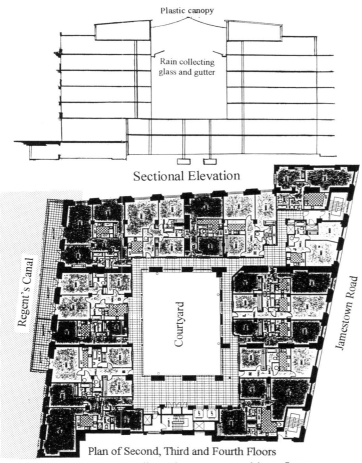

Sectional Elevation

Plan of Second, Third and Fourth Floors

William Huck's Bottling Plant converted into flats

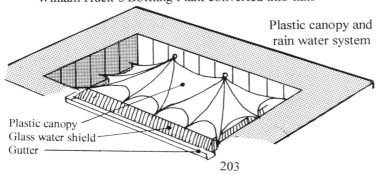

Redeveloping the Parkway/Inverness Street Block

For years this large block of buildings facing the Camden Town Tube Station has been in limbo. It was once a fine department store called Marshall Roberts, which older people will remember. Later it became a large London Co-operative Society shop, but local all-purpose stores had become uneconomical and the building was divided into smaller units. The shops at the Inverness Street corner were opened up into an open market and a supermarket. Behind the shops was a nondescript area, mostly of bungalow storage for the market and shops.

In 1998 the architects Chapman Taylor submitted a £20 million plan to redevelop the whole site. The Inverness Street corner will be extended almost as far as the cinema and developed as shops and offices. These will have their entrances in the bustle of the market and have cafés at the door.

A new building in Parkway, with offices below and flats above, can be seen in the plan. An extra floor has been added, but stepped back so that it will be almost invisible from the opposite pavement (Section BB). The floor levels in the Parkway facade copy those of the corner building and so reduce the contrast between the style of the new building and the ones on either side. The new luxury flats above, laid out with a cloistered garden and apparently isolated from the world below, will bring people right into the centre of Camden Town. Business and residential life will mix and yet be apart, as happens in Paris. Separation of work and homes, which was the first thought of all planners when they redesigned London immediately after 1945, is being reversed. A return to the city, which began in the nineteen-sixties to places like Islington and is now much in the air with the rebuilding on brown-field sites, is speeding up. It is no longer fashionable to spend half one's life commuting.

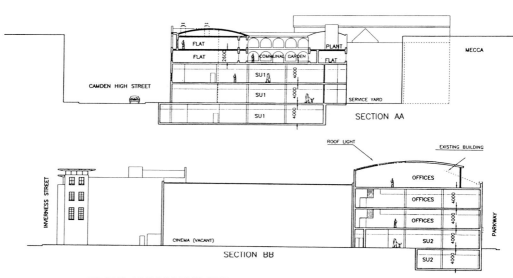

SECTIONS ACROSS THE SITE PARALLEL TO CAMDEN HIGH STREET

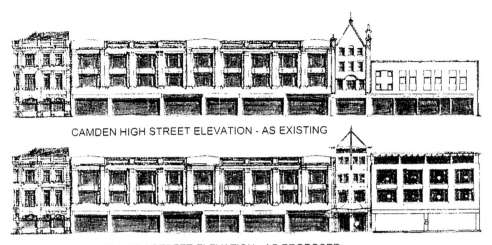

CAMDEN HIGH STREET ELEVATION - AS EXISTING

CAMDEN HIGH STREET ELEVATION - AS PROPOSED

PARKWAY ELEVATION - AS PROPOSED

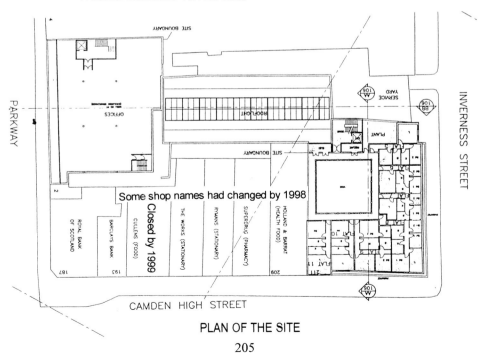

PARKWAY

INVERNESS STREET

SITE BOUNDARY

OFFICES

ROOFLIGHT

SERVICE YARD

PLANT

SITE BOUNDARY

Some shop names had changed by 1998

Closed by 1999

ROYAL BANK OF SCOTLAND

BARCLAYS BANK

CULLENS (FOOD)

THE WORKS (STATIONARY)

RYMANS (STATIONARY)

SUPERDRUG (PHARMACY)

HOLLAND & BARRAT (HEALTH FOOD)

187

193

209

CAMDEN HIGH STREET

PLAN OF THE SITE

Revitalizing the Roundhouse in 1998

There was no shortage of ideas for the renewal of the Round House, as an article in the Ham & High of 17 April 1992 showed.

The Greater London Enterprise/ Camden Town Development Trust proposed to fuse local art, fashion, theatre and retail interests. The development drawing shows a new spiral walkway sweeping round the old turntable space and a new spiral staircase linking three floors. A new piazza was to give a bright, festival entrance where it is now bleak. The multiplicity of uses is delightfully illustrated.

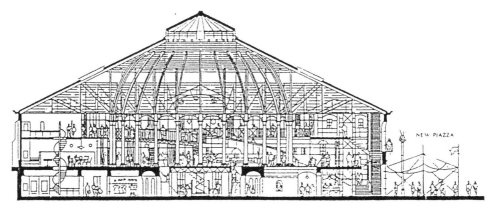

Greater London Enterprise and Camden Town Development Trust Scheme
Development drawing by McFarlane Phillips, 1992

Roundhouse Renewal Ltd suggested a 'participative arts centre', 'a place to paint rather than to look at paintings, a place to sing or play an instrument, rather than to listen to a concert'. There was to be a bar, a cafe, a creche, a small recording studio and a room for children's activities in the basement. Restoration costs were estimated at £3 to £3.5 million.

Royal Exchange Theatre, Manchester, put in a bid, also to cost £3.5 million, but financed by a low-rent homes development which depended on council permission. Rehearsals and sets for the 750 seat theatre would be paid for in Manchester, so the theatre would have broken even on only 55% capacity. It is interesting that in 1997 a roughly similar project was being planned in Islington for the rebuilt Collins Music Hall.

The Environmental Awareness Trust, an educational charity, planned to build a permanent Earth Focus exhibition on the environment, including a 50 foot globe housing an 'explanatorium' with a 360⁰ cinema. Estimated cost £4 million.

Other organizations put forward similar schemes, including a wide-screen cinema, and a hotel owner wanted to fill the building with restaurants and bars.

In the event, the property firm Placegate bought the building for £900,000 in 1993 and cleaned the brickwork, expecting to sell it on after it had been made more presentable. Only two years later they were asking £2 million,, but never achieved anything like that sum.

Some developers, including Placegate, hoped to make the Roundhouse into a venue for discos and other noisy entertainment. This would have drawn in large crowds, caused parking problems and noise late into the night, disturbing the peace of the neighbours. When Camden sold the building in 1993 they imposed a restrictive covenant forbidding the use of the building after 11.30 p.m. on weekdays and 11 p.m. on Sundays. This, with all the other restrictions connected with a Grade II* listed building, made commercial development difficult. Many producers have spoken glibly of converting it into a large theatre but, as we have seen, this is impossible as the building is listed. A number of small stages are feasible, but not one large one..

The Royal Institute of British Architects and the Roundhouse[5]

In 1995 the Royal Institute of British Architects offered £1.25 million for the building to Placegate Properties, but at first the offer was rejected. RIBA wanted to rehouse its unrivalled collections of architectural drawings in this spacious and historic building which was itself a notable piece of architecture. The collections of drawings, models and photographs, which include works by Palladio, Inigo Jones and Christopher Wren, are the finest of their kind in the world. They are housed on four separate sites, are seldom seen by the public and are kept in conditions which must be a real threat to their long-term survival. One of the sites is a beautiful house in Portman Square where space is so limited that it is necessary to remove one drawing from the table in order to open the next. It can be a nightmare when three people are working side by side, each trying to examine delicate drawings without harming them. Drawings are laid over other drawings in order to make room. The thought of the all that space at the Round House was tantalizing.

The drawing by Michael and Patty Hopkins shows how the old steam engine bays would provide radiating storage and ample study room. Structural change would have

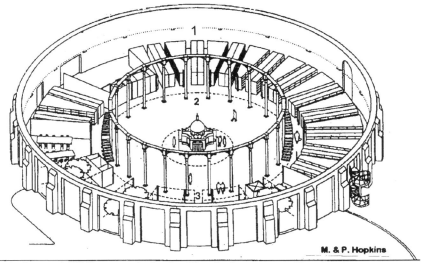

In the round: RIBA's proposals showing (1) main storage space; (2) main exhibition space; (3) readers and staff areas.

been kept to a minimum, although external staircases added in the 1960s were to have been removed. In December 1995 Placegate accepted the RIBA offer.

The Save London Theatres Campaign protested vigorously at the prospect of losing 'one of the most dazzling and extraordinary venues in Britain, if not in Europe', and promised to protest to the Planning Committee.[6,7] Peter Brook said that 'It was not just the loss of space but the loss of *that* space' and recalled his success with The Midsummer Night's Dream. The pop star Jean-Jaques Burnel of The Stranglers, remembered the building as unique. The only pop venue equal to it was in Amsterdam, but then went on to say that The Stranglers had not been spat on at the Roundhouse. Some might think this rather a negative triumph.

The Round House would have provided an ideal site for the RIBA collection. Close to train, tube and road, near to the new British Library at King's Cross and the RIBA Library in Portland Place, the choice could not be bettered. RIBA applied to the National Heritage Lottery Fund for money, and English Heritage supported the application.

If purchase had gone ahead, work would have started on the Roundhouse in March 1998 and the collections moved during the summer, but the National Heritage Memorial Fund concluded that Roundhouse 'was not ideal to house the collection'. The National Lottery refused money and the Roundhouse was blighted once again.

Theatre groups were, of course, delighted. 'Get Back Productions' planned to make their own appeal to the Lottery in order to turn the Roundhouse into a multi-media centre and 'give the Roundhouse back to the people'.

The New Plan in 1997

In the event it was bought for exactly this purpose and with a bias towards the encouragement and involvement of young people. In September 1996, the Roundhouse was bought by Torquil Norman, a millionaire who had made his money from selling toys to children. Educated at Eton, he read Economics and Law at Trinity College, Cambridge. After National Service, when he flew as a Fleet Air Arm pilot, he read more Economics at Harvard from 1953-57. From there he moved to J. P. Morgan & Co. in New York. In 1980 he formed Bluebird Toys, and was Chairman until retirement in 1996.

The same year he bought the Roundhouse, with the aim of turning it into a place where young people can be creative in art, music and drama, and have access to the expensive modern equipment. Torquil Norman pledged £6 million to the project, a sum which included the price of the Roundhouse. Ownership is secure.

In May 1997 a new charitable company, The Roundhouse Trust, was formed to take over a long-term lease of the building and to undertake its restoration. Major names from the arts are involved and Norman Foster was named as the architect..

The first production of the new regime was a spectacular theatre show from Belgium. The Roundhouse was transformed into a vast dodgems track to stage 'Bernadetje', the story of eleven young people. The director/choreographer, Alain Platel, is a remedial educationalist by training. At the same time the play is the start of a link being forged between the young people of Camden and those of Ghent, in Belgium, where Alain Platel works.

The National Theatre brought 'Oh What a Lovely War' to packed houses. The building was ready for long-term redevelopment.

Revitalizing the Roundhouse in 1998

In November 1998, revised plans by architect John McAslan were unveiled for a new, exciting Roundhouse – a centre for creativity in theatre, art, film, TV and fashion. It could cost £24 million and be completed by AD 2002. Encouraging the creative energy of young people is one of the main purposes behind the building.

The Roundhouse will be developed on four separate levels; the Undercroft at street level; the Main Theatre above; a new Balcony Level running round two thirds of the building; and 'The Lid', a new performance area in the conical roof. Altogether there will be four performance areas, with seating for up to 1200 people. For pop concerts, with seats removed and using the Balcony and Lid as well to create a huge open sound-box, the building could absorb 2,500.

The existing entrance staircase will be removed and a new glass-fronted entrance, with a spiral glass staircase and a glass restaurant, will be built to give a bright, welcoming presence. The present, drab front will be transformed

The general public is familiar with the main auditorium of the Roundhouse, with its circle of pillars which used to enclose the heavy turntable mechanisn, and the radiating bays outside which held the pairs of railway lines and inspection pits where the trains used to stand. Today the pits have been filled in to give a level floor and the steel lines have gone. However, very few people have seen the Undercroft, the floor below, which supports all this. In discussing the redevelopment of the building, let us start there and work upwards to the roof.

The undercroft was built entirely below ground level. The massive yellow brick retaining wall which was described earlier, extended along Chalk Farm Road to support the immense weight of the railway marshalling yards (now the car park). The undercroft was there to contain the turntable in the centre and to support the weight of the engines in their bays. It was simply a weight-bearing raft resting on the London Clay. Later, when the trains had gone and entrance was made from Chalk Farm Road, the space below was of very little use as it was full of solid wedges of brick, with narrow, barrel-vaulted passages between them.

The model of the Undercroft showing the engine support segments

When Gilbey's used the Roundhouse as a bonded store, goods were lowered by crane to carts below. The present outside staircase is a recent addition and will be removed.

The central circular room in the undercroft, which used to contain the turntable, is an impressive space which will become a performance area and meeting place. Its outside wall is the circular foundation for the ring of pillars above and must be retained.

On the other hand, the wedge-shaped brick blocks outside the ring, which housed the engine pits, serve no purpose today as the trains have gone. With the permission of English Heritage they will be removed completely, to make room for performance areas, music practice rooms, TV and video studios, offices and work-rooms.

Displaying the History of the Building

Removing the wedge-shaped segments will mean removing the floor of the main auditorium, as it stands on the top of them. I would make a personal plea for **one** of the wedges to be retained as a continuing example of how the building used to function. In the undercroft this would leave two large flat surfaces, ideal for display. One surface could display the history of the building – all the etchings and engravings of the building in its different states – while the other could be a huge mural telling the modern story. They could become wonderful story boards.

The wedge of floor above would also be retained so that people would be able to understand the size of the tiny engines which were in use when the Roundhouse was opened. One might even consider reopening the inspection pit, with its steps down at each end, replacing a pair of lines and placing a large photograph of one of George Stephenson's engine opposite, on the outside wall. Perhaps some railway museum might be willing to display one of its old locomotives at the Roundhouse. It would be living history, reminding visitors of how the building was first used and startling them by the tiny size of the engine. Photographers would use it in a hundred ways and every child would want to drive the engine. Incidentally, it would be a good advertisement for the museum. Wouldn't it be loverly!

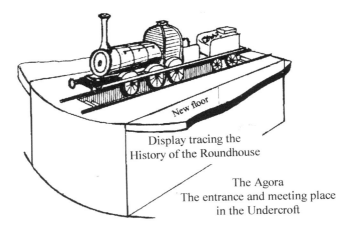

One supporting sector retained, the inspection pit reopened, and perhaps an old engine on loan from some railway museum.

Let us return to the current plans.

The New Roundhouse

The Roof

The 'Lid'
with the staircase from
the balcony level

The new Balcony level

Lifts to Balcony
and 'Lid' levels.

The Main Auditorium
set with a central stage

The Undercroft

The Main Entrance
with a staircase
to all levels

The New Balcony Level

A new balcony floor stretching round about two thirds of the building will be created around the central ring of pillars. As one enters the auditorium from the street, the nearest third will open into a huge space clear to the roof. With the immense circular window running round the roof and light able to flood in, this will give a sense of space and exhilaration. The balcony floor will provide seating for large audiences, or promenade space at other times. Opening from this will be costume-making and wardrobe departments, studios of different types, offices and other facilities.

The Lid

Ever since Thelma Holt first introduced it, theatre companies have tended to suspend some sort of canopy over the top of the central ring of pillars to contain the sound. They have also draped the columns, so that performances have taken place in a marquee inside the main building. Through this tent they have had to insert their overhead lighting.

In place of this there will be a solid circular roof suspended within the central circle of cast iron pillars on an elegant daddy-long-legs. Thin steel tubes will rise just inside alternate pillars and curve inwards to support the new floor and performance area, for the new roof wlll itself become a small theatre and rehearsal space. The steel tubes will be so fine and so close to the original pillars that they will become invisible.

The circular roof will act as an acoustic barrier, absorbing and reflecting sound; house the lighting grid, air conditioner and other technical equipment; and support the acting area above, for the Lid will become an acting/ rehearsal area in its own right. It will not be possible to give performances in both spaces at the same time, but one could be used for rehearsals while a performance is taking place in the other. The Lid will be approached by stairs from the Balcony and by lift to give disabled access.

The Roof

The roof, which is made of wooden rafters and slates, was built to shelter railway engines. It is not insulated against heat or sound. Noise from inside pollutes the local streets, while traffic noise from outside interferes with the performances. In 'O What a Lovely War', for example, the actors were forced to use microphones. It is clear that the roof must be insulated.

Secondly, the roof was not designed to hang things from. It will support itself, but nothing more. These problems will be tackled by removing the slates and adding a strong conical grid of 30 cm steel bars, in the form of a coolie's hat, adding thermal and sound insulation, and replacing the slates. The only sign of change will be a very slight raising of the roof.

The circle of windows, at present lost in the roof space, will be exposed and allow in light to the Lid and the building in general.

Redevelopment depends on Heritage Lottery Board and Arts Council funding, but when it opens the new Roundhouse, with its multiple stages and room for all the creative arts, could become the model for many other artistic centres here and abroad. For Camden Town, it will ensure a future for its best known and most extraordinary building. Robert Benson Dockray who built it, and a dour man from all accounts, must be revolving in his grave, but as an engineer and designer he would have been delighted by the imagination shown here.

Torquil and Anne Norman have set up the Roundhouse Trust The Trust invested £6.2 million pounds, which included the purchase of the Roundhouse, but the vast majority will become an endowment to secure the future of the scheme. Torquil Norman said:-

"This is a unique project which will see young people from the local and wider community learning from and being inspired by professionals in the arts industry. The Roundhouse is a beautiful building with an extraordinary history and we hope through this redevelopment we will underpin its pre-eminence as an arts venue. When we have proved the success of this unique combination of young people and professionals, the Government will want 'Roundhouses' in every part of the country"

It is the latest of a string of projects designed to find a new future for this unique building, but this time the people who own the building are making the plans, instead of merely trying to make money out of the building. This time it should work. At last the dinosaur may be restored to life.[3]

---

[1] Stanford's map of 1862
[2] Letter Guardian 12.12.1995
[3] 10 and 17 Oct. 1997, Ham & High
[5] 26 May 1995 Ham & High
[6] Ham & High 7 December, 1995.

The Camden Music Scene

The Camden music scene began for me way back in 1958. I was in a new, exciting comprehensive school, the first of its kind, when the skies were blue and we seemed set to transform the London educational scene. Complications were to arise later, but those first years were like wine.

This was the period of Skiffle, that pre-electronic form of noise, long forgotten. Guitars were the rage and we began making guitars in the school workshops. It was perfectly normal to see a class of teachers and older pupils making guitars in the evening. Some quite respectable instruments were made by people who had no idea they could achieve such a standard. Most were in thin plywood, but the bellies of some guitars were in Oregon Pine which could only have come from our school drawing boards. We put a stopper on that, but those particular instruments bore the marks of drawing pin holes for ever.

At lunch times my large classroom became a venue for a never-ending concert. While I sat marking exercise books, crowds of pupils came in from all over the school. Three double-bases made from tea chests stood permanently in the corner of the room, together with a couple of washboards and an African drum. Together with three or four guitars, these could drown out conversation along the whole corridor. The advantage was that almost anyone with a sense of rhythm could join in and beat or bang on something, while those who had no rhythm could become lost in all the din. Barbara Windsor had come from Our Lady's Convent, only half a mile away, and some of the pupils knew Helen Shapiro, who was their age and still at Skinner's, the next school along. Barbara Windsor was already a star: Helen Shapiro was becoming famous by the day. If they could do it, so could our young hopefuls and any group of them might suddenly become famous.

When the pips went for the start of afternoon school, there was absolute silence. They put everything away and filed out with a quiet word of thanks. The music may not have been very good, but the therapy was wonderful. These boys, with their DA haircuts and their hair in a quiff held rigid with sugar water, used to haunt the small clubs and venues in Hackney and Camden Town.

The Beatles crept up on us on a school journey. Two girls had been told of this new band on the train. My wife and the two girls spent a morning scouring the shops of Lucerne for their records, but nobody had ever heard of them.

Much later, Dougie Trendle and others of the 'Bad Manners' band were in our school. Trendle became 'Buster Bloodvessel', the lead singer, Brian Tuitt was on drums, and several others appeared with them on occasion. They played Two-tone music and SKA, the black rhythm from Jamaica, at a period when music was being polarized into different camps. Theirs was a mixture of skin-head punk and two tone/ska. Totally anarchic. The band became big, with twelve records in the top 100 between March 1980 and 1983, and two songs at No. 3.

Things moved on, but the atmosphere changed little. A couple of years ago a young man said:-

"Below the railway arch in Chalk Farm Road was the Carnarvon Castle, now the Fusiler & Firkin, a seething mass of Mods and Rockers, mopeds and motorbikes, threee-piece suits and leather jackets, but never on the same night. Outside the pub the bikes and mopeds would always be parked. Mopeds for Mods and bikes for Rockers. There were always a few bikes around as the bouncers on the door were Rockers. I remember them as large, aggressive men, older and heavier than us, smelling of petrol and leather, and wondered how they could stand so many Mods. Because Friday night was Mod night. It was quite rare for a club to play host to two opposing cultures. Give them your two quid and get in safely.

You entered by the left-hand door into a long thin room. The left side was raised, with tables on either side of the narrow stage. On the right were a long bar and a cigarette machine. The atmosphere generated in there was electric. The first reason was the crush. You were so squashed up against each other that you couldn't help mirroring your neighbour's gyrations. The second was the Rhythm and Blues – loud, fast and familiar. There was always a rip-roaring harmonica careering through every song like an out of control steam train. Bands kept the audience jumping by the fast tempo, speeding up classics like 'Louie, Louie' and 'Green Onions'. Twanging guitars and booming drums would sometimes be drowned by the singer's powerful voice, but the tempo never slowed and we never stopped dancing."

"In the late eighties, Parkway, the one-way road from Regent's Park, had the Jazz cafe, and still has. It is one of the major jazz clubs in London. All of the world's best play there when they are in London. Further up is the Dublin Castle. A large trad pub with thick stair carpet and old wallpaper. At the back is a small door which led to a back room with a bar at one end and a second bar at the other. Always full, it was the place to be in the 1980s and still may be. I remember coming out of the pub one evening and seeing the band 'Madness' sitting at a large round table. It was said to be always their table.

Further up, next to Mornington Crescent is the Camden Palace, the biggest club in Camden. Each evening it set a different style – 60s, 70s Gay, House, etc. Wednesday evenings were Sixties Nights, when the whole area became alive with people dressed to the nines in their best 1960s clothes."

Thus, in the 1980s, young people were copying their parents of the early sixties, wearing their clothes and sporting their hair styles. Fashions go round and round.

Buster Bloodvessel opened an hotel in Margate called 'Fatty Towers', designed for the larger person - with big chairs, strong beds which would not collapse under the weight, and generous portions on the plates. He also promoted the town's lowly football club.

Helen Shapiro has sung with Humphrey Lyttleton for fifteen years. Jazz at its best.

Ann Scanlon has told the story of Camden Town music in detail in, 'The Rock and Roll Guide to Camden Town.' It is a mine of information.

Canal Boats Today

John Jones had started running passenger trips from Camden Lock in 1951, but the great change came over the Canal in the freeze of 1962. When the canal goods-carrying trade collapsed, it gave a great impetus to trip boats and the use of the waterways as a playground. With boats at give away prices, owners looked around for some way of making a living. One boat, the Ben Lawers, was owned by one of the horse-drawn barge families and was often used as a floating stage by Northside. Barges have been opened as restaurants or picture galleries, but the vast majority disappeared.

Canal Boat Trips

British Waterways used to run barge trips from Camden Lock to Little Venice for six weeks of the year. About 1986, Northside took over the line and began to run them for 52 weeks in the year. Ten years later they were carrying 50,000 passengers a year. To achieve these figures, Northside built up a fleet of their own which now plies regularly between Camden Town and Little Venice.

The Perseus and Gardenia, both built in 1937, and The Jason, built in the 1960s, are narrow boats, The Jason was a wooden-bottomed working boat converted into a trip boat, while Perseus once carried coal. Both were converted into trip boats.

Northside commissioned Knight of Norfolk to build a glass-fibre boat called The Water Buffalo, to seat eighty. Gardenia and Perseus were completely overhauled and refurbished during the winter of 1994/95 and redecorated by signwriter and illustrator Barbara Card. After a weekend service during the winter, the boats began a daily service to and from Little Venice, each hour, on the hour. There are also day trips to more distant places like Limehouse, Three Mills, on the River Lee, and to Brentford via Little Venice.

All this movement is very leisurely. The old horse-drawn barges travelled at four miles an hour, the pace of a horse. Today, with a 24 horse powered engine instead of one horse, speed is still restricted by law to the same four miles an hour, but now it is to reduce erosion of the banks.

The Canal Towpath

Over the years the towpath has been opened up as a traffic-free footpath. In 1972 the stretch from Camden Town to the Zoo was opened and now there is free passage from the tunnel at Islington, through Camden Town and past the Zoo, to the tunnel mouth under the Edgware Road at Maida Hill. Beyond this tunnel again, the towpath is open, by way of Little Venice, to Kilburn and beyond.

Water Buffalo

Gardenia

Paddy Walker and the Jenny Wren

Paddy Walker, who died in January 1998,[1] was a wonderful character, dynamic and vital. He was an art student at Kensington and later at Westminster School of Art. In 1928 he began as a student at the Workingman's College in Camden Town and was soon teaching woodcarving and sculpture. By 1939 he was a governor of the College and remained so for the rest of his life. For him the College was to be run by teachers and students as they wished, without any outside interference.

During the second World War he made perfect scale models of newly designed ships to be made by men, skilled, but unable to read drawings. After 1945 he helped to restore St Paul's Cathedral by creating wood-carvings to replace ones damaged by bombing. He returned to Camden Town to become a furniture restorer and carver, opening Walker's Antiques in Camden High Street and living above the shop for the rest of his life.

He fought fiercely against the planned motorway, standing against the Conservatives as an anti-motorway candidate. With Viscount St David, he started the Pirate's Club, the boating club for children. In 1968 he commissioned the famous Jenny Wren and set up the Jenny Wren Canal Cruises, with their offices at Hampstead Road Bridge. Later he bought a second boat, 'My Fair Lady' and converted her into a floating restaurant. The Jenny Wren offices too were recently converted into the Waterside Restaurant, with splendid views over the canal. Shop, home, restaurant and boats, all within a couple of hundred yards. A truly Camden Town man.[1] In April 1998, the College in Crowndale Road opened a a newly refurbished art studio in his memory and named it 'Paddy's Room'.[2]

The Jenny Wren, with Paddy Walker, left, and Giles Baker who built her.

---

[1] Obituary, Ham & High, 16 January 1998
[2] Ham & High, 3 April, 1998.

Paddington Basin 1997

Over the years the 'Jenny Wren' has carried thousands of passengers from Camden Town to Little Venice, turning in the wide water at each end for the return trip. While Little Venice is very beautiful and tourists love to visit it, nobody would have wanted to go the few hundred yards further into Paddington Basin. Once this was the centre of the area, the very hub of activity. Trade had been enormous, but it faded and for years the basin has lain empty and neglected. However, during the next decade the Basin will be redeveloped. It will be transformed, with new houses, flats, shops, offices, short-stay boat moorings and become a centre for water-based activities. Barges will moor for a few days to visit the West End theatres and then move on.

The Canal Basin itself will be reshaped, widened here and narrowed there, but the total water area will stay about the same. The plan on the next page shows a restaurant and shops at the far end, looking out on a display of Historic Craft. A new Harbour Master's Building narrows the Basin, only for it to widen immediately to form visitors' moorings. This will also be the new mooring for the tour barge, next to a widened Turning Circle, so that she can reverse for the return trip. Then come further moorings and, beyond the bridge at Bishop's Bridge Road, will be a Facilities Building for visiting boats.

One end of this new building, itself built like one half of a ship, with a curved awning roof, will be the much earlier canal loading building. This has the huge overhanging roof which allowed barges to be loaded and unloaded in the dry.

The Henry Milbourne drawing below shows the original loading building in 1801, the year the Grand Union Canal reached Paddington. Wooden, with a crane and an overhanging roof, it stood alone beside an unfenced Basin, the very first of all the buildings. This was replaced at some time with a similar building but in brick and slate, which is now listed Grade II*. When the photograph on page 220 was taken, in 1996, it had long been out of use. In the builder's yard next door they were moving

The First Barge-loading Building
Paddington Canal Basin 1801, drawn by Henry Milbourne and engraved by Joseph Jeakes.

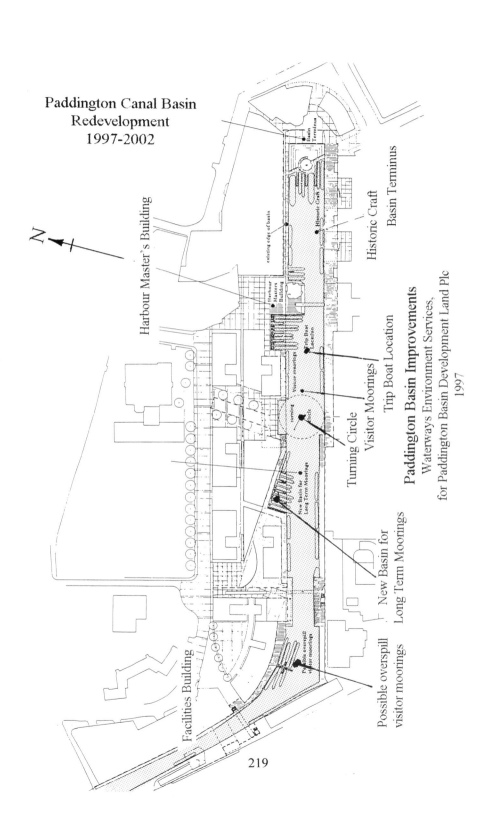

Paddington Canal Basin
Redevelopment
1997-2002

N

Harbour Master's Building

Historic Craft

Basin Terminus

Paddington Basin Improvements
Waterways Environment Services,
for Paddington Basin Development Land Plc
1997

Turning Circle
Visitor Moorings

Trip Boat Location

New Basin for
Long Term Moorings

Possible overspill
visitor moorings

Facilities Building

materials with fork-lift trucks and transporting them by road.. Apparently the useful life of the listed canal building had ended, but a new one has been found.

It will be dismantled carefully, recorded, and moved from one end of the Basin to the other. There it will become the canal-boat facilities building mentioned before, with shops, showers and a cafe. Somehow it is fitting that barges visiting in the 21st century should be first greeted and made welcome by a survivor from a much earlier age.[1]

There may have been some buildings at Camden Town with overhanging roofs early on, but the single storey building, constructed over and around the railway/canal wharf at Camden Town, and the 1912 three-storey Interchange Building which replaced it, were much more sophisticated than anything ever to have been found at Paddington. At Camden Town, canal, rail and road traffc could be transferred in one building. At Paddington, the rail and canal were too far apart for any such interchange building to be practicable. An extended roof, which allowed barges to be unloaded in the dry, was sufficient. After that goods had to be carried to Paddington Station by road.

The Second Barge-loading Building

The Grade II listed building in Paddington Basin in 1996. It was photographed from the Metropole Hotel, which stands at the head of the Basin and will tower over the new development.

---

[1] Information from Chelsfield plc and Terry Farrell & Company.

At the Start of the New Millennium

Over the years, as more and more people have been attracted to Camden Lock, the value of local property has soared. Vast warehouses have become TV studios. Old buildings, notably William Huck's Bottling Plant in Jamestown Road, have been converted into expensive flats. The Interchange Building has developed a new life as World Wide Television. Shops in Chalk Farm Road used to include butchers, bakers, fresh fish shops, small ironmongers, and the odd half shop selling vacuum cleaner parts. Almost all are gone. Instead, the shops have been opened out, basements dug out and back yards built over to form deep, narrow, selling-caverns. Jeans, tops, boots, leather jackets and still more leather jackets, as far as the eye can reach. Each year the shops become longer and deeper to hold all the merchandise.

With the crowds have come even more street stalls selling anything that came to hand, from temporary pitches. The fronts of established shops and pubs are taken over by stalls, more and more closely packed. It is legal for shopkeepers to use their fronts, or 'curtilages' for sales, but it causes obstruction, making access for emergency vehicles difficult. There have been running battles for years between shopkeepers, vendors, and the Council. Shop rents in the 'Golden Half Mile', the stretch from the Underground Station to the Lock, have risen to as much as £150,000 a year, as high as some parts of Oxford Street. Tiny pitches can cost £400 a week, so shopkeepers are only too willing to let their fronts to help pay their own rocketing rents.

In the 1970s Camden Council was trying to tackle the problem of short-term traders on temporary, unauthorized pitches. The law is so complicated and time consuming, involving individual court appearances for each case and the medieval rights of a pedlar to sell in public places on a certain number of days a year. But how many days, and which, and where, and who counted them, and who was selling on that day, and

Camden Town High Street, circa 1900

was it the man in the dock, or was it his brother? The whole subject is a minefield. Camden regulates the market as well as they may, concerned for safety, while at the same time anxious not to destroy the vitality and bustle which is the whole driving force of the area.

Then, on two Sundays the 'Save Our Streets' Campaign', which aims to reduce car traffic, completely blocked the road. On one occasion a broken down car was dumped in the roadway outside Camden Town Tube Station and children were invited to take it to pieces. An immense street party developed. Buses had to be diverted along Prince of Wales Road, while crowds took over the whole roadway. For an hour no cars could use the street at all. What would have happened in the event of a fire, nobody knows.

Perhaps as a result of this, perhaps as part of general traffic management, Camden Council narrowed the roadway in 1997 from four lanes to two. Pavements have been widened and the roadway narrowed between the Tube Station and the Railway Bridge, to make the traffic safer and allow the crowds to spread.

Camden Town is still a great place for people-watching: no two couples seem the same and every language may be heard. There are long trails of obedient tourists from a dozen countries, following their hectoring guides, and rugged individuals with backpacks, carrying their houses on their backs. Rugged, but not necessarily poor. A backpack and three credit card accounts is not unknown. The variety is intoxicating.

People still invent new dress. Anything can be worn at Camden Lock. Caftans, smocks, open-toed sandals, enormous boots for trudging across the Arctic, or metalized slippers too light for Cinderella. Hairdressers watch how young people do their hair and copy the styles. In an old G.K.Chesterton story, a murderer was on the run. He ordered a hairdresser to change his hairstyle, the simplest of all forms of disguise. The hairdresser recognized him, but was too frightened to arrest him, or even to utter a word. Instead, he gave the man a special shampoo. A day later the man's hair had turned bright green. The police were warned and promptly arrested him. Today they would have to arrest half Camden Lock.

Camden Town High Street, 1998.

222

Index

The Growth of St Marylebone & Paddington:
From Hyde Park to Queen's Park
by
Jack Whitehead
ISBN 0 9509362 5 1. 138 pages, 70 maps and over 150 illustrations
£7.50

Traces the development of the Bishop of London's Estate, Bayswater, Paddington Green, Little Venice, to Kilburn Bridge, and on the other side of the Edgware Road, Lisson Green up to St John's Wood.

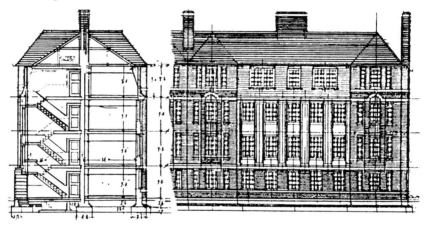

Local Authority Housing in St Marylebone

In country districts cottages were built, but in towns where land values were so high, blocks were the norm. This is a typical Local Authority development of 1924---

Stories – stories – stories –

Did Eliza Dolittle live in Lisson Grove and go to Bell Street School? Was she the centre of a child abduction scandal? Why did a Queen's Park School have the first woodwork classes in Britain? Can you find the 300 million year old corals in the Marks & Spencer's wall, now well past their sell-by date? The book is full of stories, including a dinosaur living in an eighth-floor flat in Edgware Road.

A coral surrounded by
crinoid fragments in a
wall near Edgware Road.

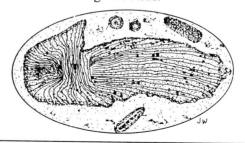

'This book is an exemplar.'   Heritage Outlook (THE CIVIC TRUST).

'This book is a wonderful rich mixture of visual and written information.'
Streetwise (organ of the NATIONAL ASSOCIATION FOR URBAN STUDIES).

228

The Growth of Muswell Hill by Jack Whitehead

ISBN 0 9509362 4 3

248 pages, 245mm x 165mm, many maps and drawings. £9.95

In 1924 the author moved to Muswell Hill to find a countryside full of butterflies and enormous trees. He saw many of the trees disappear under crops of houses., watched the men as they built them and was fascinated by the skills of the different craftsmen. Later he researched the history of the district and shows how the buildings had been spreading form the end of the Napoleonic Wars, engulfing fields and woods, to change a rural lndscape into a vibrant suburb.

Anyone interested in the development of London, its periodical building explosions and their different building styles, will enjoy this book.

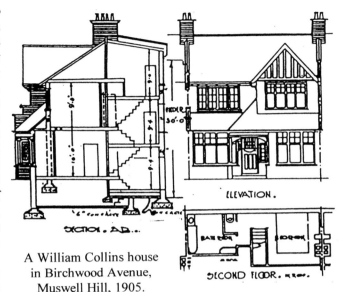

A William Collins house in Birchwood Avenue, Muswell Hill, 1905.

The Glacial Drifts of Muswell Hill & Finchley
by Henry Walker, F.G.S., 1874
Reprinted with a foreword by Jack Whitehead and a postscript by
Eric Robinson giving the interpretation of a modern geologist
£1.50

In 1926, as a young boy, Jack Whitehead was amazed and enchanted to hear that Muswell Hill was once covered with glaciers. This is the pamphlet about the 1835 finds made in Coldfall Woods which brought it all to light and gives a description of North London perhaps 12,000 years ago. Dr Eric Robinson, Librarian of the Geologists' Association, has added a postscript which gives the modern view and shows that this was not a fantastic dream, but good science, which can be proved any day by digging in Muswell Hill gardens.

COMMON FOSSILS OF THE FINCHLEY GLACIAL CLAY.

The Growth of Stoke Newington: a model for other studies
by Jack Whitehead
ISBN 0 9509362 0 0. Many maps and illustrations, 78 pages, A4   £4.50

A history of the district from Palaeolithic times to today – flints to reinforced concrete. The book shows how the first houses were built on gravel and only later, when all the gravel had been occupied, did the builders venture on to the clay. Thus changes in date and design of houses can reveal geology hidden below.

Stoke Newington Common, now built over, is one of the most important Palaeolithic sites in North Europe. In the 1860s, when the houses were being built, G. Worthington Smith, a colourful character in a flowing cloak, began to discover an old world, lost under his feet, -----

Lordship Park, 1860s.

Trimmed flake tool found
in Abney Park Cemetry

'If this book does not encourage both children and teachers to appreciate their local heritage, then nothing will.'   LONDON TOPOGRAPHICAL NEWS

From Ragged School to Comprehensive:
A brief history of a site in Marylebone and its Grade II* liisted building
by Jack Whitehead, 1998,
ISBN 0-9509362-8-6, 245mm x 165 mm, 64 pages.   £3.00

North Westminster Community School
Marylebone Lower House, Penfold Street, NW1

On one site in Marylebone, near the flyover, there have been a Ragged School, a London School Board School, a Secondary Modern, and now a Comprehensive School. Their histories are wrapped round each other, one leading on to the next

In 1998 the new Comprehensive School building, which had been built as Rutherford School in 1960 by Leonard Manasseh, was listed Grade II*. This book celebrates the achievement, describes the new building and its effect on planning in the surrounding area. It was a catalyst in a dozen different ways.

The Paddington Almshouse Stone
by
Jack Whitehead

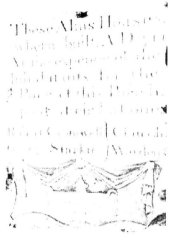

The Paddington Almshouse stone

In 1980, an inscribed stone with the date of 1714, was found lying on a school playground in Paddington. 1714 was the year Queen Anne died and George 1 succeded to the throne. This is the oldest engraved stone in Paddington and one of the oldest Georgian stones in the country. It stood on Paddington Green, high on the chimney of Paddington Alms Houses. This stone has a longer history than the British Empire.

Besides tracing the history of the stone, the booklet includes local paintings by T. Hosmer Shepherd, Charles Ginner, and Algernon Newton, engravings by Chatelaine, and the Bishop of London's Estate map of 1742, and reveals that the church wardens paid a bounty of a shilling for each polecat caught   A fascinating picture of a distant world.

The RTZ Geological Garden
At North Westminster School, Elgin Avenue, W9
by
Eric Robinson and Jack Whitehead

This booklet describes a unique display of geological stones built as an outdoor garden, or theatre, in a North London school play-ground. Built by Cullum & Nightingale and funded by Rio Tinto Zinc, the Garden is a familiar, friendly place, yet full of exotic stones. The booklet describes them, and other building materials, so that it is a guide to stones found in any London street.

This 'garden' idea can be copied anywhere and at any level of complexity by schools, or by town planners and architects who are setting out local parks or courtards. There is no reason, except lack of imagination, why paths should be dull. This booklet is full of interesting ideas and building history, while the Garden itself can be viewed by appointment during term time.

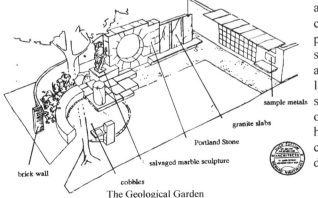

sample metals
granite slabs
Portland Stone
salvaged marble sculpture
brick wall
cobbles
The Geological Garden